MULTI-ACTOR HUMAN RIGHTS PROTECTION AT THE INTERNATIONAL CRIMINAL COURT

Conversations about the involvement of States in the workings of the International Criminal Court often focus on the role of State cooperation in enabling the ICC to carry out criminal trials. However, there is a dimension to this cooperation that is underexplored. Whenever the ICC relies on the assistance of States, or States otherwise become involved in its functioning, the human rights of accused and witnesses involved in proceedings may be adversely affected. The simultaneous involvement of the ICC, ICC States Parties, and the ICC host State – whilst essential and unavoidable – can insert ambiguity and uncertainty into the protection of individuals, leaving the door open for human rights violations. This book explores this phenomenon of multi-actor human rights protection at the ICC. By setting out the relevant obligations of the different actors, the book highlights potential problems in human rights protection and proposes ways to mitigate them.

EMMA IRVING is Assistant Professor of Public International Law at the Grotius Centre for Legal Studies of Leiden University.

MULTI-ACTOR HUMAN RIGHTS PROTECTION AT THE INTERNATIONAL CRIMINAL COURT

EMMA IRVING
Leiden University

CAMBRIDGE
UNIVERSITY PRESS

University Printing House, Cambridge CB2 8BS, United Kingdom

One Liberty Plaza, 20th Floor, New York, NY 10006, USA

477 Williamstown Road, Port Melbourne, VIC 3207, Australia

314–321, 3rd Floor, Plot 3, Splendor Forum, Jasola District Centre,
New Delhi – 110025, India

79 Anson Road, #06–04/06, Singapore 079906

Cambridge University Press is part of the University of Cambridge.

It furthers the University's mission by disseminating knowledge in the pursuit of education, learning, and research at the highest international levels of excellence.

www.cambridge.org
Information on this title: www.cambridge.org/9781108481069
DOI: 10.1017/9781108646291

© Emma Irving 2020

This publication is in copyright. Subject to statutory exception and to the provisions of relevant collective licensing agreements, no reproduction of any part may take place without the written permission of Cambridge University Press.

First published 2020

Printed in the United Kingdom by TJ International Ltd. Padstow Cornwall

A catalogue record for this publication is available from the British Library.

Library of Congress Cataloging-in-Publication Data
Names: Irving, Emma, 1989– author.
Title: Multi-actor human rights protection at the International Criminal Court / Emma Irving.
Description: New York : Cambridge University Press, 2020. | Includes bibliographical references and index.
Identifiers: LCCN 2019029328 (print) | LCCN 2019029329 (ebook) | ISBN 9781108481069 (hardback) | ISBN 9781108646291 (epub)
Subjects: LCSH: International Criminal Court. | Human rights.
Classification: LCC KZ7312 .I78 2020 (print) | LCC KZ7312 (ebook) | DDC 345/.01–dc23
LC record available at https://lccn.loc.gov/2019029328
LC ebook record available at https://lccn.loc.gov/2019029329

ISBN 978-1-108-48106-9 Hardback

Cambridge University Press has no responsibility for the persistence or accuracy of URLs for external or third-party internet websites referred to in this publication and does not guarantee that any content on such websites is, or will remain, accurate or appropriate.

For you Ewoud
Always

CONTENTS

Introduction *page* 1

0.1 Understanding Multi-Actor Human Rights Protection at the ICC   3

0.2 Approach and Structure   7

1 The Human Rights Obligations of the ICC   10

1.1 Within the Rome Statute Protection Framework   11

1.2 Beyond the Rome Statute Protection Framework   20

1.3 The Limits of the ICC's Human Rights Law Obligations   22

1.4 The Approach to the ICC's Obligations Adopted in Parts I and II   24

1.5 Conclusion   25

PART I **Multi-Actor Human Rights Protection: The ICC and States Parties**   27

2 The Human Rights Obligations of States Parties to the Rome Statute   29

2.1 Within the Rome Statute Protection Framework   29

2.2 Human Rights Obligations in Particular Provisions   30

2.3 Beyond the Rome Statute Protection Framework   34

2.4 Obligations of States Not Party to the Rome Statute   35

2.5 Conclusion   38

3 Suspects, Accused, Convicted, and Acquitted   39

3.1 Interrogation   40

3.2 Arrest and Surrender   48

3.3 Interim Release prior to and during ICC Proceedings   65

3.4 Treatment in the Enforcement State   78

3.5 Acquittal and Release   93

3.6 Conclusion   99

4 Witnesses   101

4.1 Witnesses Located in the Situation State   102

4.2 Relocating Witnesses to a Third State   120

4.3 Conclusion   133

PART II **Multi-Actor Human Rights Protection: The ICC and Its Host State**   137

5 The Human Rights Obligations of the ICC Host State   139

5.1 Within the Rome Statute Protection Framework   140

5.2 Beyond the Rome Statute Protection Framework   140

5.3 Conclusion   144

6 Accused, Convicted, and Acquitted   146

6.1 Interim Release   146

6.2 Removal to the Enforcement State   149

6.3 Acquittal and Release   155

6.4 Conclusion   162

CONTENTS

7 Detained and Non-Detained Witnesses   164

   7.1 Detained Witnesses: Right to Life, Protection from Inhuman Treatment, and Fair Trial   166

   7.2 Detained Witnesses: Right to Liberty   183

   7.3 Non-Detained Witnesses   197

   7.4 Conclusion   203

PART III   Evaluation and Proposals   207

8 Evaluation and Proposals for Change   209

   8.1 Summary of the Problems Identified in the Situations of Multi-Actor Human Rights Protection   210

   8.2 Changes to the Law   213

   8.3 Practical Solutions for Particular Problems   223

   8.4 Mechanism for Choosing between Actors   226

   8.5 Mechanism to Pinpoint a Volunteer State   230

   8.6 Reasons for States to Volunteer   233

   8.7 Conclusion   235

9 Conclusion   237

Bibliography   242
Index   263

Introduction

The International Criminal Court (ICC) was envisaged as a beacon of international criminal justice, but it cannot exist or operate in splendid isolation. Rather, it is inextricably linked to, and reliant on, the international community of States. Such reliance has long been a feature of international criminal justice: speaking of the International Criminal Tribunal for the Former Yugoslavia, Antonio Cassese once wrote that the Tribunal was 'like a giant without arms and legs'.[1] The artificial limbs the Tribunal needed to walk and work were state authorities, whose cooperation was key to the Tribunal's functioning.

Conversations about the involvement of States in the workings of international criminal courts and tribunals often focus on the role of State cooperation in enabling these bodies to effectively carry out criminal trials. Evidence, accused persons, and witnesses will, almost exclusively, be under the control of a State, or present on its territory, meaning that courts and tribunals require State assistance to access such evidence, accused, and witnesses. However, there is a dimension to this cooperation that is less well explored. When international criminal courts and tribunals call on the assistance of States, or States otherwise become involved in aspects of their functioning, this can have an impact on the human rights of individuals involved in proceedings before these courts and tribunals. This simultaneous involvement of States and courts, whilst essential and unavoidable, can insert ambiguity and uncertainty into the protection of individuals, leaving the door open for human rights violations.

The potential problems posed by the involvement of multiple actors in the work of international criminal courts and tribunals can be illustrated by a situation that arose at the ICC in 2011. Four individuals travelled

---

[1] Antonio Cassese, 'On the Current Trends towards Criminal Prosecution and Punishment of Breaches of International Humanitarian Law' (1998) 9 *European Journal of International Law*, 2, 13.

from the Democratic Republic of Congo (DRC) to The Hague to act as witnesses before the Court. This was done pursuant to special arrangements, due to the fact that the four witnesses were themselves imprisoned in the DRC for crimes under domestic law. These special arrangements required that the witnesses remain detained while at the seat of the ICC, and that they be returned to the DRC as soon as their testimony was complete. However, once they concluded their testimony, the four witnesses submitted asylum claims to the Dutch authorities, claiming that if they were returned to the DRC they would face an unfair trial, torture, and summary execution. The ensuing back-and-forth took several years to resolve, during which time the witnesses remained detained in the ICC Detention Centre.

By presenting asylum claims to the Dutch authorities, the four witnesses added further complexity to an already complex situation. The protection of witnesses is invariably a task that involves multiple actors, as protection is arranged through cooperation between the ICC and a State. The State is often the witness's home State (which, in this case, was also the detaining State), but could also be a safe third State to which the witness will be relocated. By involving the Netherlands through the asylum claims, the four witnesses added yet another actor to the cooperation mix. Each of the three actors involved in the witnesses' situation had their own understanding of their respective obligations, and their own ideas on how the situation should be resolved. The DRC requested that the witnesses be returned, and offered assurances as to their protection; the ICC indicated that it could not return the witnesses until the Netherlands had made a decision regarding their asylum, and requested that the Netherlands take over custody of them; and the Netherlands determined that the witnesses could not be processed as regular asylum seekers given their status as ICC witnesses, and refused the invitation to take over custody of them. The fact that multiple actors were involved in this situation, each with its own role to play in protecting the witnesses' human rights, created such uncertainty as to who was responsible for their protection that the witnesses' rights almost went unprotected. Indeed for a period they did, as the years that the witnesses spent in ICC detention while the legal questions were resolved was itself arguably a violation of the right to liberty.[2] Ultimately, both the Netherlands and the ICC determined that the assurances offered by the DRC were

---

[2] The situation of the detained witnesses is examined in detail in Chapter 7.

sufficient to manage and mitigate the risks faced by the witnesses, leading to their return to the DRC.

The case of detained Congolese witnesses served as the catalyst for this book. The unusual circumstances – and the responses of the DRC, the ICC, and the Netherlands – highlighted the complex questions that can arise when multiple actors play a role in protecting individuals involved in ICC proceedings. Yet the particular situation described in the preceding paragraphs is by no means the only instance where this phenomenon is present. The range of situations where States are involved in protecting individuals appearing before the ICC is diverse. The objective of this book is to identify these situations of multi-actor involvement, understand the respective obligations of the different actors, and examine how the multi-actor nature of a situation can affect the human rights of individuals. In this way, potential problems can be identified before they arise, and the possibility arises to make arrangements to mitigate them.

The book examines multi-actor human rights protection as it manifests at the ICC. While the phenomenon is not absent from other international criminal courts and tribunals, the universal nature of the ICC makes it – at present – the central actor in the international criminal justice landscape. Furthermore its intended permanency makes examining the potential problems caused by multi-actor human rights protection a forward-looking and worthwhile endeavour. The experiences of other courts and tribunals are considered to the extent that they shed light on the challenges facing the ICC.

0.1 Understanding Multi-Actor Human Rights Protection at the ICC

The situations where multiple actors are involved in human rights protection can be broadly distinguished into two categories, based on the actors: those involving the ICC and State Parties, and those involving the ICC and its host State.[3]

The first category encompasses situations where the ICC has a task or function which it cannot accomplish without the assistance of a State Party. Consider the example of arrests: in order to conduct a trial the ICC must secure the presence of a defendant, meaning that the accused must

---

[3] Non-States Parties to the Rome Statute play a very limited role in this study, as is explained in Chapter 2.

be arrested and transferred to the Court. The ICC, however, lacks the legal and factual capacity to carry out arrests, given that it has no police force of its own and cannot carry out enforcement measures on the territory of a sovereign State. Consequently, the ICC relies on States to arrest suspects on its behalf and surrender them to the Court. There are numerous other instances where the ICC requires the assistance of States to carry out functions and tasks: when conducting an investigation on the territory of a State, when an accused has been convicted and must serve a prison sentence in a State, when a witness needs protecting in their home country, and so on.

These ICC functions and tasks place the individuals they concern – whether suspect, accused, or witness – in a position where their human rights could be compromised. In arrest proceedings, an accused will be taken into custody and deprived of their freedom; if proper procedures are not followed, this can result in a violation of their right to liberty. When the act of testifying before the ICC places a witness at risk, in seeking protection from the Court the witness will be concerned with safeguarding their physical and psychological wellbeing (and that of their family). Importantly, any time that the ICC relies on States Parties to help it carry out functions and tasks, it also relies on those States to help it protect the human rights (potentially) affected by these functions. In this way the situations of the first category come to involve multiple actors in human rights protection.

The second category covers situations in which, by virtue of the fact that the ICC is situated and conducts activities on the territory of the Netherlands, its host State, the latter becomes involved in the protection of the human rights of individuals present at the seat of the Court. An example of how this occurs is as follows: witnesses who come to the ICC to provide testimony in ICC trials may require protection from reprisals. Generally speaking, responsibility for protecting witnesses falls to the ICC. However, there have been instances where, not trusting the ICC to fully protect them, witnesses have applied to the Dutch authorities for asylum once they arrived on the territory of the Netherlands (as was the case with the detained witnesses from the DRC). In so doing, these witnesses engaged the obligations of the Netherlands under international human rights and refugee law, resulting in a situation where both the Netherlands and the ICC became involved in protecting the witnesses from harm.

These two categories of situation, while being dissimilar in many ways, have an important commonality: they encompass instances where multiple actors are involved in protecting the human rights of individuals caught up in ICC proceedings. Each situation will engage a complex web of obligations and responsibilities that overlap and interact.

The involvement of multiple actors in human rights protection can give rise to a unique set of problems. The precise contours of these problems will differ from one situation to another, depending on the factual circumstances and on the different obligations (or lack thereof, as the case may be) and attitudes of the actors involved. The problems range from a lack of clarity about the existence and content of obligations, to deliberate avoidance of obligations, to a lack of relevant obligations. Despite these differences, the problems encountered in situations of multi-actor human rights protection at the ICC can generally be characterised as either implementation problems or structural problems.

The term 'implementation problem' describes a set of circumstances in which there will be a higher chance than normal that an actor (or actors) will fail to implement an obligation. As the obligation will have a direct or indirect effect on human rights protection, this failure to implement can have a negative effect on an individual's human rights. Two prominent causes of implementation problems in situations of multi-actor human rights protection at the ICC are a lack of clarity about the obligations, and/or deliberate 'buck passing'.

Beginning with the issue of clarity, if an actor is not clear on what the law requires and what protection it is required to provide, the actor may fail to properly perform its obligations, to the detriment of an individual's rights. As multi-actor situations can be particularly complex, with different sets of obligations and different actors, this is a highly plausible problem. Consider the following: when a State carries out an arrest on the ICC's behalf, certain safeguards must be provided. The ICC might assume that the arresting State will check whether human rights protections were provided during the arrest, whereas the State might assume that this role falls instead to the ICC. The result of this confusion can be a failure to guarantee the human rights of the suspect. While the problem of obligations being improperly implemented is not exclusive to multi-actor situations, the complexity resulting from the involvement of multiple actors in these situations makes clarity more elusive, and ambiguity more likely.

The implementation issues associated with a lack of clarity are generally not deliberate; 'buck passing', however, is a more cynical implementation problem. Here the actors, instead of being unclear as to what they must do and when, use the fact that there is another actor who also has an obligation to justify refraining from acting themselves: 'why should I be the one to act, if the other actor is also obliged to do so? Why should the other not act instead?'[4]

The circumstances in which buck passing can occur arise when two or more actors have, at the same time, obligations relating to the protection of an individual. The precise content of the obligation need not be identical, just that the protective actions of one actor would render action by the other unnecessary. The situation described at the start of this Introduction, of ICC witnesses seeking asylum in the Netherlands, provides a helpful illustration. The ICC has an obligation to protect all witnesses involved in ICC proceedings; the Netherlands has an obligation, under human rights law and refugee law, to not remove individuals from its territory if to do so would place them at risk of harm. If the ICC performs its obligation, it renders protective action by the Dutch State unnecessary, because the witnesses' rights are safeguarded, and vice versa. This overlap creates a situation in which the ICC and the Netherlands could potentially both attempt to avoid complying with their obligations by claiming that the other should be the one to act. The result can be that neither will protect the witness. Buck passing in these circumstances is by no means inevitable, but it is a possibility that the law at present cannot prevent and has no tools to deal with.

Structural problems occur when the multi-actor nature of a situation produces a gap in legal protection. Such gaps arise in situations where the ICC needs assistance to safeguard human rights, but there is no corresponding obligation on any State to provide this assistance. In these circumstances, the ICC is the only actor with an obligation to protect a right, but because of its institutional structure, it lacks the legal or factual capacity to do so. The result is a gap in protection. The situation of interim release illustrates this scenario well. An important safeguard of the right to liberty and the presumption of innocence is that individuals accused of a criminal offence should not be remanded in custody unless the circumstances so warrant. These circumstances may include flight risk or a risk that the accused would interfere in the investigation. The ICC, for its part, has an obligation that reflects this. However, the ICC does not itself possess a territory into which accused can be released when

---

[4] In psychology literature, this phenomenon has been termed 'diffused responsibility', denoting that the existence of multiple potentially responsible actors decreases the likelihood that any will act. John Darley and Bibb Latane, 'Bystander Intervention in Emergencies: Diffusion of Responsibility' (1968) 8 *Journal of Personality and Social Psychology*, 377.

they are granted interim release; for this, the ICC is dependent on States for assistance. For their part, States have no obligation to assist the Court by accepting onto their territory accused persons granted interim release. Such assistance must be rendered voluntarily. The result can be that an accused who is entitled to interim release may have to remain detained.

The chapters of Part I and Part II of this book set about disentangling the obligations and responsibilities incumbent upon each actor in different situations of multi-actor human rights protection at the ICC. Doing so leads to three overarching insights. The first is that the involvement of multiple actors in the work of the ICC can render human rights protection at the Court particularly complex. In some cases this complexity can be unpicked by examining the legal framework in detail, whereas in other situations the unpicking reveals that the legal framework is itself the problem. The second insight is that the multi-actor nature of human rights protection at the ICC has the potential to lead to problems in the protection of these rights, including to the extent that rights are left unprotected. That being said, while the potential for problems is there, it is not inevitable that concrete negative effects will arise for individuals in every situation. In many instances, cooperation and protection proceeds smoothly. However, in order to mitigate and prevent potential problems, it is important to understand how and when they might arise. This awareness is the foundation for the third insight of this book, namely that through changes in the approach to the applicable law – some big, some small – and institutional innovations, the challenges of multi-actor human rights protection at the ICC could be overcome. This is addressed in Part III.

0.2 Approach and Structure

The book is divided into three parts, and the first two parts reflect the two categories of situations identified in Section 0.1. Part I comprises the situations involving the ICC and States Parties, and Part II comprises the situations involving the ICC and its host State. Before delving into the particularities of these situations, Chapter 1 discusses, at a general level, the human rights obligations of the ICC both under the Rome Statute and other ICC documents, as well as under general international law more broadly. The obligations discussed in Chapter 1 are of relevance for both Part I and Part II, and as such are placed at the beginning.

Part I and Part II follow the same overall structure. They each begin with one general chapter followed by two substantive chapters. For Part I the general chapter is Chapter 2, which describes the sources of human rights obligations of State Parties. For Part II the general chapter is Chapter 5, which concerns the sources of the human rights obligations of the ICC host State.

Following these general chapters, each Part contains two substantive chapters that analyse specific situations of multi-actor human rights protection, and in particular, situations concerning ICC witnesses and accused. Witnesses and accused are the focus of this book because it is in relation to these individuals that most situations of multi-actor human rights protection arise. To the extent that multiple actors may be involved in protecting victims participating in ICC proceedings, the relevant framework is the same as that for witnesses, and so separate consideration is not needed. Situations involving multi-actor protection of accused are discussed in Chapters 3 and 6, while situations involving witnesses are discussed in Chapters 4 and 7.

The structure employed to analyse the situations of multi-actor human rights obligations in the substantive chapters is the same throughout the book. Following an introduction, each section discusses first the obligations of the ICC, and second the obligations of either the State Party or the host State, depending on whether the chapter is under Part I or Part II. The discussion of obligations is not all encompassing, in the sense that it does not purport to be a comprehensive description of the entirety of the obligations incumbent on each actor in a particular situation. Instead, the discussion is focused on setting out the obligations that relate to the protection of human rights. For an obligation to fall into this category, it may be phrased in human rights terms – such as 'the accused must be given a fair trial' – but it need not be. The only requirement is that the obligation be directly or indirectly relevant to protecting a witness or accused's human rights.

In each of the examined situations, a myriad of individual rights can be affected, the particularities of which will naturally depend on the specific circumstances. Taking witness protection as an example, when a witness is in such danger that they need to be relocated to a safe third State, their right to life and to protection from inhuman treatment is clearly at stake. However, given that their relocation can mean separation from family members, the right to family life is also engaged. It was not feasible to undertake an analysis of all potentially affected rights. Instead, the choice was made to concentrate on the right most likely to be compromised in a given case; the right which would always be at risk regardless of the particular circumstances of the individual. For instance, because arrest will always restrict an individual's liberty, the right focused on for that stage of proceedings is the right to liberty. The result of this delimitation is a focus on four human rights overall: the right to liberty, the right to a fair trial, the right to protection from torture, inhuman and degrading treatment and punishment, and the right to life.

Once the obligations of the actors to protect a given right (or rights) are set out, the analysis in each section of the substantive chapters identifies the problems for human rights protection that may arise as a result of the involvement of multiple actors. By looking at the totality of the obligations relevant in a multi-actor situation, potential implementation and structural problems that would affect human rights protection can be identified and discussed.

Concluding the book is Part III. This part contains a series of proposals to mitigate the negative effects that the involvement of multiple actors has on human rights protection (Chapter 8), covering proposals relating to changes in the law, changes in the way the law is interpreted, and the introduction of institutional mechanisms. Chapter 9 is the concluding chapter.

1

The Human Rights Obligations of the ICC

When examining multi-actor human rights protection at the International Criminal Court (ICC), there is one constant: the ICC itself. Part I of this book considers situations involving States Parties, and Part II situations involving the ICC's host State; the ICC is present in all situations. As such, the sources of the ICC's human rights obligations are considered prior to, and outside of, the three-Part arrangement that structures the rest of this book.

In Part I and Part II, the discussion will zoom in on specific ICC obligations applicable in situations of multi-actor human rights protection. The purpose of the present chapter is broader, and instead generally sets out the sources of the ICC's obligations. The aim is not to comprehensively address the full range of ICC obligations, but rather to identify the sources of the ICC's human rights obligations in particular, and to explain which sources of law will be most relevant in the chapters that follow.

The chapter is divided into obligations arising *within* the Rome Statute protection framework and obligations arising *beyond* this framework, a distinction that will be used throughout this book, including with respect to the obligations of ICC States Parties and the ICC host State. The term 'Rome Statute protection framework' is a collective term encompassing the Rome Statute, the instruments that derive their binding force from the Rome Statute (including the Rules of Procedure and Evidence (RPE), the Regulations of the Registry, and the Regulations of the Court), and agreements made between the ICC and States (such as the Headquarters Agreement, agreements on the protection of witnesses, and agreements on the enforcement of sentences). Obligations that stem from these sources will be termed obligations arising within the Rome Statute protection framework. Obligations arising from other sources, such as international human rights law treaties, domestic law, etc., are said to arise beyond the Rome Statute protection framework.

The distinction between sources is drawn, in large part, for the sake of analytical clarity. It allows the different obligations to be separated out and allows for an understanding of how the different obligations might contribute to, or mitigate, problems in human rights protection. However, there is a further reason. All obligations arising within the Rome Statute protection framework are subject to Article 21(3) of the Rome Statute which, as will be discussed in Section 1.1, is of importance for understanding the nature and content of the human rights obligations of the ICC, States Parties, and the ICC host State. Obligations arising beyond the Rome Statute protection framework are not subject to the same interpretative requirements.

1.1 Within the Rome Statute Protection Framework

The Rome Statute tells readers specifically where to look to find the obligations of the ICC. Article 21 dictates the law to be applied by the Court, and was one of the innovative developments of the Rome Statute. Article 21 states as follows:

1. The Court shall apply:
   a. In the first place, this Statute, Elements of Crimes and its Rules of Procedure and Evidence;
   b. In the second place, where appropriate, applicable treaties and the principles and rules of international law, including the established principles of the international law of armed conflict;
   c. Failing that, general principles of law derived by the Court from national laws of legal systems of the world including, as appropriate, the national laws of States that would normally exercise jurisdiction over the crime, provided that those principles are not inconsistent with this Statute and with international law and internationally recognized norms and standards.
2. [...]
3. The application and interpretation of law pursuant to this article must be consistent with internationally recognized human rights, and be without any adverse distinction founded on grounds such as gender as defined in article 7, paragraph 3, age, race, colour, language, religion or belief, political or other opinion, national, ethnic or social origin, wealth, birth or other status.

By setting out in detail the law to be applied by the ICC, the aim of Article 21 was to increase legal certainty by restricting judicial discretion.[5] Although the provision's complexity and ambiguity means that this goal was only partly achieved,[6] Article 21 provides a useful structure for examining the human rights obligations of the ICC within the Rome Statute protection framework. This section will work through Article 21, considering whether the Court is bound to apply human rights law under its different subparagraphs.[7]

Not only did Article 21 set out the sources of applicable law for the ICC, it also established a hierarchical relationship between them. As one might expect, Article 21(1)(a) stipulates that 'in the first place' the Court must apply the 'internal' sources of law:[8] the Rome Statute, the Elements of Crimes, and the RPE. Within these instruments there are a number of important provisions detailing the ICC's obligations to protect human rights. One clear example is Article 55, which lists a number of rights for suspects that must be respected during an investigation, including the right to an interpreter and the right to remain silent. Another example is Article 67 which, mirroring Article 14 of the International Covenant on Civil and Political Rights (ICCPR), lists the rights of an accused during trial, including to be tried without undue delay and to adequate time and facilities to prepare a defence. Of a more general character is Article 64(2), which imposes on the ICC the overarching human rights obligation to 'ensure that a trial is fair and expeditious and is conducted with full respect for the rights of the accused'. In addition to the provisions that are phrased in human rights terms, there are provisions that safeguard rights more indirectly, such as Article 40 on the principle of the independence of ICC judges. Even though they are not listed in Article

---

[5] Gudrun Hochmayr, 'Applicable Law in Practice and Theory: Interpreting Article 21 of the ICC Statute' (2014) 12 *Journal of International Criminal Justice*, 655, 656; Leena Grover, 'A Call to Arms: Fundamental Dilemmas Confronting the Interpretation of Crimes in the Rome Statute of the International Criminal Court' (2010) 21 *European Journal of International Law*, 543, 559.

[6] Hochmayr, 'Applicable Law in Practice and Theory', 656; see further Robert Cryer, 'Royalism and the King: Article 21 of the Rome Statute and the Politics of Sources' (2009) 12 *New Criminal Law Review*, 390, who argues that the distrust of judges that led to the inclusion of Article 21 has resulted in distorted definitions of the ICC crimes.

[7] For many parts of this chapter I am greatly indebted to the work of Krit Zeegers. The research in chapters 2 and 3 of his book entitled Krit Zeegers, *International Criminal Tribunals and Human Rights Law: Adherence and Contextualisation*, International Criminal Justice Series (T. M. C. Asser Press, 2016) has been instrumental and provides the basis on which much of this section of the chapter is written.

[8] For example, Hochmayr, 'Applicable Law in Practice and Theory', 656; Gilbert Bitti, 'Article 21 and the Hierarchy of Sources of Law before the ICC' in Carsten Stahn (ed.), *The Law and Practice of the International Criminal Court* (Oxford University Press, 2015), 411, 414; Zeegers, International Criminal Tribunals and Human Rights, 65.

21(1)(a), the author considers that the Regulations of the Court and the Regulations of the Registry should also be considered internal law, and applied 'in the first place', as long as they are read subject to the Statute and RPE.[9]

One tier down in the hierarchy, and to be applied 'in second place' and 'where appropriate', are the sources listed in Article 21(1)(b): applicable treaties and the principles and rules of international law. These are 'external' sources of law. As to applicable treaties, this clearly includes treaties to which the ICC is a party, such as the Headquarters Agreement with the Netherlands, and the relationship agreement with the United Nations.[10] The Vienna Convention of the Law of Treaties 1969 (VCLT), in particular Articles 31 and 32, has also been found to be 'applicable' in this sense.[11] Beyond this though, it is not obvious what makes a treaty 'applicable', and whether the Court can apply human rights treaties under this provision. When the provision was drafted, a change was made from 'relevant treaties' to 'applicable treaties',[12] which could indicate that a narrower approach was preferred. One suggestion is that a human rights treaty is applicable if the State with respect to which the ICC is exercising jurisdiction has ratified it. However, as Zeegers points out, this would give rise to problems regarding the equality of ICC defendants from different countries.[13] Another suggestion is that

---

[9] In this respect, the author agrees with authors such as Hochmayr (Hochmayr, 'Applicable Law in Practice and Theory', 660) and deGuzman (Margaret deGuzman, 'Article 21: Applicable Law' in Otto Triffterer and Kai Ambos (eds.), *Rome Statute of the International Criminal Court: A Commentary* (C. H. Beck, 2016), 933). The Regulations of the Court were adopted pursuant to Article 52 Rome Statute, and importantly for this study, contain provisions relevant to interim release. The Regulations of the Registry were adopted pursuant to Rule 14 RPE, and contain provisions relevant to the protection of witnesses. Article 52(1) and Rule 14(1) stipulate that both sets of Regulations must be read subject to the Rome Statute and the RPE.

[10] William Schabas, *The International Criminal Court: A Commentary on the Rome Statute* (Oxford University Press, 2010), 390.

[11] *The Prosecutor v. Germain Katanga*, ICC-01/04-01/07-3436-tENG, Judgment Pursuant to Article 74 of the Statute, 7 March 2014 (Trial Chamber II) §43. Although the Trial Chamber does not explicitly state that the VCLT is an applicable treaty pursuant to Article 21(1)(b), Hochmayr offers a convincing explanation of why this is the case (Hochmayr, 'Applicable Law in Practice and Theory', 667).

[12] Zeegers, International Criminal Tribunals and Human Rights, 68.

[13] Zeegers, International Criminal Tribunals and Human Rights, 69, footnote 116. Hochmayr also points out that 'the ICC does not derive its sanctioning powers from those States normally holding jurisdiction over the case. Thus the criterion cannot depend on which treaties these States have ratified' (Hochmayr, 'Applicable Law in Practice and Theory', 666).

a treaty's applicability turns on the appropriateness of its application, as the wording of Article 21(1)(b) suggests. This is a matter left to the discretion of judges, and with respect to human rights treaties, it will depend on the substantive relevance of the standards set out in the treaty in question.[14]

Turning to what is encompassed by the term 'principles and rules of international law' in Article 21(1)(b), there is also a degree of ambiguity. A common approach among a number of academics is to see this as referring to international law generally, including customary law and general principles.[15] Rule 72 *bis* of the Rules and Procedure and Evidence of the Special Court of Sierra Leone (SCSL), which was passed after the Rome Statute and is said to be modelled on Article 21 of the Statute, is more specific, and refers to 'applicable treaties and the principles and rules of international customary law'. In line with this approach, where human rights constitute custom, the ICC could apply them under this provision.

Yet another tier down in the hierarchy, and to be applied only if the sources in subparagraphs (a) and (b) do not yield an answer, Article 21(1)(c) empowers the ICC to apply 'general principles of law derived by the Court from national laws of legal systems of the world'. The provision is the 'awkward' result of compromise during the drafting process,[16] and leaves a clear potential for overlap between the principles referred to in (b) and those referred to in (c). This problem can be averted if (b) is deemed to refer to international law principles, and (c) to principles derived from a comparative study of national law. This seems to be supported by the wording of Article 21(1), academic commentary,[17] and the drafting history.[18] While it remains to be seen whether this provision will be used to import human rights into the law and practice of the ICC, it is certainly a possibility.

---

[14] Sergey Vasiliev, *International Criminal Trials: A Normative Theory* (Academisch Proefschrift, 2014), 105.

[15] DeGuzman provides an overview of different scholars who share this view (deGuzman, 'Article 21', 939) as does Zeegers (Zeegers, International Criminal Tribunals and Human Rights, 70, footnote 121).

[16] DeGuzman, 'Article 21', 942.

[17] Raimondo lists a number of these scholars. See Fabian Raimondo, *General Principles of Law in the Decisions of International Criminal Courts and Tribunals* (Academisch Proefschrift, 2007), 45.

[18] Zeegers explains that during the drafting process the Working Group stated that the phrase 'international law' in Article 21(1)(b) should be understood to mean public international law (Zeegers, International Criminal Tribunals and Human Rights, 69).

It is clear from this discussion of Article 21 that a number of questions surrounding Article 21(1)(b) and (c) remain unanswered. This is perhaps exacerbated by the fact that the Court refers to sources of law without explaining under which section of Article 21(1) it is doing so.[19] While it is desirable that these questions be addressed, it is not necessary to consider them in detail here, given that Article 21(3) provides a necessary and sufficient gateway for the application of human rights in the multi-actor situations to be addressed in the following chapters.

Article 21(3) requires that 'the application and interpretation of law pursuant to this article must be consistent with internationally recognised human rights', and for those endeavouring to interpret the Rome Statute protection framework the provision is both a great ally and a challenging nemesis. By academics it has been described variously as 'one of the more important provisions of the Rome Statute',[20] with 'significant potential in shaping the practice before the ICC', yet somewhat 'mind-boggling'.[21] Its importance quickly became clear in ICC case law, with Article 21(3) being invoked – among other things – to broaden the notion of victims who can participate in proceedings to include deceased victims,[22] allow a stay of proceedings when a fair trial cannot be achieved,[23] and compel the Court to fund family visits for indigent defendants.[24] And yet, the provision has also given rise to contrasting academic opinion, particularly with respect to how its various vague terms – 'application', 'interpretation', 'consistent', 'internationally recognised' – should be understood in practice.[25]

---

[19] Zeegers, *International Criminal Tribunals and Human Rights*, 71.
[20] DeGuzman, 'Article 21', 948.
[21] Vasiliev, *International Criminal Trials*, 132; see generally Rebecca Young, '"Internationally Recognised Human Rights" before the International Criminal Court' (2011) 60 *International and Comparative Law Quarterly*, 189.
[22] *The Prosecutor v. Jean-Pierre Bemba Gombo*, ICC-01/05-01/08-320, Fourth Decision on Victims' Participation, 12 December 2018 (Pre-Trial Chamber III).
[23] *The Prosecutor v. Thomas Lubanga Dyilo*, ICC-01/04-01/06-1486, Judgment on the Appeal of the Prosecutor against the Decision of Trial Chamber I Entitled 'Decision on the Consequences of Non-Disclosure of Exculpatory Materials Covered by Article 54(3)(e) Agreements and the Application to Stay the Prosecution of the Accused, Together with Certain Other Issues Raised at the Status Conference on 10 June 2008', 21 October 2008 (Appeals Chamber) (*Lubanga*, 21 October 2008).
[24] *The Prosecutor v. Germain Katanga and Mathieu Ngudjolo Chui*, ICC-RoR217-02/08-8, Decision on 'Mr Mathieu Ngudjolo's Complaint under Regulation 221(1) of the Regulations of the Registry against the Registrar's Decision of 18 November 2008', 10 March 2009 (The Presidency) (*Katanga/Ngudjolo*, 10 March 2009).
[25] For an overview of different issues and opinions, see for example Young, 'Internationally Recognised Human Rights' and Sergey Vasiliev, 'Proofing the Ban on "Witness Proofing": Did the ICC Get It Right?' (2009) 20 *Criminal Law Forum*, 193, 214–19.

While there are a range of views on the precise place afforded to human rights in the Rome Statute protection framework, the author agrees with those who consider that Article 21(3) places human rights law in the position of *lex superior* as regards the rest of the sources in Article 21.[26] The formal hierarchy of sources set out in Article 21(1) is overlaid by another hierarchy, but this hierarchy is based not on the source of the law but on the subject matter of the norms.[27] In other words, Article 21(3) does not establish a hierarchy of sources, but a substantive hierarchy of norms.[28] This view of Article 21(3) is supported by the ICC Appeals Chamber: 'Article 21(3) makes the interpretation as well as the application of the law applicable under the Statute *subject to* internationally recognised human rights', with the consequence that 'human rights underpin the Statute; every aspect of it' (emphasis added).[29]

That Article 21(3) creates a *lex superior* has a number of consequences. Firstly, it means that if a written provision is capable of multiple interpretations, Article 21(3) requires that the interpretation that best protects human rights be preferred.[30] Secondly – and whether a provision is

---

[26] For example Alain Pellet, 'Applicable Law', in Antonio Cassese, Paola Gaeta, and John R. W. D. Jones (eds.), *The Rome Statute of the International Criminal Court: A Commentary* (Oxford University Press, 2002), 1051; Daniel Sheppard, 'The International Criminal Court and "Internationally Recognized Human Rights": Understanding Article 21(3) of the Rome Statute' (2010) 10 *International Criminal Law Review*, 43; Zeegers, International Criminal Tribunals and Human Rights; Schabas, A Commentary on the Rome Statute, 390; Hochmayr, 'Applicable Law in Practice and Theory'; Göran Sluiter, 'Human Rights Protection in the Pre-Trial Phase' in Carsten Stahn and Göran Sluiter (eds.), *The Emerging Practice of the International Criminal Court* (Martinus Nijhoff Publishers, 2009), 459. For opposing views, see for example Kenneth Gallant, 'Individual Human Rights in a New International Organisation: The Rome Statute of the International Criminal Court', in Mahmoud Cherif Bassiouni (ed.), *International Criminal Law – Volume II: Enforcement* (Transnational Publishers, 1999), 693; Gerhard Hafner and Christina Binder, 'The Interpretation of Article 21(3) ICC Statute Opinion Reviewed' (2004) 9 *Austrian Review of International and European Law*, 163; Joe Verhoeven, 'Article 21 of the Rome Statute and the Ambiguities of Applicable Law' (2002) 33 *Netherlands Yearbook of International Law*, 2.
[27] Pellet, 'Applicable Law', 1077.
[28] Zeegers, International Criminal Tribunals and Human Rights, 78.
[29] *The Prosecutor v. Thomas Lubanga Dyilo*, ICC-01/04-01/06-772, Judgment on the Appeal of Mr Thomas Lubanga Dyilo against the Decision on the Defence Challenge to the Jurisdiction of the Court pursuant to Article 19(2)(a) of the Statute of 3 October 2006, 14 December 2006 (Appeals Chamber) §37.
[30] Hochmayr, 'Applicable Law in Practice and Theory', 673; Hafner and Binder, 'Interpretation of Article 21(3)', 171.

capable of multiple interpretations or not – all interpretations of the applicable law must be subject to a compulsory review, to ensure that they are consistent with human rights. In this sense, Article 21(3) has been referred to as a 'mandatory principle of consistency'.[31] Throughout the present book, this is termed the 'Article 21(3) test', and is the final stage in the interpretative process for all obligations whose source is within the Rome Statute protection framework.

The third consequence of human rights being *lex superior* is that if, on applying the Article 21(3) test, it is found that a provision of the applicable law is not consistent with human rights, then adjustments must be made to make it so. For example, if a provision is phrased so as to give an actor *discretion* in whether to protect rights, Article 21(3) can require that this be interpreted as an *obligation* to protect rights. Sometimes the modifications made in order to ensure consistency with human rights are quite substantial. For this reason, Article 21(3) has been described as having 'generative powers', meaning that Article 21(3) empowers the Court to go beyond the provisions of the Statute, for example by creating a new procedural remedy. During the *Lubanga* trial, the Prosecution created a situation where full disclosure of exculpatory evidence to the Defence was hampered, as evidence had been given to the Prosecution on the basis of confidentiality.[32] Deciding that a fair trial was no longer possible, the judges of Trial Chamber I unconditionally stayed proceedings against the defendant.[33] Nothing in the Rome Statute protection framework mentions stay of proceedings as an available remedy.[34] However, the Appeals Chamber upheld the Trial Chamber decision, holding on the basis of Article 21(3) that not only was the Court

---

[31] Zeegers, International Criminal Tribunals and Human Rights, 78 (citing Vasiliev, 'Proofing the Ban', 216); Gallant, 'Individual Human Rights in a New International Organisation', 704; and Young, 'Internationally Recognised Human Rights', 207.

[32] The Prosecution had acquired evidence through Article 54(3)(e) of the Rome Statute, which permits confidentiality on the condition that the evidence is used solely for the purpose of generating new evidence.

[33] Trial Chamber I decided that the Prosecution had misused Article 54(3)(e), 'with the consequence that a significant body of exculpatory evidence which would otherwise have been disclosed to the accused is to be withheld from him' (*The Prosecutor v. Thomas Lubanga Dyilo*, ICC-01/04-01/06-1401, Decision on the Consequences of Non-Disclosure of Exculpatory Materials Covered by Article 54(3)(e) Agreements and the Application to Stay the Prosecution of the Accused, Together with Certain Other Issues Raised at the Status Conference on 10 June 2008, 13 June 2008 (Trial Chamber I) §§92–4).

[34] In the words of the Appeals Chamber: 'neither the Rome Statute nor the Rules of Procedure and Evidence provides for a "stay of proceedings" before the Court' (*Lubanga*, 21 October 2008, §77).

empowered to grant a stay where justice could not be done but that two types of stay were possible: permanent and conditional.[35] This has led at least one commentator to suggest that these powers arose entirely out of Article 21(3) and demonstrate judicial acceptance of the provision's generative effect.[36]

While the potential for Article 21(3) to expand human rights protection beyond what is contained in the Rome Statute protection framework is clear, the author would dispute the assertion that it can generate powers and/or remedies with no basis in the framework whatsoever. The remedy of stay of proceedings identified in the *Lubanga* decision, while not linked by either Chamber to a specific statutory provision, could arise out of an interpretation of Article 64(2) of the Rome Statute, which obliges the Court to ensure that the trial as a whole is fair.[37] Interpreting Article 64(2) in light of Article 21(3) could certainly lead to the remedy of stay of proceedings on facts such as those in the *Lubanga* case.[38] Allowing Article 21(3) to generate powers with no grounding whatsoever in the Rome Statute protection framework is not supported by the text of that provision, which refers to the 'interpretation and application of law'. Furthermore, in a previous decision, the Pre-Trial Chamber in *Lubanga* stated:

> The Chamber considers that prior to undertaking the analysis required by article 21(3) of the Statute, the Chamber must find a provision, rule or principle that, under article 21(1)(a) to (c) of the Statute, could be applicable to the issue at hand.[39]

---

[35] *Lubanga*, 21 October 2008, §§79–8. Trial Chamber I had ordered a permanent stay of proceedings and ordered that the accused be released. The Appeals Chamber substituted the permanent stay for a conditional once, and reversed the release order. The trial later resumed.

[36] Sheppard, 'Understanding Article 21(3)', 62.

[37] Vasiliev, 'Proofing the Ban', 218–19.

[38] Another case that is often cited in this regard concerned whether the Court was obliged to fund the family visits of indigent defendants detained at the ICC Detention Centre. The Presidency held that there was a positive obligation under the right to family life to provide this funding. However, this decision can also be formulated as Article 21(3) being used to add substance to certain provisions of the Regulations of the Registry that would not otherwise be there, rather than being a completely free-standing obligation (*Katanga/Ngudjolo*, 10 March 2009). See also chapter 8 of Denis Abels, *Prisoners of the International Community: The Legal Position of Persons Detained at International Criminal Tribunals* (T. M. C. Asser Press, 2012).

[39] *The Prosecutor* v. *Thomas Lubanga Dyilo*, ICC-01/04-01/06-679, Decision on the Practices of Witness Familiarisation and Witness Proofing, 8 November 2006 (Pre-Trial Chamber I), §10.

As such, it is proposed that the correct role of Article 21(3) is in adding human rights protections to existing provisions, and not in creating entirely new, free-standing obligations. That being said, there are key provisions in the Rome Statute that are sufficiently general that, as far as the ICC is concerned, this is not of great significance. As the substantive chapters will demonstrate, the same is not true when it comes to the obligations of States.

The fourth and final consequence of Article 21(3) placing human rights in the position of *lex superior* is that if a particular provision is not consistent with human rights, and cannot be made so through the process just described, then the Court cannot apply the provision at all. There is broad support for this position in academic literature,[40] and the ICC has taken this approach in practice. As will be discussed in Chapter 7, Trial Chamber II refused to apply Article 93(7) of the Rome Statute because on the facts it could not be applied in a manner consistent with human rights.[41]

There are, of course, a number of other issues surrounding Article 21(3) – the discussion so far does not purport to be a comprehensive examination of the provision. The focus has concentrated on those aspects of the provision that are most relevant to the present study. Issues such as how to determine which human rights are 'internationally recognised' are important,[42] but as few would contest that the rights included in this research[43] would meet any

---

[40] See Pellet, 'Applicable Law', 1079–81; Mahnoush Arsanjani, 'The Rome Statute of the International Criminal Court' (1999) 93 *American Journal of International Law*, 22, 29; and Sheppard, who states that 'even a conservative interpretation of the Article could support the proposition that, in the case of a conflict between the Statute and a human rights norms, the court could decline to apply the statutory rule' (Sheppard, 'Understanding Article 21(3)', 62). However, not all academics agree, see Hafner and Binder, 'Interpretation of Article 21(3)', 173–5.

[41] *The Prosecutor* v. *Katanga and Ngudjolo*, ICC-01/04-01/07-3003-tENG, Decision on an Amicus Curiae Application and on the 'Requête tenant à obtenir présentations des témoins DRC D02 P 0350, DRC D02 P 0236, DRC D02 P 0228 aux autorités néerlandaises aux fins d'asile' (Articles 68 and 93(7) of the Statute), 9 June 2011 (Trial Chamber II) (*Katanga/Ngudjolo*, 9 June 2011), §73.

[42] Judge Pikis did little to clarify the term when he said that internationally recognised human rights are those 'acknowledged by customary international law and international treaties and convention' (*The Prosecutor* v. *Thomas Lubanga Dyilo*, ICC-01/04-01/06-424, Decision on the Prosecutor's 'Application for Leave to Reply to "Conclusions de la défense en réponse au mémoire d'appel du Procureur"', 12 September 2006 (Appeals Chamber), §3). Zeegers provides a succinct overview of this debate at 91–9 (Zeegers, *International Criminal Tribunals and Human Rights*).

[43] The rights to life, fair trial, liberty, and protection from torture and inhuman and degrading treatment and punishment are common to all major human rights treaties and instruments.

definition of that term, further discussion of the complexities of Article 21(3) is left to other work.

1.2 Beyond the Rome Statute Protection Framework

As an actor on the international stage, the ICC does not operate in a legal vacuum. While the obligations that are found within the Rome Statute protection framework are the most pertinent, it is also relevant to consider any human rights law obligations that the ICC may have beyond the Rome Statute protection framework, under general international law.

In understanding the ICC's relationship with general international law, it is useful to take as a starting point the proposition that the ICC qualifies as an international organisation. While the ICC, being an international court, does not look like a traditional international organisation, it does possess the characteristics that are generally attributed to international organisations. In terms of the definition set out in the International Law Commission (ILC) Articles on the Responsibility of International Organisations,[44] the ICC meets the requirements of being established by treaty and possessing international legal personality. Its personality is explicitly provided for in Article 4 of the Rome Statute ('The Court shall have international legal personality'), and is confirmed by the fact that the ICC is capable of concluding international agreements with other international actors (both States and international organisations), and is granted privileges and immunities.[45] Furthermore, while some organs of the ICC may not be of a type we are familiar with in the context of international organisations (in particular Chambers and the Office of the Prosecutor), the Assembly of State Parties and the Presidency are organs that do not look out of place among the myriad of international organisations.

Understanding the ICC as an international organisation allows us to understand its position vis-à-vis international law more easily. It is a widely accepted proposition in practice and legal theory that international organisations are bound by international law.[46] Indeed, as Zeegers

---

[44] Article 2(a), 'Draft Articles on the Responsibility of International Organisations' (2011) Vol. II, Part 2, *Yearbook of the International Law Commission*.

[45] These being two of the four markers of international legal personality, see for example Dapo Akande, 'International Organisations', in Malcolm D. Evans (ed.), *International Law* (Oxford University Press, 2014), 248, 253–4; and James Crawford, *Brownlie's Principles of Public International Law* (Oxford University Press, 2012), 115–16.

[46] Zeegers, International Criminal Tribunals and Human Rights, 20; August Reinisch, 'The Changing International Legal Framework for Dealing with Non-State Actors' in Philip Alston (ed.), *Non-State Actors and Human Rights* (Oxford University Press, 2005),

points out, it is difficult to find evidence in practice or scholarship that contradicts this.[47]

The sources of obligations for international organisations are the same as those of States, namely treaties, customary international law, and general principles of law. As with States, international organisations derive obligations from treaties as a result of their membership of those treaties. The ICC is party to a number of treaties, for example the Headquarters Agreement with the Netherlands and the Relationship Agreement with the UN. However, since the ICC is not party to any human rights law treaties, we must look elsewhere to ascertain what human rights obligations the ICC has under general international law.

Unlike with treaty law, for other sources of international law there is no express basis for applicability to international organisations, and unlike with States, the role of international organisations in the formation of these types of law is a debated issue.[48] That being said, the proposition that international organisations are bound by general international law was clearly endorsed by the International Court of Justice (ICJ) in its *WHO/Egypt* Advisory Opinion:

> [i]nternational organisations are subjects of international law and, as such, are bound by any obligations incumbent upon them under general rules of international law, under their constitutions, or under international agreements to which they are parties.[49]

46; Philippe Sands and Pierre Klein, *Bowett's Law of International Institutions* (Sweet & Maxwell, 2009), 461; Andrew Clapham *Human Rights Obligations of Non-State Actors* (Oxford University Press, 2006), 65; Moshe Hirsch, *The Responsibility of International Organizations Towards Third Parties* (Martinus Nijhoff, 1995), 17; Henry Schermers and Niels Blokker, *International Institutional Law: Unity within Diversity* (Brill, 2011), 997; Olivier de Schutter, 'Human Rights and the Rise of International Organisations: The Logic of Sliding Scales in the Law of International Responsibility' in Jan Wouters, Eva Brems, Stefaan Smis, and Pierre Schmitt (eds.), *Accountability for Human Rights Violations by International Organisations* (Intersentia, 2010), 68.

[47] Zeegers, International Criminal Tribunals and Human Rights, 12. However, Zeegers does go on to note that 'many theories that justify the binding effect of international law vis-à-vis international organizations walk a thin line between the "is" and "ought" and fail to clarify the formal legal source of the obligations that they allege exist'.

[48] Kristina Daugirdas, 'International Organizations and the Creation of Customary International Law' (2018) University of Michigan Public Law Research Paper No. 597, available at http://dx.doi.org/10.2139/ssrn.3160229, last accessed 25 April 2019; Jean d'Aspremont and Sufyan Droubi (eds.), *International Organizations and the Formation of Customary International Law* (Manchester University Press, forthcoming 2019).

[49] *Interpretation of the Agreement of 25 March 1951 between the WHO and Egypt*, Advisory Opinion, ICJ Reports 1980, 20 December 1980, 73, §37.

General international law is understood to refer to the unwritten sources of international law, namely custom and general principles. It is to these that one must turn for applicable human rights law obligations.

The situations of multi-actor human rights protection examined in this book touch on four rights: the right to life, the right to a fair trial, the right to liberty, and the right to protection from inhuman treatment. These rights are included, without exception, in all the principal human rights law treaties, and in the Universal Declaration of Human Rights. To state that each of these rights is protected under customary international law is not a controversial proposition, and as such, the ICC is subject to international law obligations to protect these rights. What is less well accepted is the precise nature and scope of these obligations when they are applied to the ICC. As we will now examine, even though international organisations can be bound by general international law, the content of these obligations is not necessarily the same for organisations as it is for States.

1.3 The Limits of the ICC's Human Rights Law Obligations

The ICC is bound by human rights law, both under the Rome Statute protection framework and beyond it, but there are limits to these obligations that follow from the fact that the ICC is an international organisation and not a State. As the ICJ stated in the *Reparation for Injuries* advisory opinion: '[w]hereas a State possesses the totality of international rights and duties recognised by international law, the rights and duties of an entity such as the [UN] must depend on its purposes and functions'.[50] The ICJ's position supports a functional approach to the obligations of international organisations, support for which Zeegers discerns in the scholarship.[51] According to this approach, the only general international law obligations that bind international organisations are those that pertain to the functions exercised by that organisation. So, for example, the ICC is not bound by norms relating to drilling for oil on the high seas, because such norms are unconnected to its functions.

If an organisation's obligations are limited by its institutional *functions*, the logical corollary is that an organisation's obligations are also limited by its institutional *capacities*. This follows from the idea that there

---

[50] *Reparation for injuries suffered in the service of the United Nations*, Advisory Opinion, ICJ Reports 1949, 11 April 1949, 174.
[51] Zeegers, International Criminal Tribunals and Human Rights, 24.

is no obligation to do the impossible (*impossibilium nulla obligatio est*). In other words, an organisation can only be bound by obligations which it has the capacity to carry out. For instance, while the ICC may be bound by certain elements of refugee law, it cannot be subject to an obligation to actually host refugees in the way that States are, because it lacks the territory, and therefore the capacity, to do so.

The case law of the European Court of Human Rights (ECtHR) supports this position with respect to obligations under human rights law. In two cases involving Poland and Russia, defendants in criminal proceedings argued that their Article 6 right to a fair trial had been violated. Part of the evidence used in the trials was from witnesses who, at the time of the trials, could not be located. As such, the defendants did not have an opportunity to challenge the witnesses. The ECtHR held that the State's failure to secure the witnesses' presence at the trial was not per se a violation of the defendants' right to challenge adverse witnesses under Article 6, as long as the State had exercised its best efforts and due diligence to find the witness.[52] If the witness still cannot be found, the State cannot be obliged to do the impossible and produce the witness. The circumstances converted the State's obligation from an obligation of result (to produce the witness) to an obligation of conduct (due diligence and best effort).

In interpreting the ICC's obligations under the Rome Statute protection framework, this capacity limitation must be borne in mind. For an illustrative example we can consider the position of accused persons who are entitled to interim release. The right to liberty requires that, when an individual is arrested and charged with a criminal offence, they should only be detained prior to and during their trial if there are pressing reasons (such as the danger that the accused would abscond). Because an accused person is innocent until proven guilty, to keep them detained should be the exception and not the norm. The ICC is obliged to assess the situation of every accused person and determine whether they should be granted interim release or not. However, if the Court finds that the accused is so entitled, it is limited in its ability to secure interim release and by extension the right to liberty. The ICC does not have a territory of its own into which it could release the accused person temporarily, and is entirely reliant on States for assistance. There are two ways of interpreting the ICC's obligation in this case. Either, the Court has the obligation

---

[52] *Case of Mirilashvili v. Russia*, Application no. 6293/04, Judgment, 11 December 2008, §163; *Case of Biełaj v. Poland*, Application no. 43643/04, Judgment, 27 April 2010, §56.

to fulfil the right in the way a State would have to, and is responsible if it fails to do so; or the obligation is limited by capacity. In the former case, the ICC would be obliged to release the person even if no State came forward to host them; in the latter case the ICC would be obliged to exercise its best efforts to secure State cooperation and the interim release of the accused, but would not be responsible for breaching an obligation if these efforts ultimately failed. The latter approach is the one followed in this study: it best reflects the reality of international organisations' limited functions and capacities, and accords with the general notion of *impossibilium nulla obligatio est*.

This is not altered by Article 21(3). As noted in Section 1.1, the potential of Article 21(3) is significant, but it cannot change the fundamentals of the ICC's institutional capacities. Firstly, it cannot, for example, provide the ICC with a territory it does not have. Secondly, while it may be true that rights would be better protected if the ICC were under an unconditional obligation to secure them (in the sense that, at the very least, affected individuals would have an actor against which to bring a claim), Article 21(3) cannot alter key aspects of how international legal obligations work. This provision, while highly significant, does not alter the limitations to the ICC's obligations set out in this section.

1.4 The Approach to the ICC's Obligations Adopted in Parts I and II

To summarise the previous sections of this chapter, there are four bases on which the ICC has obligations under international human rights law:

i. Where a specific provision of the Rome Statute protection framework obliges the ICC to protect human rights (Article 21(1)(a));
ii. Where human rights law applies by means of Article 21(1)(b) and/or (c) of the Rome Statute;
iii. Where human rights law shapes the interpretation and application of the law through Article 21(3) of the Rome Statute;
iv. Where the ICC has human rights obligations under general international law.

The analysis of the ICC's obligations in Part I and Part II focuses on the obligations stemming from bases i) and iii). While the human rights obligations stemming from bases ii) and iv) will, at times, be important, in the situations of multi-actor human rights protection addressed in this book, they do not add to or alter the analysis of the ICC's obligations.

The sources of law in Article 21(1)(b) and (c) are of limited importance for two reasons. First, because the wording of Article 21 places them on the lower rungs of the hierarchy of sources, to be applied 'where appropriate' and only where the sources listed in subparagraph (a) do not produce an answer. Second, according to Pre-Trial Chamber I in the *Al-Bashir* case, the sources in Article 21(1)(b) and (c) are only to be used where there is a lacuna in the law that 'cannot be filled by the application of the criteria provided for in articles 31 and 32 of the VCLT and Article 21(3)'.[53] As far as the situations addressed in Part I and Part II are concerned, the times when Article 21(3) cannot provide an answer are those when no other source of law can either. This is because the lacuna exists due to a lack of capacity on the part of the ICC, and as the previous section explained, neither the sources listed in Article 21(1)(b) and (c), nor general international law, can be interpreted so as to oblige the Court to do something which it lacks the capacity to do. As such, the situations in which it would be necessary and appropriate to look at the sources in ii) and iv) are the situations where those sources will be of no assistance. The discussions that follow on the ICC's human rights obligations therefore centre around those found in the provisions of the Rome Statute protection framework, as interpreted and applied in light of Article 21(3).

1.5 Conclusion

The ICC is the central actor that is common to all situations of multi-actor human rights protection addressed in this book. Establishing the sources of the ICC's obligations, and the limits of these obligations, is therefore the logical first step. Obligations to protect human rights arise for the ICC in a variety of ways. Within the Rome Statute protection framework, Article 21 of the Rome Statute opens up many potential avenues for the ICC to apply human rights norms, and the normative hierarchy created by Article 21(3) ensures that human rights underpin all aspects of the Court's work. Beyond the Rome Statute protection framework, general international law contains customary human rights norms that bind the ICC as an international organisation, and so offers a further avenue for human rights to shape the work of the Court.

---

[53] *The Prosecutor v Omar Hassan Ahmad Al Bashir*, ICC-02/05-01/09-3, Decision on the Prosecution's Application for a Warrant of Arrest against Omar Hassan Ahmad Al Bashir, 4 March 2009 (Pre-Trial Chamber I), §126.

There is then, no shortage of bases on which the ICC can be said to be bound by obligations to protect human rights. However, the precise nature and scope of the Court's human rights obligations will inevitably be shaped by the limitations of the ICC's institutional capacity. Regardless of whether an obligation to protect human rights stems from within the Rome Statute protection framework or beyond it, and despite the far-reaching power of Article 21(3) of the Rome Statute, the ICC has no obligation to do the impossible. As a result, the substantive chapters that follow in Part I and Part II will describe a number of situations where the legal framework of the ICC stops short of providing comprehensive human rights protection for witnesses and accused. This, combined with the limitations on the obligations of States Parties to the Rome Statute (as will be discussed in Chapter 2), results in the existence of structural gaps in protection.

PART I

Multi-Actor Human Rights Protection

The ICC and States Parties

PART I

Multi-Actor Human Rights Protection

The ICC and Statte Parties

2

The Human Rights Obligations of States Parties to the Rome Statute

When States become parties to the Rome Statute, they signal their support for the global fight against impunity, and in so doing, accept that the time may come when they will play a role in this fight. This role can take the form of carrying out arrests on the ICC's behalf, conducting interrogations, collecting and handing over evidence, and protecting witnesses who testify in ICC trials. In order to form a full picture of how human rights are protected in situations involving multiple actors at the ICC, it is necessary to understand the States Parties' side of the story. Such is the aim of this chapter, which will set out the sources of obligations incumbent upon States Parties.

As was the case in relation to the ICC's obligations in Chapter 1, the purpose of this chapter is to identify, in a general way, the source of State Party human rights obligations. These sources will then be referred to in the substantive analysis of multi-actor human rights protection contained in Chapters 3 and 4. The focus on human rights obligations means that these sections are not a comprehensive inventory of all obligations that State Parties might have under different legal regimes, but are instead limited to those pertaining – whether directly or indirectly – to the protection of human rights.

States Parties have obligations arising both within the Rome Statute protection framework and beyond it, and these are considered in turn. Section 2.4 addresses the obligations of States that are not parties to the Rome Statute. While it is true that such States are not bound by the Statute, there are a number of situations where non-States Parties may become involved in the work of the ICC, and so may develop obligations that are connected to the Rome Statute.

2.1 Within the Rome Statute Protection Framework

The Rome Statute protection framework contains two types of human rights obligations applicable to States Parties: those expressly set out in the provisions of the framework itself, and those that result from the operation of the ICC cooperation regime. This section will address these two types in turn. Given the relevance of Article 21(3) whenever the Rome Statute protection framework is considered, this section concludes with an examination of the role of this article in this context.

2.2 Human Rights Obligations in Particular Provisions

The Rome Statute protection framework contains provisions that are especially designed to create obligations for State Parties to respect human rights. Article 55 of the Rome Statute, for example, enumerates the rights to be granted to persons during an investigation, including during an interrogation. The list of protections includes the right to an interpreter, to not be subject to arbitrary arrest, to remain silent, and so on. As will be elaborated on in Chapter 3, where a State Party is involved in the interrogation of potential suspects, it is required to secure the rights enumerated in Article 55. A similar arrangement can be seen in Article 59 of the Rome Statute, which requires that States protect the rights of suspects during arrest and surrender proceedings.

2.2.1 Human Rights Obligations and the ICC Cooperation Regime

In addition to provisions of the Rome Statute protection framework that expressly create human rights obligations for States in specific situations, obligations can also arise from the operation of the ICC cooperation regime. When States become parties to the Rome Statute, they agree to cooperate with the Court pursuant to the provisions in Part 9 of the Statute. Article 86 contains an overarching cooperation obligation: 'States Parties shall, in accordance with the provisions of this Statute, cooperate fully with the Court in its investigation and prosecution of crimes within the jurisdiction of the Court.' Article 87 bestows the corresponding authority on the Court to 'make requests to States Parties for cooperation'. When referring to State cooperation with the ICC, the language used refers to cooperation *requests*. However, the compulsory nature of these requests is evident from the wording of Article 86, as well as from the fact that a failure to comply with a cooperation request can result in a referral to the Assembly of State Parties (ASP) (Article 87(7)). Where the situation was referred to the ICC by the UN Security Council, the non-compliance is referred to the Security Council.

The content and framing of a cooperation request can result, directly or indirectly, in the creation of obligations for State Parties to protect human rights. For example, in relation to ICC witnesses, the Court may issue a general request to a State to protect the human rights of witnesses residing in its territory; alternatively, the ICC could issue a more concrete protection request, such as asking a State to post a police officer outside of a witness' home. The latter cooperation request does result, indirectly, in the protection of a witness' human rights, even though it is not explicitly framed in those terms.

The cooperation regime in Part 9 of the Rome Statute is relatively detailed. In addition to cooperation relating to arrest and surrender (for which provision is made in Articles 89, 91, and 92), Article 93 lists a range of other forms of cooperation that States may be asked to provide to the ICC, including the provision of documents, the protection of witnesses and victims, and the execution of searches and seizures. Article 93(1)(l) indicates that the list is not exhaustive, as it provides for cooperation in 'any other type of assistance' that could facilitate the investigation and prosecution of crimes within the ICC's jurisdiction.

Despite the non-exhaustive nature of Part 9 of the Statute, there are limits to the types of cooperation that the ICC can request, on a compulsory basis, from States Parties, even when it comes to cooperation in human rights protection. An attempt to draw the precise boundaries of Part 9 need not be made here; however, there is one particular limitation that is relevant to a number of the multi-actor situations addressed in Chapters 3 and 4: the cooperation provisions in Part 9 of the Statute cannot be used to impose an obligation on a State Party to allow entry of a non-national onto its territory.

The relevance of this limitation can be illustrated by the following example from ICC practice. For the period prior to the beginning of the trial of Jean-Pierre Bemba Gombo, Pre-Trial Chamber II determined that the accused should be granted interim release.[54] As such, it became necessary for the ICC to release Bemba from custody, which in turn required that a State be found willing to host him for the interim period. The only State that would be obliged to receive Bemba would be the

---

[54] *The Prosecutor v Jean-Pierre Bemba Gombo*, ICC-01/05–01/08–475, Decision on the Interim Release of Jean-Pierre Bemba Gombo and Convening Hearings with the Kingdom of Belgium, the Republic of Portugal, the Republic of France, the Federal Republic of Germany, the Italian Republic, and the Republic of South Africa, 14 August 2009 (Pre-Trial Chamber II) (*Bemba* 14 August 2009), 35.

Democratic Republic of Congo (DRC), as his State of nationality.[55] However, Bemba did not request release to the DRC, acknowledging that his release to an African country would cause concern because of his proximity to trial witnesses.[56] The States that Bemba did request interim release to[57] voiced 'objections and concerns' at the idea of hosting him,[58] and ultimately no State was found that was voluntarily willing to host him. As will be explained further in Chapter 3, there is no obligation in the Rome Statute protection framework, nor under general international law, that would oblige a State to accept an ICC accused granted interim release onto its territory. The question therefore arises whether the general cooperation obligations in Part 9 of the Rome Statute could form the basis for such an obligation.

If the ICC were to issue a binding cooperation request to a State, under Part 9, requiring it to accept a non-national onto its territory, this would involve the ICC exercising control over who can enter and reside on the territory of a State. Such a power would be a significant inroad into a core tenet of State sovereignty. While States are not precluded from granting this power to an international organisation, the intrusiveness of it would require express consent from the States involved. Interpreting the words 'any other type of assistance' in Article 93(1)(l) as bestowing on the ICC the power to interfere with State sovereignty in this way would exceed the consent of the States Parties. This is confirmed if one looks to the drafting history of Part 9. The whole of Part 9 was subject to great debate during the drafting of the Rome Statute, with some States not convinced that cooperation should be an obligation at all. The entire State cooperation regime was carefully negotiated in order to take into account State concerns about sovereignty.[59] In light of this history of delicate compromise, it would not be appropriate to interpret the Statute so as to create

---

[55] Paul Weis, *Nationality and Statelessness in International Law* (Sijthoff & Noordhoff, 1979), 45.

[56] *The Prosecutor v Jean-Pierre Bemba Gombo*, ICC-01/05–01/08-T-13-ENG, Transcript of proceedings, 29 June 2009 (Pre-Trial Chamber II), 23, lines 12–15.

[57] These States were Belgium, Portugal, France, Germany, Italy, and South Africa (*Bemba* 14 August 2009, 35).

[58] Jonathan O'Donohue, 'Conditional Release of Bemba Gombo? States object to cooperating with the conditional release of Jean-Pierre Bemba Gombo – another sign of a cooperation crisis?', Amnesty International (reposting from Coalition for International Criminal Court blog (no longer available)), 10 September 2009 available at www2.amnesty.se/icc.nsf/ffc3926fc473d909c12570b90033f05f/89bba55aea0 d9a4c0025763500516453, last accessed 26 April 2019.

[59] Schabas, A Commentary on the Rome Statute, 973.

onerous obligations on States that are not explicitly set out in the Rome Statute protection framework. As such, there is a limit to human rights protective obligations that can be generated using the Rome Statute cooperation regime.

Ultimately, the dilemma facing the ICC with respect to Bemba's interim release was resolved in this instance when the Appeals Chamber reversed the Pre-Trial Chamber's decision to grant said release.[60] However the situation did illustrate the problems that the multi-actor nature of human rights protection at the ICC can cause, and demonstrated that the cooperation regime in Part 9 of the Rome Statute was limited in its reach.

2.2.2 State Obligations and Article 21(3) of the Rome Statute

Wherever obligations under the Rome Statute protection framework are at issue, Article 21(3) of the Rome Statute comes into play. As established in Chapter 1, Article 21(3) requires that provisions of the Rome Statute protection framework be interpreted consistently with internationally recognised human rights. Just as when interpreting the obligations of the ICC to protect human rights, Article 21(3) can have an important effect on the scope of obligations for States Parties also. For example, the legal framework setting out the standard of human rights protection to be afforded to ICC suspects during an arrest are ambiguously formulated, such that it is not clear whether the relevant standard is to be derived from domestic law or international law. Reading the relevant provisions in light of the Article 21(3) consistency test requires, it will be argued in Chapter 3, that international standards be upheld and adhered to. This potentially expands the protective measures that States must put in place during an arrest.

While Article 21(3) can have far-reaching effects, it cannot be used to sidestep the limitations of the cooperation regime discussed in the previous section. It is true that the rights of accused granted interim release would be best protected if Part 9 of the Rome Statute were interpreted so as to allow the ICC to oblige a State to accept accused on its territory. This would avoid a situation such as Bemba would have faced, had the

---

[60] *The Prosecutor v. Bemba Gombo*, ICC-01/05–01/08–631-Red, Judgment on the appeal of the Prosecutor against Pre-Trial Chamber II's 'Decision on the Interim Release of Jean-Pierre Bemba Gombo and Convening Hearings with the Kingdom of Belgium, the Republic of Portugal, the Republic of France, the Federal Republic of Germany, the Italian Republic and the Republic of South Africa', 2 December 2009 (Appeals Chamber).

decision to grant him interim release not been reversed on appeal: that his right to liberty would be compromised because the interim release could not be implemented. However, as was set out in Chapter 1, Article 21(3) does not provide for the creation of entirely new obligations that have no basis in the Rome Statute protection framework. Furthermore, it cannot be used to sidestep the constraints of State consent. As was noted in Section 2.2.1, the intrusive nature of obliging a State to permit entry to a non-national, and the fact that this touches on a core element of State sovereignty, would require the express consent of States. As was the case with Part 9 therefore, there are limits to the obligations which can be read into the Rome Statute protection framework on the basis of Article 21(3).

2.3 Beyond the Rome Statute Protection Framework

Apart from obligations to protect human rights that a State may have under the Rome Statute protection framework, any individual on a State Party's territory is entitled to protection under general international law. A State must protect the human rights of all those on its territory and subject to its jurisdiction,[61] whether or not they are an ICC suspect or witness. States do not assist the ICC in a legal vacuum; when providing assistance to the ICC, their actions may activate other obligations the State has under international law, including human rights obligations. Therefore, to understand and disentangle the full range of obligations incumbent upon States in multi-actor situations at the ICC, it is essential to understand the human rights obligations that arise for States Parties beyond the Rome Statute protection framework.

Treaties and custom are the sources of international law from which the human rights obligations of States derive. The relevant treaties will differ depending on the State in question, but the four rights that are key to the issues explored in this book – the right to life, liberty, protection from inhuman treatment, and fair trial – are included in all major human rights treaties. Due to its wide ratification and universal nature, the International Covenant on Civil and Political Rights 1966 (ICCPR) is the human rights treaty most often referred to in this book when discussing the obligations of States Parties (and by extension, reference is made to the decisions of the Human Rights Committee). Even though the

---

[61] Article 2(1) International Covenant on Civil and Political Rights 1966: 'Each State Party to the present Covenant undertakes to respect and to ensure to all individuals within its territory and subject to its jurisdiction the rights recognized in the present Covenant.'

European Convention on Human Rights (ECHR) is a regional treaty, the case law of the European Court of Human Rights (ECtHR) contains important developments in human rights law that are influential beyond the borders of the Council of Europe. As such it is also referred to.

2.4 Obligations of States Not Party to the Rome Statute

By virtue of the principle that treaties do not bind third parties (*pacta tertiis nec nocent nec prosunt*), non-States Parties to the Rome Statute derive no benefit and undertake no obligations with respect to the ICC, whether human rights obligations or otherwise. That being said, there are three situations where non-States Parties may become involved in situations of multi-actor human rights protection, and for this reason, it is worthwhile to dedicate some attention to this group of States. The three avenues for involvement, and the associated obligations to protect human rights, are considered here in turn.

The distinction between obligations that arise within the Rome Statute protection framework and beyond it is less helpful when considering the obligations of non-States Parties. While non-States Parties to the Rome Statute always retain their general international law obligations to protect human rights, the following paragraphs highlight how the avenue through which a non-State Party becomes involved with the ICC can lead to different relationships between that State and the Rome Statute. A clear dichotomy between being bound by the Rome Statute and not bound by the Rome Statute is therefore harder to draw.

The first way in which non-States Parties may become involved in multi-actor human rights protection at the ICC is where they submit an Article 12(3) of the Rome Statute declaration accepting the Court's jurisdiction. Through this mechanism, States can accept the jurisdiction of the ICC over a situation on their territory without becoming parties to the Rome Statute.[62] The ICC has seen declarations of this type submitted by Ivory Coast, Uganda, Ukraine, and Palestine.[63]

Where a non-State Party becomes involved in multi-actor human rights protection at the ICC by means of an Article 12(3) declaration,

---

[62] While Article 12(3) uses the expression 'with respect to the crime' to denote what a non-State Party is accepting the ICC's jurisdiction over, Rule 44 RPE, as well as the practice of the Court, indicate that Article 12(3) is used to grant jurisdiction over a situation in the sense used elsewhere in the Statute, rather than over a specific crime (Schabas, A Commentary on the Rome Statute, 358)

[63] Schabas, A Commentary on the Rome Statute, 359

they agree to cooperate with the Court with respect to the subject matter covered by the declaration.[64] The terms of Article 12(3) stipulate that the State making the declaration 'shall cooperate with the Court without any delay or exception in accordance with Part 9'. The State would therefore not be bound by the Rome Statute as a whole, but would have the same cooperation obligations as a State Party with respect to the subject matter covered by the declaration.[65] As per Section 2.2.1, these obligations may include obligations to protect human rights.

The second way non-States Parties may become involved in the activities of the ICC is where the UN Security Council refers a non-State Party to the Court, thereby granting the latter jurisdiction. Provision for UN Security Council referrals is made in Article 13(b) of the Rome Statute, and requires the Council to act under Chapter 7 of the UN Charter. The situations in Libya and Sudan came within the Court's jurisdiction in this way.[66]

Where the UN Security Council refers a non-State Party to the ICC, the referring resolutions have to date always included an obligation on the referred State to cooperate with the Court.[67] The binding force for this cooperation obligation derives from the UN Security Council resolution – and by extension Chapter 7 of the UN Charter – rather than from Part 9 of the Rome Statute, although there is not thought to be a relevant difference between the content of the obligations.[68] By subjecting a non-State Party to cooperation requests from the Court, a Security Council referral also subjects the non-State Party to obligations to protect human rights that result from such requests. States other than the State that is the subject of the referral are encouraged by the Security

[64] Dominik Zimmerman (revised by Mark Klamberg), 'Article 12(3)' (Case Matrix Network), available at www.casematrixnetwork.org/cmn-knowledge-hub/icc-commentary-clicc/commentary-rome-statute/commentary-rome-statute-part-2-articles-11-21/, last accessed 24 April 2019.
[65] Zimmerman, 'Article 12(3)'.
[66] Libya referral: UN Security Council Resolution 1970 (2011), S/RES/1970 (2011), 26 February 2011; Sudan referral: UN Security Council Resolution 1593 (2005), S/RES/1593 (2005), 31 March 2005.
[67] Resolution 1970 on Libya: 'Decides that the Libyan authorities shall cooperate fully with and provide any necessary assistance to the Court and the Prosecutor' (operative paragraph 5); Resolution 1593 on Sudan: 'Decides that the Government of Sudan and all other parties to the conflict in Darfur, shall cooperate fully with and provide any necessary assistance to the Court and the Prosecutor' (operative paragraph 2).
[68] Dapo Akande, 'The Effect of Security Council Resolutions and Domestic Proceedings on State Obligations to Cooperate with the ICC' (2012) 10 *Journal of International Criminal Justice*, 299, 309–11.

Council to cooperate with the Court, but the respective resolutions each acknowledge that 'States not party to the Rome Statute have no obligation under the Statute'.[69]

Thirdly, a State may choose to become involved in human rights protection at the ICC voluntarily. An example of this occurred when, in March 2013, Bosco Ntaganda walked into the US embassy in Rwanda and handed himself in.[70] Ntaganda was by that time subject to two ICC arrest warrants. Neither Rwanda nor the United States are parties to the Rome Statute, and yet all actors cooperated so as to see Ntaganda transferred to the ICC within five days of his surrender. Given that Ntaganda was in their custody, those involved in his arrest and surrender were also involved in protecting the human rights affected by this process.

Where involvement with multi-actor human rights protection at the ICC arises from the voluntary action of a non-State Party, the obligations that result depend on the agreement reached between the Court and that State. Article 87(5) of the Rome Statute allows the ICC to invite a non-State Party to provide assistance on the basis of an ad hoc arrangement, an agreement between the ICC and the State, or 'any other appropriate basis'. Any obligations to protect human rights that may result depend on the content of these arrangements.

Outside of this section, non-States Parties to the Rome Statute are not afforded special consideration in the remaining chapters of this book. Where a non-State Party becomes involved with the ICC through the first or second avenue described in this section, their obligations connected to the Rome Statute are substantively the same as those of States Parties. Where a State becomes involved in the third way described in this section, the nature of the obligations depends on the agreements made between the ICC and the State. The ad hoc nature of this means that general conclusions cannot be drawn without access to these agreements. Finally, beyond non-States Parties' relationship to the Rome Statute, obligations that arise under general international law are the same regardless of whether a State is a party to the Rome Statute or not, and so in this respect further consideration of non-States Parties is also not warranted.

---

[69] Operative paragraph of Resolution 1970 on Libya and operative paragraph 2 of Resolution 1593 on Sudan.

[70] Jenny Clover, 'Congo ICC war suspect surrenders at U.S. Embassy in Rwanda', Reuters, 18 March 2013; Emma Irving, 'The Surrender of Ntaganda to the ICC: A Story of Shared Responsibility Success', Shares Project Blog, 3 April 2013.

2.5 Conclusion

Understanding multi-actor human rights protection at the ICC begins with understanding, in a general sense, the sources of obligations of the actors involved. This chapter adds to the picture that was started in Chapter 1 (and which will be finished by Chapter 5) by identifying the sources of State Party obligations to protect human rights. Obligations arising within the Rome Statute protection framework stem from either specific statutory provisions or from cooperation requests issued by the ICC pursuant to its powers under Part 9 of the Rome Statute. In both cases, the obligations need not be framed directly in human rights terms, but rather can result in the protection of human rights more indirectly. Beyond the Rome Statute protection framework, States have a wide range of obligations to protect human rights, stemming from the variety of human rights law treaties and customary law norms.

Non-States Parties do not play a notable role in the analysis of multi-actor human rights protection undertaken in this book. While they do at times, and in different ways, become involved in the work of the ICC – and consequently in the protection of witnesses and accused before the ICC – the nature and scope of their obligations in these cases do not differ significantly from those of ICC States Parties. Detailed separate consideration of these States is therefore not necessary.

With the foundations in place, it is now possible to turn to the first substantive analysis of multi-actor human rights protection at the ICC. Beginning with suspects, accused, convicted, and acquitted, and moving on then to witnesses, Chapters 3 and 4 set out to disentangle the complex sets of obligations at play in multi-actor situations, and identify the problems that this complexity can cause for the protection of human rights.

3

Suspects, Accused, Convicted, and Acquitted

Once a person comes to the attention of the ICC as a potential perpetrator of international crimes, their association with the Court will move through a number of different stages. Initially, the person will be the subject of an ICC investigation, during which interviews and interrogations can take place. This is followed by the issuance of an arrest warrant, leading to the arrest and surrender of the person to ICC custody. The time between surrender to the Court and the start of the trial can be lengthy, meaning that the possibility of release pending trial must be considered. If at the end of the trial the person is convicted, they will be transferred to a State Party to serve their sentence; if the trial concludes in an acquittal, the person will be released from custody to continue on with their lives.

From this narrative, five distinct stages of proceedings can be discerned: investigation, arrest and surrender, interim release, enforcement of sentence, and acquittal and release. Each of these is a situation involving multiple actors, as each requires the involvement of both the ICC and States Parties. For an *investigation* to be effective in gathering evidence, identifying suspects, and acquiring information from suspects and witnesses, the ICC must work with the State in which the investigation is taking place. For suspects at large to be *arrested and surrendered* to the ICC for trial, the Court must ask States to carry out arrests on its behalf. For those individuals who are in custody to be granted *interim release* where appropriate, the ICC must secure the cooperation of a State willing to host the accused for the duration of their release. Where an accused is convicted, a State must be found that is willing to *enforce* the resulting custodial sentence. Where an accused is *acquitted and released*, a State must be found that is willing to allow them to enter and reside on their territory. These are all functions that the Court must carry out, and they all require the involvement of a State.

In each of these multi-actor situations, the actions undertaken by the ICC and States touch upon the human rights of the individuals concerned.

The interrogation of a suspect on the territory of a State engages the right to a fair trial. If fair trial is not respected at this early stage, it can cause irreparable harm to the fairness of the proceedings as a whole. For arrest and surrender and interim release the right to liberty is central. In any situation where an individual is being deprived of their liberty, the proper processes and procedures must be followed to ensure that the detention is neither arbitrary nor unnecessary. Where a convicted person is transferred to a State to serve their sentence, it is important to ensure that their detention complies with certain minimum standards, to ensure that they are not subject to inhuman treatment. Protection from inhuman treatment is also at stake for acquitted persons, as it can be challenging to identify a safe place for an acquitted person to reside once their involvement with the ICC concludes.

The remaining sections of this chapter examine each of the five situations in turn, setting out the obligations that the ICC and States Parties have to protect the rights affected in those situations. Following this discussion of obligations, each section will look at the potential implementation and structural problems that the multi-actor nature of the human rights protection can give rise to.

3.1 Interrogation

3.1.1 Introduction

Every criminal trial begins with an investigation. It is the time when ICC investigating teams are sent out to collect information, identify potential suspects, and gather evidence. An ICC investigation into a particular situation can be opened following a State or UN Security Council referral, or through the *proprio motu* powers of the Prosecutor.[71] By the twentieth anniversary of the Rome Statute in 2018, the ICC had investigated eleven situations.

Conducting investigations is a crucial function of the ICC, and yet a great many investigative activities cannot be carried out by the ICC acting alone. If the ICC requires a search warrant, official documents, or needs to interrogate a suspect, it must seek the assistance of the State Party where the investigation is taking place (hereafter the 'investigation State'). All these activities are intrusive and have the potential to compromise the human rights of the suspect. At this stage in proceedings, the most pressing human rights concern for many accused is the right to

---

[71] Article 13 of the Rome Statute.

a fair trial. Measures taken during this time can jeopardise the fairness of a possible future trial: 'the rights of the accused during the trial would have little meaning in the absence of respect for the rights of the suspect during the investigation'.[72] This is particularly true of the interrogation element of the investigation phase, when the suspect is particularly vulnerable[73] and a lack of safeguards can lead to self-incrimination. For this reason, and because the investigation stage in general would be worthy of an entire study in and of itself,[74] the focus of this section will be on the interrogation part of the investigative phase.

An important preliminary matter that must be addressed is whether fair trial protections apply to interrogations conducted during the investigation phase, at a time when a formal charge has not yet been brought. The issue is not without contention. Article 14(2) and (3) ICCPR list many of the substantive protections that make up the right to a fair trial (such as the right not be to compelled to testify against oneself, the right to an interpreter, etc.). These two paragraphs are prefaced with 'everyone charged with a criminal offence' and 'in the determination of any criminal charge' respectively, which points to the protections only being applicable once a charge has been brought. This is also true for the wording of Article 6 ECHR. However, the practice of the ECtHR does not endorse such an interpretation.

The ECtHR largely asserts the view that a lack of protection in the pre-trial phase renders trial protections meaningless.[75] It does acknowledge that not all of Article 6 ECHR can be relevant to the pre-trial phase, by which it is surely referring to rights very much linked to a charge, such as time and facilities for the preparation of a defence. With this caveat, the ECtHR jurisprudence supports the position that Article 6 is applicable to interrogations in the investigation phase if the fairness of the trial would otherwise be greatly prejudiced.[76] Building on this in the ICC context, De Meester uses the ECtHR case law to convincingly argue that Article 6(1)

---

[72] International Law Commission, 'Report of the Commission to the General Assembly on the work of its forty-fifth session' (1993) Vol. 2, Part 2, *Yearbook of the International Law Commission*, 113.
[73] *Case of Pakshayev v. Russia*, Application no. 1377/04, Judgment, 13 March 2014, §28.
[74] And indeed has been, although the focus was not on the multi-actor dimension of investigations: Karel de Meester, *The Investigation Phase in International Criminal Procedure: In Search of Common Principles* (Academisch Proefschrift, 2014).
[75] 'Guide on Article 6: Right to a Fair Trial (Criminal Limb)', European Court of Human Rights, 2014.
[76] *Case of Imbrioscia v. Switzerland*, Application no. 13972/88, Judgment, 24 November 1993, §36.

applies from the moment a person is considered a suspect by the ICC Prosecutor.[77] It is submitted that this is the correct stance; while not all fair trial protections can apply prior to a charge being brought, there are many that must apply. To find otherwise would contradict the often-pronounced notion that human rights should be practical and effective, and not merely theoretical or illusory.[78] As such, it is proposed that this approach is not limited to the ECHR, but applies to the right to fair trial more generally.

Having determined that fair trial protections apply to the interrogation phase, it is now possible to proceed to a discussion of the relevant obligations to protect this right. The two actors involved in this situation are the ICC and the investigation State. As the suspect is still on the territory of the investigation State (generally speaking), this is the only State involved. Following this discussion, the obligations as a whole will be considered in order to determine whether any problems arise as a result of the multi-actor nature of human rights protection at this stage.

3.1.2   Obligations of the ICC

The Rome Statute constituted an innovation in detailing the rights of persons under investigation; Article 55 is entirely dedicated to this.[79] While the Statute of the Special Tribunal for Lebanon (STL) (enacted eight years after the Rome Statute) also has detailed investigation stage rights, the Statutes of the International Criminal Tribunal for the Former Yugoslavia (ICTY), International Criminal Tribunal for Rwanda (ICTR), and the Special Court for Sierra Leone (SCSL) do not. Provision at these tribunals for rights at this stage was made in the RPE, and they were not as comprehensive as the Rome Statute.[80]

Article 55 is not phrased in terms of obligations, but rather in terms of rights for the individual suspect. The provision was designed to provide seamless protection for the suspect at all stages of the investigation.[81]

---

[77] de Meester, The Investigation Phase, 369.
[78] This is often said by the ECtHR. See for example *Airey* v. *Ireland*, Application no. 6289/73, Judgment, 9 October 1979, §24.
[79] Schabas, A Commentary on the Rome Statute, 684
[80] ICTY RPE Rule 42; ICTR RPE Rule 42; SCSL RPE Rule 42; STL Statute Article 15.
[81] Schabas, A Commentary on the Rome Statute, 685. Article 55 grants more than just the traditional fair trial rights. Article 55(1)(b) also prohibits the use of coercion, duress, or threats during the investigation, including any form of torture, cruel, inhuman, or degrading treatment. Also covered in Article 55(1)(d) is a prohibition on arbitrary detention or arrest. These additional protections, designed to enhance fair trial, are not replicated in the other international criminal tribunal statutes.

SUSPECTS, ACCUSED, CONVICTED, AND ACQUITTED 43

It is structured in a pyramidal way:[82] paragraph (1) grants rights to all persons involved in an investigation, and paragraph (2) grants additional rights to suspects in an interrogation. Together they cover all elements of fair trial that are relevant to this stage: right to counsel, right to an interpreter, right against self-incrimination, and the presumption of innocence. The latter right is supported in Article 55 through the right to remain silent. The obligations created by this article are those that correlate to the listed rights. For instance, the obligation correlating to the right to counsel is the obligation to ensure that the suspect has counsel present during an interrogation if they so choose.

In contrast to the *rights*-based phrasing of Article 55, the Rome Statute protection framework also contains provisions that are worded as *obligations* for the ICC. In connection with the right to legal assistance in Article 55(2)(c), Rule 21(2) RPE requires that the Registry keep a list of counsel from which the suspect can choose, and Rule 128 of the Regulations of the Registry (RoR) requires that the Registry assist any person to whom Article 55(2) applies and who is in need of legal assistance. Furthermore, Article 69(7) requires the ICC to deem inadmissible evidence collected in an interrogation that did not comply with Article 55, if the violation casts doubt on the reliability of the evidence, or if to admit the evidence would damage the integrity of the proceedings.[83] Such exclusionary measures have been taken at the ICTY, where an interview with Zdravko Mucić conducted by Austrian authorities was excluded because Austrian law did not allow for the assistance of counsel at the investigation stage.[84]

In some instances, the ICC will conduct the interrogation of a suspect alone,[85] in which case the only assistance that the ICC requires from the

---

[82] Salvatore Zappalà, 'International Criminal Proceedings, Investigation' in Antonio Cassese, Paola Gaeta, and John R. W. D. Jones (eds.), *The Rome Statute of the International Criminal Court* (Oxford University Press, 2002), 1200.
[83] Article 69(7) of the Rome Statute.
[84] Schabas, A Commentary on the Rome Statute, 689.
[85] At the ad hoc tribunals there was some disagreement on whether the test for labelling an individual as a suspect was objective or subjective (de Meester, The Investigation Phase, 364). If subjective, the determination would fall entirely to the discretion of the Prosecutor. The Rome Statute sidestepped this debate with the unambiguously objective wording of Article 55(2): a person is a suspect where 'there are grounds to believe that a person has committed a crime within the jurisdiction of the Court'. This provides a higher degree of protection for the individual because it is harder for the Prosecution to argue that the person was not a suspect at the time of the interrogation (Mihail Vatsov, 'Security Council Referrals to the ICC and EU Fundamental Rights: A Test for ECJ's Stance in Kadi I' (2012) 25 *Hague Yearbook of International Law*, 79, 87).

investigation State is a grant of permission to operate on its territory.[86] In these circumstances, the obligations of the Court are clear: the Court must be the one to ensure that the suspect is provided with all the necessary fair trial guarantees. However, when both the ICC and the investigation State have a role to play in an interrogation, the conduct required from the ICC is less clear. To show why this is the case, it is necessary to discuss the investigation State's obligations.

3.1.3 Obligations of States

As mentioned in Section 3.1.2, sometimes the extent of the assistance required from the investigation State is the granting of permission to operate independently on its territory. At other times, the State is more involved, either because it carries out an interrogation on the ICC's behalf, or because it conducts the interrogation alongside ICC staff members.

From the phrasing of Article 55(2), it is clearly envisaged that a State may carry out an interrogation on the ICC's behalf, and that when it does so, it must be the one to provide the Article 55(2) protections:

> Where there are grounds to believe that a person has committed a crime within the jurisdiction of the Court and that person is about to be questioned *either by the Prosecutor, or by national authorities* pursuant to a request made under Part 9, that person shall also have the following rights of which he or she shall be informed prior to being questioned. (emphasis added)

Article 55(1) does not begin as unequivocally, and does not specifically mention 'national authorities'. Instead it simply states '[i]n respect of an investigation under this Statute, a person', and lists the rights (including the right to an interpreter and the right not to be compelled to self-incriminate). This could mean that there is a deliberate difference between the two subparagraphs, and that the rights listed in Article 55(1) are always the responsibility of the ICC regardless of who carries out the interrogation. Alternatively, the difference could be attributed to the pyramidal structure of Article 55, and the fact that the first set of rights is of a more general nature that is always applicable, and the second set is specific to

---

[86] An example of such an arrangement can be found in a Cooperation Agreement between the DRC and the ICC Office of the Prosecutor (Judicial Cooperation Agreement between the Democratic Republic of the Congo and the Office of the Prosecutor of the International Criminal Court, 6 October 2004, Part 4, §19).

interrogations. There is little guidance on this question in the drafting history or practice; however, scholarly opinion supports the idea that when States carry out interrogations on the ICC's behalf, they must comply with Article 55 (even if the modalities of the interrogation are left to the State).[87]

In line with Article 21(3), where multiple interpretations are possible, the one that best protects human rights should be favoured. In this case that means interpreting Article 55, in its entirety, as imposing obligations on the investigation State to protect the listed rights whenever it conducts an interrogation on the ICC's behalf. This follows from the fact that the investigation State, as the actor in charge of the interrogation, is the one best placed to effectively protect the right to fair trial in those circumstances.

Turning to a different case scenario, one can imagine a situation where an ICC suspect is being interrogated, and both ICC and investigation State representatives are involved. For example, it could be that an ICC staff member is asking the questions, but an investigation State judge is present in the room. Or the investigator might be from the investigation State, but a member of the ICC Office of the Prosecutor (OTP) is present during the interrogation. In this multi-actor scenario, which actor must provide the Article 55 protections?

The wording of Article 55(2) suggests that which actor carries out the interrogation will be an 'either/or' situation: the suspect will be questioned '*either* by the Prosecutor, *or* by the national authorities' (emphasis added). The 'either/or' phrasing suggests that only one of the multiple actors should be responsible at any one time, and that it was not envisaged that both actors would have protection obligations simultaneously. One interpretation could be that the actor in charge of the interrogation – the one leading it – must provide the Article 55 protections. This has a certain common sense appeal: in charge of the interrogation, in charge of the protection. Militating against such an interpretation is the existence of Rule 21 RPE and Rule 128 RoR, which suggest that the ICC is always responsible when it comes to providing legal assistance. However, it is submitted that these rules should not be read too strictly, as it would also mean that the ICC should be solely responsible for legal assistance even when the investigation State is carrying out the interrogation autonomously. Article 21(3) does not provide any guidance as to which interpretation should be preferred, as in each of the alternatives the rights are

---

[87] de Meester, The Investigation Phase, 376–7.

protected one way or another. The author therefore proposes that obligations should concentrate in the actor leading the interrogation. Which actor this is will be determined on a case-by-case basis.

Moving to a different issue, where a State Party is carrying out an investigation entirely on its own behalf, and not as part of an ICC situation, Article 55 creates no obligations for that State (although, as noted later in this section, this is not say that the State has no obligations at all in this situation). This is so even if the suspect is also of interest to the ICC. The wording of Article 55 indicates this, and it has been confirmed in ICC practice. As Pre-Trial Chamber I held in the *Gbagbo* case, Article 55:

> must be understood to encompass any investigative steps that are taken either by the Prosecutor or by national authorities at his or her behest. Conversely, an investigation conducted by an entity other than the Prosecutor, and which is not related to proceedings before the Court, does not trigger the rights under article 55 of the Statute.[88]

If a State conducts an interrogation separately from any ICC investigation, and this interrogation did not comply with the requirements of Article 55, can evidence acquired from such interrogations be used in subsequent ICC proceedings? This potential loophole in fair trial protection is dealt with in Article 69(7), which declares evidence obtained in violation of internationally recognised human rights as inadmissible. Such was the situation in the *Katanga* case. Evidence had been obtained during an interrogation in which there had been a violation by national authorities of the suspect's right to remain silent. Even though this interrogation was unrelated to ICC proceedings, the violation contravened international human rights norms and the evidence was therefore inadmissible before the Trial Chamber.[89]

Both when a State conducts an interrogation independently, and when it does so at the behest of the ICC, it is bound by obligations stemming

---

[88] *The Prosecutor v. Laurent Gbagbo*, ICC-02/11-01/11-212, Decision on the 'Corrigendum of the Challenge to the Jurisdiction of the International Criminal Court on the Basis of Articles 12(3), 19(2), 21(3), 55 and 59 of the Rome Statute Filed by the Defence for President Gbagbo (ICC-02/11-01/11-129)', 15 August 2012 (Pre-Trial Chamber I) (*Gbagbo*, 15 August 2012), §96. Furthermore, in the *Katanga* case, Trial Chamber II noted that 'Article 55(2) does not impose procedural obligations on States acting independently of the Court' (*The Prosecutor v. Germain Katanga and Mathieu Ngudjolo Chui*, ICC-01/04-01/07-2635, Decision on the Prosecutor's Bar Table Motions, 17 December 2010 (Trial Chamber II) (*Katanga/Ngudjolo*, 17 December 2010), §59).

[89] *Katanga/Ngudjolo*, 17 December 2010, §§60–5.

from beyond the Rome Statute protection framework. States are bound by their obligations under international human rights law, whether contained in treaties or under customary international law. Article 55 is comprehensive in the safeguards it provides, and so human rights law does not add substantially to the protections that must be provided during interrogations to which that Article applies. However, where Article 55 does not apply, human rights law will supply the minimum standards that States must adhere to.

3.1.4 Problems in Human Rights Protection

The way that Article 55 is set up means that the obligation to provide human rights protection during an interrogation always falls to one actor, and one actor only. This is an appealing conclusion, as the fact that there is no overlap in the actors' obligations means that implementation problems such as buck passing should, for the most part, be avoided.

That being said, this stage of proceedings is not without difficulties. Even though the author has proposed that the actor leading the interrogation should be the one to provide the Article 55(2) guarantees, there is a lack of guidance in the law as to how the interrogation leader is to be identified. This means that, in the situation where both the ICC and the investigation State are involved in the interrogation, there is the potential for implementation problems to arise. If the actors are not clear between themselves as to who is in charge, then it will not be clear who is responsible for, inter alia, providing an interpreter, informing the suspect of the grounds to believe that they have committed a crime, informing the suspect of the right to remain silent, etc. On a more sceptical note, this ambiguity leaves space for the actors to deliberately obscure which one of them is in charge, in order to obscure who must provide the relevant protections. Either way, this state of affairs may leave the suspect vulnerable to violations of the right to a fair trial.

3.1.5 Conclusion

To successfully investigate crimes within its jurisdiction, the ICC requires the assistance and cooperation of the State within whose borders it seeks to investigate. When it comes to interrogating suspects, the degree of assistance required can differ. On the one hand, it could be that the ICC requires only the permission of the investigation State to conduct interrogations on its territory; with that granted, the ICC conducts the interrogation and is responsible for any human rights protections that may be required. On the other hand, the ICC may request more intensive assistance from the investigation State, ranging from asking the national authorities to be involved in the interrogation alongside the ICC, to asking the national authorities to carry out the interrogation on the ICC's behalf.

The right to fair trial is protected at this stage of ICC proceedings by Article 55 of the Rome Statute. This provision navigates the multi-actor nature of the situation by ensuring that regardless of which actor is interrogating a suspect, certain fair trial safeguards are provided. These protections represent a comprehensive protection of the right to a fair trial at the investigation stage. The actor that must provide these protections is the one that leads (i.e. is in charge of) the interrogation. Implementation issues may arise where the circumstances make it unclear who the leader is. If both actors assume that the other is leading the interrogation, then it is possible that neither actor will provide the necessary fair trial protections to the suspect.

Investigations and interrogations will lead the Prosecutor to a handful of suspects, those suspected of the greatest involvement and/or responsibility for the crimes. Where there are reasonable grounds to believe that an individual has committed a crime within the jurisdiction of the Court,[90] an arrest warrant may be issued, followed by a request to States to arrest and surrender the individual to the ICC.

3.2 Arrest and Surrender

3.2.1 Introduction

The arrest of an accused is a prerequisite for any ICC trial to take place;[91] however, it cannot be accomplished without the assistance of States. The Court lacks both the legal and factual capacity to arrest suspects itself; it does not have the power, either legal from the provisions of the Rome Statute, or factual in terms of resources, to send representatives into a State to carry out an arrest, and to do so would be a violation of State sovereignty. The ICC therefore relies on States to physically apprehend the subjects of ICC arrest warrants and surrender them to the Court. All States Parties of the ICC are under an obligation to comply with requests for arrest and surrender.

---

[90] Article 58(1)(a) of the Rome Statute.
[91] As per Article 63 of the Rome Statute, trials in absentia are not a possibility at the ICC.

Being involved in the arrest of suspects means that a State (hereafter 'the arresting State') is also involved in the protection of the rights affected by that arrest. Arrest signals the beginning of an individual's deprivation of liberty, making the right to liberty an important concern at this stage of proceedings. This right embodies the principle that a person should not be detained unless absolutely necessary and only following the proper procedures. The particular gravity of the crimes of which ICC suspects are accused does not justify any form of arrest or detention that does not respect international human rights law. The proper guarantees must at all times be afforded: suspects must be lawfully detained, informed of the reasons for the detention, brought promptly before a judge, be able to challenge their detention, and be afforded compensation where the deprivation of liberty was unlawful.[92]

Given the intrinsically multi-actor nature of the arrest and surrender stage of proceedings, it is pertinent to ascertain how the respective obligations of the arresting State and the ICC operate in this situation. In order to do so, this section deals with the two types of arrest that can be requested by the Court: standard arrest and provisional arrest.

With the exception of arrest and surrender, all the multi-actor situations analysed in this study begin with a discussion of the obligations of the ICC, followed by the obligations of States. For the present situation, it is helpful to invert this order. The arresting State is the principal actor here, carrying out the greater part of the relevant conduct. The obligations of the ICC are designed to complement the obligations of the State. As such, the obligations of the State will be considered first.

3.2.2 Obligations of States: Standard Arrest

Obligations relating to arrest and surrender are scattered in provisions throughout the Rome Statute protection framework.[93] Part 9 of the Rome Statute contains the articles that oblige States Parties to comply with an ICC request for arrest and surrender.[94] The wording of Article 89(1) makes this compulsory nature clear: 'State Parties *shall*, in accordance with the provisions of this Part and the procedure under their national

---

[92] Article 9 ICCPR.
[93] Bert Swart, 'Arrest and Surrender', in Antonio Cassese, Paola Gaeta, and John R. W. D. Jones (eds.), *The Rome Statute of the International Criminal Court* (Oxford University Press, 2002), 1688.
[94] For detail on the content of the duty to arrest and surrender, see Swart, 'Arrest and Surrender', 1680 onwards.

law, comply with requests for arrest and surrender' (emphasis added).[95] Such requests also fall under the general duty to cooperate in Article 86.[96] Several ICC decisions are evidence of the compulsory nature of this cooperation, with formal findings of non-compliance being issued against Chad, Malawi, and Kenya for their failure to arrest Omar Al-Bashir.[97]

In carrying out an arrest at the ICC's request, two provisions are relevant to protecting the arrested person's right to liberty: Articles 55 and 59(2) of the Rome Statute. Article 55 has been considered in detail in Section 3.1 in relation to interrogations, but also contains important right to liberty protections. Article 55(1)(d) states that an individual under investigation shall not be arbitrarily arrested or detained, imposing a corresponding obligation on States to refrain from doing so. While the title of Article 55 is 'Rights of persons during an investigation', it should be interpreted as continuing to apply during arrest proceedings. A person does not cease to be under investigation just because they are under arrest, and it is possible that more interrogations will be conducted. Scholarship supports this interpretation, which allows Article 55 and Article 67 (rights of an accused during trial) to provide seamless protection at all stages of proceedings.[98] This is also in line with Article 21(3).

---

[95] On this point, see Christopher Hall and Cedric Ryngaert, 'Article 59: Arrest Proceedings in the Custodial State', in Otto Triffterer and Kai Ambos (eds.), *Rome Statute of the International Criminal Court: A Commentary* (C. H. Beck 2016), 1462.

[96] Hall and Ryngaert, 'Article 59', 1462.

[97] For an overview of decisions up until December 2014, see Annex I of Assembly of States Parties, 'Report of the Bureau on Non-Cooperation', ICC-ASP/13/40, 8–17 December 2014. Some have resulted in legal findings of non-compliance, where the ICC held that the State was in violation of Articles 89 and 97 of the Rome Statute. On this see the Chad, DRC, and Malawi decisions: *The Prosecutor v. Oman Hassan Ahmad Al Bashir*, ICC-02/05-01/09-139, Decision Pursuant to Article 87(7) of the Rome Statute on the Failure by the Republic of Malawi to Comply with the Cooperation Requests Issued by the Court with Respect to the Arrest and Surrender of Omar Hassan Ahmad Al Bashir, 12 December 2011 (Pre-Trial Chamber I); *The Prosecutor v. Oman Hassan Ahmad Al Bashir*, ICC-02/05-01/09-151, Decision on the Non-Compliance of the Republic of Chad with the Cooperation Requests Issued by the Court Regarding the Arrest and Surrender of Omar Hassan Ahmad Al-Bashir, 26 March 2013 (Pre-Trial Chamber II); *The Prosecutor v. Omar Hassan Ahmad Al Bashir* ICC-02/05-01/09-195, Decision on the Cooperation of the Democratic Republic of the Congo Regarding Omar Al Bashir's Arrest and Surrender to the Court, 9 April 2014 (Pre-Trial Chamber II).

[98] Schabas, A Commentary on the Rome Statute, 685. See also Karim Khan, 'Article 60: Initial Proceedings Before the Court' in Otto Triffterer and Kai Ambos (eds.), *Rome Statute of the International Criminal Court: A Commentary* (C. H. Beck 2016), 1474.

Article 59(2) regulates the manner in which the State is to carry out the arrest, and does so by indicating the factors against which the domestic courts of the arresting State must review the arrest. The provision is crucial because it organises the relationship between the ICC and domestic authorities in arrest proceedings, and establishes the division of labour between the Court and the arresting State for protecting the right to liberty.[99] While the article imposes obligations on both the arresting State and the ICC, the hands-on task of protecting the individual's rights is aimed at the arresting State given that this is the actor actually carrying out the arrest. Article 59(2) states as follows:

> A person arrested shall be brought promptly before the competent judicial authority in the custodial State which shall determine, in accordance with the law of that State, that:
>
> (a) The warrant applies to that person;
> (b) The person has been arrested in accordance with the proper process; and
> (c) The person's rights have been respected.

The first line of the provision already contains an important right to liberty protection: to be brought promptly before a judge. This creates a corresponding obligation on the arresting State to ensure that this takes place. After this basic protection, Article 59(2) sets out three elements that the judicial authority of the State must check. While the first of these – establishing that the person arrested is indeed the correct person – is self-evident and straightforward, the other elements of Article 59(2) are less clear. As the content of the arresting State's obligations to protect the right to liberty depends on how the component elements of Article 59(2) are understood, the ambiguities in the provision will be explored in turn, with some proposals for their resolution.

First is the reference to 'in accordance with the law of' the arresting State. One could describe this as the *chapeau* of Article 59(2). The meaning of this phrase will affect the content of the rest of Article 59(2), in particular the meaning of 'person's rights' and 'proper process', and as such should be addressed first. The wording of the provision does not indicate whether these terms are to be given an entirely domestic meaning, or whether they include international law protections.

---

[99] Mohamed M. El Zeidy, 'Critical Thoughts on Article 59(2) of the ICC Statute' (2006) 4 *Journal of International Criminal Justice*, 448, 450.

The ICC Appeals Chamber made some ambiguous statements on this subject in a decision issued in the *Lubanga* case. The Defence argued that the right to liberty violations Lubanga suffered in the Democratic Republic of the Congo (DRC) rendered any proceedings at the ICC an abuse of process, and that it fell to the ICC to review the arrest proceedings in the arresting State. To reach a decision on whether this was a proper role for the ICC to play, the Appeals Chamber examined the role assigned to the Court by Article 59(2). While this is principally relevant to Section 3.2.3 on the obligations of the ICC, the decision is relevant to the extent that, at first glance, it appears to support the position that only national law is relevant in interpreting Article 59(2):

> The enforcement of a warrant of arrest is designed to ensure, as article 59(2) of the Statute specifically directs, that there is identity between the person against whom the warrant is directed and the arrested person, secondly, that the process followed is the one envisaged by national law, and thirdly that the person's rights have been respected. The Court does not sit in the process, as the Prosecutor rightly observes, on judgment as a court of appeal on the identificatory decision of the Congolese judicial authority. Its task is to see that the process envisaged by Congolese law was duly followed and that the rights of the arrestee were properly respected. Article 99(1) of the Statute lays down that the enforcement of the warrant must follow the process laid down by the law of the requested state. In this case, the Pre-Trial Chamber determined that the process followed accorded with Congolese law.[100]

The Appeals Chamber seems to limit the ICC's role in reviewing the execution of the arrest warrant, and appears to decide that domestic law, which is the exclusive realm of the State, is the only relevant law when applying Article 59(2). This reading was adopted in a subsequent decision of Pre-Trial Chamber I in the *Gbagbo* case, where the Chamber held that the role of the Chamber 'with respect to proceedings under article 59 of the Statute is limited to verifying that the basic safeguards envisaged by national law have been made available to the arrested person'.[101]

The author submits that the Pre-Trial Chamber's reading of the Appeals Chamber decision was incorrect. Despite first appearances, the Appeals Chamber did not rule out the relevance of international law for Article 59(2). In the excerpt provided in the previous paragraph, the Appeals Chamber tied the *process* of the arrest to national law; however, in tasking the ICC with checking that the 'rights of the arrestee were

---

[100] *Lubanga*, 14 December 2006, §41.
[101] *Gbagbo*, 15 August 2012, §104.

properly respected', no domestic law link is made. It is therefore proposed that the Appeals Chamber intended the rights of the arrested person to have a meaning independent from domestic law. This would tie in with Sluiter's argument that a proper interpretation of Article 59(2) would be one in which the procedural aspects of an arrest are governed by national law, but the substantive protections for the arrested persons should have an international meaning.[102] In other words, domestic process, international substance.

The distinction between procedure and substantive rights is reinforced by the distinction in Article 59(2) itself, which lists 'proper process' and 'person's rights' as two separate elements that a domestic court must examine. If this proposed interpretation of Article 59(2)'s *chapeau* is accepted, then this also resolves the remaining ambiguities in Article 59(2): the meaning of 'proper process' (Article 59(2)(b)) and 'person's rights' (Article 59(2)(c)). The arresting State has an obligation to ensure that it follows its own procedures under national law when arresting an ICC suspect (proper process), and an obligation to respect the substantive rights of the suspect under international human rights law (person's rights).[103]

An additional argument can be made which gives even the notion of 'proper process' an internationalised meaning. It can be argued that references to the national law of a State should include its international human rights law obligations, as States are obliged to apply these standards in their domestic proceedings.[104] As such, the procedures are dictated by domestic law, but the content of the domestic law should be seen as informed by human rights.

The author argues that tying the interpretation of Article 59(2) to international standards (at least as far as 'person's rights' is concerned) is the only interpretation that complies with the Article 21(3) test, as only this approach ensures that the Rome Statute protection framework is

---

[102] Sluiter, 'Human Rights Protection in the Pre-Trial Phase', 474.
[103] There is much academic support for the idea that an individual's rights during an arrest are to be given an international meaning. See Bert Swart, 'Arrest Proceedings in the Custodial State', in Antonio Cassese, Paola Gaeta, and John R. W. D. Jones (eds.), *The Rome Statute of the International Criminal Court* (Oxford University Press 2002), 1253; Hall and Ryngaert, 'Article 59', 1465.
[104] Article 2 of the ICCPR: 'Each State Party to the present Covenant undertakes to respect and to ensure to all individuals within its territory and subject to its jurisdiction the rights recognized in the present Covenant, without distinction of any kind, such as race, colour, sex, language, religion, political or other opinion, national or social origin, property, birth or other status.'

applied consistently with human rights. As one commentator points out, if the provision is confined strictly to domestic law, Article 59(2) would lose much of its protective force and would leave significant differences in the treatment of ICC suspects in different arresting States.[105]

The question that logically follows from this discussion is also perhaps the most difficult in terms of establishing the obligations of the arresting State. The domestic court must review the arrest in line with the requirements in Article 59(2), but what should the court order if it finds that Article 59(2) has not been complied with? Must the arresting State still surrender the suspect if proper process has not been followed or if their rights have been violated? Article 59(2) is silent on this question; however, other provisions in the Rome Statute protection framework indicate that the individual must be surrendered regardless. Article 89, detailing the obligations of States to carry out a request for arrest and surrender, makes no mention of refusing surrender because Article 59(2) has not been complied with. At most, Article 97 requires that the State communicate with the ICC about its concerns. Academic commentary agrees with this position. The opinion of one commentator is that, just as it is not open to the arresting State to review the validity of an ICC arrest warrant, it cannot be open to that State to release a person and so impede their surrender to the Court.[106] In the words of another commentator, 'neither the determination by the national judicial authority that the suspect's rights were violated nor the remedies it adopted could prevent surrender to the Court'.[107] As long as problems in the arrest are addressed by the ICC in its own process, there is no reason why this interpretation of Article 59(2) should not comply with the Article 21(3) test.

It is at this juncture that the existence of obligations beyond the Rome Statute protection framework becomes important. In this section it has been proposed that international human rights norms inform the standard of treatment to be afforded to arrested persons under Article 59(2); as such, by applying Article 59(2) properly, the State will be complying with its obligations under human rights law. However, obligations beyond the Rome Statute protection framework relate not only to the arrest proceedings themselves, but also to how a State must act when it

---

[105] Sluiter, 'Human Rights Protection in the Pre-Trial Phase', 474.
[106] Göran Sluiter, 'The Surrender of War Criminals to the International Criminal Court' (2002–2003) 25 *Loyola of Los Angeles International & Comparative Law Review*, 605, 625.
[107] Hall and Ryngaert, 'Article 59', 1465.

determines that human rights have been violated. When a violation of a particular gravity has occurred, the State must choose between its Rome Statute obligation to surrender the individual to the Court, and its human rights law obligation to release the individual. This tension was noted by the ICTR Appeals Chamber in *Kajelijeli*, when it observed that an arresting State must 'strike a balance between two different obligations under international law': on the one hand the obligation to comply with requests for arrest and surrender, and on the other hand the obligations under human rights law that the State has pursuant to its international commitments.[108]

Different States have handled this balance differently, and as a result there is a discrepancy in how arresting States handle the issue.[109] In New Zealand, a person is not eligible for surrender if proper process has not been followed or the person's rights have been violated.[110] In such a case, the person must be discharged unless they remain detained pending an appeal.[111] While Australia shares New Zealand's approach,[112] the powers of British courts are much more limited. In the UK, the arrested person must be surrendered to the ICC as long as the arrest warrant is delivered in good order.[113] While a British court is permitted to inquire into whether the arrest was lawful and the person's rights respected, where it finds a violation to have occurred, it can only make a declaration to that effect. A UK court is specifically prohibited from granting any other form of relief.[114] Ultimately the authorities of the arresting State, either through legislation or through a judicial decision, will have to decide which international obligation takes precedence over the other.

Finally, and returning to the Rome Statute protection framework, it is important to establish when Article 59 applies. This is especially relevant because in the early cases before the ICC, namely in the *Lubanga* and *Katanga* cases, the individuals were already in detention in the DRC when they became ICC suspects. They were originally arrested for crimes under domestic criminal law, and only later did the ICC arrest warrants

---

[108] *Juvénal Kajelijelo v. The Prosecutor*, Case No. ICTR-98-44A, Judgment, 23 May 2005 (Appeals Chamber), §220.
[109] El Zeidy, 'Critical Thoughts on Article 59(2)', 455–7.
[110] Section 43, International Crimes and International Criminal Court Act 2000, Public Act 2000 No. 26, 6 September 2000, New Zealand.
[111] *Ibid.*, Section 46(4).
[112] Section 23(3), International Criminal Court Act 2002, Act No. 41 of 2002, Australia.
[113] Section 5(2), International Criminal Court Act 2001, 2001 Chapter 17, 1 September 2001, Great Britain.
[114] *Ibid.*, Section 5(8).

arrive. Technically therefore, they were not arrested pursuant to an ICC arrest warrant. The question then arose whether the domestic court still had to review the arrest for compatibility with Article 59(2).

The phrasing of Article 59(2) does not answer this question, but there is practice on the point. The Pre-Trial Chamber in the *Lubanga* case held that Article 59(2) does not apply to arrest and detention predating the involvement of the ICC. The date when the request for the arrest and surrender of Thomas Lubanga was transmitted to the DRC was 14 March 2006, and so only events occurring after that date were relevant for Article 59 considerations.[115] What this essentially means is that when the arrest predates the ICC arrest warrant, the manner in which the arrest was carried out will be outside the scope of Article 59 review. This approach is consistent with the inapplicability of Article 55 to interrogations that occur before the ICC's involvement.

Does this interpretation of Article 59 comply with Article 21(3)? It is proposed that it does, on one condition: that once the arrest warrant is transmitted, the detained individual is given the benefit of all of Article 59(2)'s protections. While this condition was not expressly set out in the *Lubanga* decision discussed in the previous paragraph, the Pre-Trial Chamber judges did examine the events that took place following 14 March 2006, and concluded that there was no breach of Article 59(2).

3.2.3 Obligations of the ICC: Standard Arrest

The State might be the actor that carries out the arrest, but since this is done pursuant to an ICC arrest warrant, the Court is inextricably involved. The question therefore is: what obligations does the ICC have to protect the right to liberty of a suspect arrested in a State Party? The answer to this is not entirely clear. The author proposes that Article 59(2) obliges the ICC to (1) monitor the compliance of arresting States with their own obligations and (2) act to address any violations that occur of the rights protected by Article 59(2).

Article 59(2) does not mention the ICC, nor is it explicitly directed at the Court. Despite this, support for the idea that the ICC must monitor State compliance with Article 59(2) can be derived from

---

[115] *The Prosecutor* v. *Thomas Lubanga Dyilo*, ICC-01/04-01/06-512, Decision on the Defence Challenge to the Jurisdiction of the Court Pursuant to Article 19(2)(a) of the Statute, 3 October 2006 (Pre-Trial Chamber I) (*Lubanga*, 3 October 2006), 6.

other provisions of the Rome Statute protection framework, practice, and scholarly opinion.

The relevant other provisions in the Rome Statute protection framework are of a general nature and a more specific nature. The general provision is Article 64(2), which imposes an overarching obligation on the ICC to ensure that a trial is fair. Monitoring the arrest process, which can have an important impact on the fairness of a subsequent trial, therefore seems indicated. In terms of more specific provisions, there is Rule 117 RPE and Article 85 of the Rome Statute. These can be read as supporting a monitoring role for the Court because, without such a role, the provisions would be rendered ineffective. Rule 117(1) RPE (Detention in the custodial State) stipulates that the Court 'shall ensure' that the arrested person is provided with a copy of the arrest warrant in a language they understand. This covers an important element of the right to liberty, namely to be informed of the charge for which one is detained.[116] The language of the rule is compulsory. However, this does not mean that the ICC is obliged to send an ICC staff member into the presence of the accused person in the State's custody and read them the charges; instead it means that the ICC must monitor whether the accused has been given a copy of the arrest warrant by the arresting State. Turning to Article 85(1) of the Rome Statute, this provision grants individuals the right to compensation if they have been the victim of unlawful arrest or detention. As arrests are exclusively carried out by States, it is necessary that the ICC examine how they are carried out, as otherwise it could not be determined whether or not the arrest was lawful. Rule 117(1) and Article 85(1) may deal with specific situations, but they are indicative of a broader monitoring role for the Court.

One academic commentator takes it as 'self-evident' that the ICC has a supervisory role when it comes to compliance with Article 59(2). The role is said to derive from the fact that the Court is the only actor able to ensure the fairness of the criminal proceedings as a whole, including the arrest.[117] Another commentator sets out further arguments in favour of the ICC's monitoring role. One of these stems from the implied powers rule, and rests on the notion that the ICC must be able to rule on a violation by a State of its treaty obligation, especially when this is essential to the performance of the ICC's functions.[118] A different

---

[116] Article 9(2) and (4) respectively, ICCPR.
[117] Sluiter, 'Human Rights Protection in the Pre-Trial Phase', 470.
[118] El Zeidy, 'Critical Thoughts on Article 59(2)', 458.

argument is based on the idea that jurisdiction and primacy over the arrest have passed to the ICC, such that the arresting State is acting on behalf of the ICC. It follows that simply because Article 59(2) leaves arrest proceedings to the national authorities, does not mean that the ICC lacks competence.[119]

Support for the ICC's monitoring role can also be found in the decision from the Appeals Chamber in the *Lubanga* case discussed in detail in the previous section.[120] The Chamber stated that the ICC has a role in ensuring that the domestic court has followed its own criminal law procedure and that the individual's rights have been respected. Such a review inevitably grants the ICC some monitoring powers. In line with the procedure/substance distinction, Sluiter proposes that the Chamber should use two margins of review: a marginal one for reviewing compliance with domestic law, but a stronger one for reviewing compliance with international human rights law.[121]

The broader context surrounding Article 59(2), the decision of the Appeals Chamber, and scholarly opinion, all support the notion that the ICC must supervise the arresting State's compliance with Article 59(2). But such supervision is of little use if the ICC cannot act where it observes non-compliance, or is informed of the non-compliance by the domestic court. The next question must therefore be what the ICC is obliged to do where it notes that the arresting State is not complying or has not complied with Article 59(2).[122] There are two points in time that are relevant: while the accused is still in the custody of the arresting State, and after the accused has been surrendered to the ICC.

---

[119] El Zeidy, 'Critical Thoughts on Article 59(2)', 458.
[120] *Lubanga*, 14 December 2006, §41.
[121] Sluiter, 'Human Rights Protection in the Pre-Trial Phase', 474.
[122] El Zeidy argues, and the author agrees, that this is not a situation in which a declaration of non-compliance under Article 87 would be appropriate: 'One should not confuse the question of non-compliance with the rights of the arrested person per Art. 59(2) with the question of non-compliance to cooperate with an ICC request per Arts. 87(7) and 112(2)(f), which provide the Court with the discretionary power to "make a finding to that effect and refer the matter to the Assembly of States Parties". Article 87(7) deals with a broader question, that is, a failure to cooperate that results in "preventing the Court from exercising its functions and powers under the Statute". As to non-compliance with the prerequisites of Art. 59(2), it is not that the state fails to comply with the Court's request to cooperate, rather that the state in an effort to comply with the request of surrender violates the person's rights before the domestic courts. Accordingly, Arts 87(7) and 112(2)(f) do not seem to be applicable in this context' (El Zeidy, 'Critical Thoughts on Article 59(2)', 457, footnote 40).

During the arrest, and for the time between the arrest and the surrender to the Court, the author proposes that the ICC is obliged to enter into a dialogue with the arresting State where it notes non-compliance with Article 59(2). The object of this is to prevent a violation from occurring, or to stop a violation from continuing. As Judge Lal Chand Vohrah stated in the *Semanza* case before the ICTR:

> If an accused is arrested or detained by a state at the request or under the authority of the Tribunal, even though the accused is not yet within the actual custody of the Tribunal, the Tribunal has a responsibility to provide whatever relief is available to it to attempt to reduce any violations as much as possible.[123]

Article 59 has established a delicate balance in the division of labour between the domestic authorities and the ICC in arrest and surrender matters,[124] and only a limited form of intervention such as this would be appropriate while the individual is still on the territory of the arresting State.

Once the arrested person has been transferred to the ICC, it is a different matter. At that point, it is no longer a question of preventing a violation of the rights embodied in Article 59(2), but of remedying any prejudice done to the accused's rights by a violation that has already taken place. As on many other issues, Article 59(2) is silent on what the ICC should do if domestic authorities fail to provide the protections it lists, or indeed, on what to do if a domestic court declares that there has been a violation. As the suspect must be surrendered regardless, the author proposes that it falls to the ICC to provide a remedy. The type of remedy will depend on the seriousness of the breach, and could include a reduction of sentence if found guilty,[125] financial compensation,[126] or in case of a very egregious breach, a stay of proceedings.[127]

---

[123] Declaration of Judge Lal Chand Vohrah in *Laurent Semanza v. The Prosecutor*, Case No. ICTR-97-20-A, Decision, 31 May 2000 (Appeals Chamber), §6.

[124] El Zeidy, 'Critical Thoughts on Article 59(2)', 450.

[125] This remedy is not explicitly provided for in the Rome Statute protection framework but has been used at the ICTR. In the *Barayagwiza* case, in response to violations of the right to liberty of the accused while in pre-trial detention in Cameroon, the Appeals Chamber decided that if the accused were convicted, time would be taken off the sentence to reflect this prejudice to the accused's rights. If acquitted, the response was to be financial compensation (*Jean Bosco Barayagwiza v. The Prosecutor*, ICTR-97-19-AR72, Decision (Prosecutor's Request for Review or Reconsideration), 31 March 2000 (Appeals Chamber) (*Barayagwiza*, 31 March 2000), §75).

[126] Article 85 of the Rome Statute.

[127] The availability of this remedy in cases of pre-trial violations of rights was confirmed in the *Lubanga* case. The Defence alleged that Lubanga had been subjected to a number of

The one remaining issue to consider on the ICC's monitoring obligations under Article 59(2) is whether the proposed interpretation satisfies the Article 21(3) test. The author proposes that it does. The ICC is able to monitor compliance with human rights in the arrest and surrender process, and can remedy violations if they take place.

While Article 59(2) is an important provision, the ICC has some additional obligations that must be noted. Two other provisions of the Rome Statute protection framework are relevant to the protection of arrested persons, namely Rule 117 RPE and Article 55 of the Rome Statute. Rule 117(2) and (3) RPE are concerned with ensuring that the accused can challenge the basis of their detention, an important safeguard for the right to liberty. Such a challenge can be brought by an individual who is still detained in the arresting State, but since Article 59(4) of the Rome Statute explicitly prohibits national courts from deciding on the validity of an ICC arrest warrant, the challenge is heard before the ICC. Where a suspect challenges an arrest warrant on the ground that it was not properly issued in accordance with Article 58(1)(a) and (b), Rule 117(3) obliges the Pre-Trial Chamber to make a determination on the challenge, and requires that this be done 'without delay'. The right to challenge the grounds for detention is bolstered by Rule 117(2), whereby the arrested person can apply to the Pre-Trial Chamber for legal assistance in proceedings before that Chamber.

The final ICC obligation discussed in this section is found in Article 55(1)(d), which contains a broad obligation on the ICC to not violate the right to liberty through arbitrary arrest or detention. As stated in the previous section, the obligations correlating to the rights enumerated in Article 55 continue to apply during arrest proceedings. It is clear that this provision would apply if the ICC were detaining an individual for an extended period at the seat of the Court, but it must also be read so as to prohibit the ICC from engaging in such conduct through another actor. For example, the ICC would also violate this provision by requesting that the arresting State keep a suspect in custody on an ICC arrest warrant for an unreasonably long period of time before they are surrendered to the Court. Such an interpretation is necessary if the Article 21(3) test is to be satisfied, and is also supported by practice of the ICTR in *Barayagwiza*.

human rights abuses while detained in the DRC. Pre-Trial Chamber I and the Appeals Chamber confirmed that a stay of proceedings can be ordered where there has been an abuse of process. On the facts, it was not proved that an abuse of process had taken place. Pre-Trial Chamber: *Lubanga*, 3 October 2006; Appeals Chamber: *Lubanga*, 14 December 2006.

In the *Barayagwiza* case,[128] the suspect was arrested in Cameroon in response to extradition requests from Belgium and Rwanda. These requests were refused, but before the suspect was released, the ICTR requested that the Cameroonian authorities continue to detain him and that he be transferred to the ICTR detention unit. Nine months elapsed before he was actually transferred to the Tribunal detention unit, during which time the suspect remained detained in Cameroon. The ICTR Appeals Chamber determined that during this nine-month period the suspect had been held by Cameroon in the constructive custody of the ICTR. The ICTR was the actor with personal jurisdiction over the suspect, as he would not have been detained but for the ICTR order.[129] The nine-month period was deemed to be a serious violation of the suspect's rights, and the Appeals Chamber ordered that he be released.[130]

The constructive custody argument was used by the Defence in the *Katanga* case to try and bring violations of the right to liberty that took place before the issuance of the ICC arrest warrant within the ICC's purview. Prior to the issuance of the ICC arrest warrant, Katanga had already been detained in the DRC on other charges for approximately two years. The Defence argued that as soon as the arrest warrant and the request for arrest and surrender were communicated to the DRC, Katanga fell under the constructive custody of the ICC. The ICC therefore shared responsibility for the ongoing violation.[131] In this way, the Defence sought to engage the ICC's obligation to remedy violations of

---

[128] Trial Chamber: *Prosecutor v. Jean-Bosco Barayagwiza*, Case No. ICTR-97-19-AR72, Decision, 3 November 1999 (Trial Chamber); Appeals Chamber: *Barayagwiza*, 31 March 2000. For background on this case, see William Schabas, 'Barayagwiza v. Prosecutor (Decision, and Decision (Prosecutor's Request for Review or Reconsideration)) Case No. ICTR-97-19-AR72' (2000) 94 *American Journal of International Law*, 563; and Bert Swart, 'Commentary on ICTR Decision Barayagwiza v. Prosecutor, Case No. ICTR-97-19-AR72, A. Ch., 3 November 1999' (2001) 2 *Annotated Leading Cases*, 197.

[129] This reasoning was derived by analogy from the 'detainer' process, whereby a person already in the custody of one State is kept there at the request of another State, so that the latter State can take custody once the former States' reasons for custody are ended. The suspect in the detainer process is in the constructive custody of the requesting State, with the detaining State acting as agent (*Barayagwiza*, 31 March 2000, §§56 and 61).

[130] This order was overturned on appeal. The Appeals Chamber decided in *Barayagwiza*, 31 March 2000, that the Prosecutor was less to blame for the extended detention than previously thought, and that remedies short of terminating proceedings would be more appropriate.

[131] *The Prosecutor v. Katanga and Ngudjolo*, ICC-01/04-01/07-1263, Public Redacted Version of the Defence Motion for a Declaration on Unlawful Detention and Stay of Proceedings (ICC-01/07-01/04-1258-Conf-Exp), 2 July 2009 (Trial Chamber II), §§101–6.

the right to liberty with respect to the period of detention prior to the arrest warrant. If the ICC had agreed with these arguments, the Court would have had to remedy a violation that had been ongoing for an extended period of time, and the remedy requested by the Defence was a stay of proceedings. In light of the important points raised, it is regrettable that the Trial Chamber dismissed the motion on procedural grounds.[132] Given the approach taken to State obligations under Articles 55 and 59 for conduct undertaken prior to ICC involvement, the Defence's argument on this point would, in all likelihood, have been rejected.

3.2.4 Obligations of States and the ICC: Provisional Arrest

Putting together a full request for arrest and surrender takes time. In standard arrest proceedings, the Court must complete two steps in requesting the arrest and surrender of a suspect. First, the Pre-Trial Chamber must issue an arrest warrant, and second a formal request for arrest and surrender, containing numerous documents,[133] must be put together and transmitted. Such a lengthy procedure can be problematic when time is of the essence. In the lead-up to the issuance of an arrest warrant for Jean-Pierre Bemba Gombo, the Prosecution received information that he intended to travel within a few days' time, possibly to the DRC where he would be able to avoid capture.[134] In response, on the same day as the arrest warrant was issued, a request for provisional arrest was transmitted to Belgium where Bemba was located.[135]

Provisional arrest, provided for in Article 92 of the Rome Statute, allows the ICC to request the arrest of a suspect before having completed and transmitted the full arrest and surrender request. At the ICTY and ICTR, provisional arrest was possible even when no arrest warrant had

---

[132] *The Prosecutor v. Germain Katanga*, ICC-01/04-01/07-1666-Red-tENG, Public Redacted Version of the 'Decision on the Motion of the Defence for Germain Katanga for a Declaration on Unlawful Detention and Stay of Proceedings' of 20 November 2009 (ICC-01/04-01/07-1666-Conf-Exp), 3 December 2009 (Trial Chamber II), §§65–6.

[133] These are set out in Article 91 of the Rome Statute.

[134] *Situation in the Central African Republic*, ICC-01/05-01/08-28, Prosecutor's Application for Request for Provisional Arrest under Article 92, 23 May 2008 (Pre-Trial Chamber III), §§5–6.

[135] *The Prosecutor v. Jean-Pierre Bemba Gombo*, ICC-01/05-01/08-3, Demande d'arrestation provisoire de M. Jean-Peirre Bemba Gombo addressee au Royaume de Belgique, 23 May 2008 (Pre-Trial Chamber II).

SUSPECTS, ACCUSED, CONVICTED, AND ACQUITTED 63

been issued,[136] but this is not the case at the ICC.[137] The expedited nature of provisional arrest does not mean that the protections discussed in the previous section arising from Article 59(2) do not apply; those safeguards must be followed whether it is a provisional arrest or a standard one. But in provisional arrest situations there is an additional requirement. When a request for provisional arrest and detention is transmitted to a State in accordance with Article 92, the formal request, as required by Article 89, must follow within sixty days of the arrest. The time limit of sixty days is important. Rule 188 RPE sets the limit, and Article 92(3) provides for the release of the arrested person if the formal request is not received within that time limit. Should the time limit pass without a request being made, the suspect is no longer lawfully detained. These provisions are significant in safeguarding elements of the right to liberty, in particular the right to be brought promptly before a judge and the right to trial within a reasonable time.[138] The time limit requirement prevents a person from remaining stuck in limbo, unable to be released on the one hand, but unable to go ahead with the trial on the other.

The ICC's obligation in cases of provisional arrest and detention are fairly straightforward. The Court has an obligation to transmit the formal request for arrest and surrender within the time limit of sixty days, or otherwise arrange for the release of the suspect. The obligations on the arresting State are also straightforward. Before the expiry of the sixty-day time limit, the arresting State is detaining the arrested person on behalf of the Court, and there is a legal basis for the detention in Article 92 of the Rome Statute. Once the sixty-day period expires, so does the legal basis for the detention. In such a case, the State must release the individual or be found to be in violation of Article 55(1)(d) of the Rome Statute and international human rights law, both of which oblige States not to subject persons to arbitrary detention.

3.2.5 Problems in Human Rights Protection

Arrest and surrender proceedings are perhaps one of the most complicated situations addressed in this study, and certainly the most complicated situation involving accused. That being said, it is also the stage that, once the various obligations are set out and understood, poses the fewest

---

[136] Rules 40 and 40*bis* of the Statutes of the ICTY and ICTR.
[137] Article 58(5) of the Rome Statute stipulates that provisional arrest or arrest and surrender may be requested *on the basis of an arrest warrant.*
[138] Article 9(3) of the ICCPR.

problems for human rights protection. In terms of structural problems, there is no issue here, as there is no lack of duty bearers for the entirety of the right to liberty. In terms of implementation problems, these are associated with situations in which more than one actor has an obligation to act simultaneously, whereby each actor can argue that it is the other that must protect the right. For arrest and surrender proceedings, the actors will find it difficult to pass the buck in this way.

The division of labour between the ICC and the arresting State is clear. On the one hand, the State that carries out the arrest is responsible for providing the relevant protections, and the judicial authority of that State is responsible for checking whether these protections have been provided. If they have not, the ICC should be informed of this at the time of surrender. As arrests invariably take place on the territory of the arresting State by the authorities of that State, it is hard to argue that another actor must be in charge of protecting the accused's right to liberty. On the other hand, the ICC monitors the actions of the State to check whether the rights of the accused are being respected. Where it finds deficiencies in protection, the ICC must apply pressure on the arresting State while the accused is still in the State's custody, and/or provide a remedy for any violations once the individual is transferred to ICC custody. As the ICC is the forum in which the criminal trial will take place, it cannot be assumed that any other actor will fulfil this role.

The main challenge presented by the arrest and surrender stage does not arise from structural or implementation problems linked to the multi-actor nature of the situation, but rather from the complexity of the obligations. The solution to this lies in raising awareness among States Parties, and in promoting consistency in how the ICC approaches the obligations engaged by this situation

3.2.6 Conclusion

At the arrest stage, the ICC is particularly reliant on the assistance of States. Securing a suspect's arrest has been called the Court's 'Achilles' heel',[139] because its reliance on reluctant States is the principal reason why high-profile indictees such as Al-Bashir have not yet been tried. Such problems, while important, are entirely political, and so are not the focus of this study. Instead, this section has examined the distribution of obligations between the ICC and an arresting State when it comes to protecting a suspect's right

---

[139] Nick Donovan, 'The Enforcement of International Criminal Court', Aegis, 2009, 9.

to liberty. The arrest and surrender stage of proceedings at the ICC is right at the fault line between the national justice system and the functions of the Court.[140] The resulting regime is one that is complex, and whose content is very much open to interpretation at multiple stages.

The multi-actor nature of the arrest regime may be complicated, but the result of this complexity is that the situation in fact produces few to any implementation problems. As long as States and the Court are clear as to the content of their obligations, and the approach of the different actors to these obligations is uniform, the involvement of multiple actors during the arrest stage of ICC proceedings need not produce any distinct problems for human rights protection. This positive conclusion is rather unique among the situations examined in this study, and as the next section of this chapter will show, is certainly not the case once the arrested person arrives at the Court and requests interim release.

3.3 Interim Release prior to and during ICC Proceedings

3.3.1 Introduction

Once a suspect is arrested by a State Party and surrendered to the ICC, the individual faces a long period of detention before the proceedings against them are concluded. Detention prior to and during the trial often extends to years in international criminal trials. This tendency has continued in the cases thus far brought to a conclusion at the ICC. From the moment of surrender to the Court until the end of their respective trials, Bemba was detained for ten years, Lubanga for eight years, Katanga for seven years, and Ngudjolo for four years. For those convicted, the time spent in detention before and during the trial is deducted from their sentence as time served; for acquitted persons, such as Ngudjolo, there is no compensation mechanism.[141]

These extended periods of time in detention prior to conviction seriously compromise the right to liberty. As such, the analysis of this situation will focus on this right, and in particular, on protecting the right

---

[140] Schabas, A Commentary on the Rome Statute, 904.
[141] Article 85 of the Rome Statute allows for compensation, but only in cases of unlawful arrest or detention, or miscarriage of justice, and not simply because there was an acquittal. The claim made by Ngudjolo pursuant to this article after his acquittal was rejected on the basis that he did not suffer a miscarriage of justice (*The Prosecutor v. Mathieu Ngudjolo Chui*, ICC-01/04-02/12-301-tENG, Decision on the 'Requête en indemnisation en application des dispositions de l'article 85(1) et (3) du Statut de Rome', 16 December 2015 (Trial Chamber II).

through interim release. The right to liberty demands that pre-trial detention be the exception and not the norm. This is prominent in the ICCPR and has been succinctly put by the Human Rights Committee: 'pre-trial detention should be an exception and as short as possible'.[142] The importance of interim release stems from its connection to the presumption of innocence, and the idea that incarceration prior to conviction must be justified by compelling reasons.[143]

Interim release can be granted at the ICC during two separate stages: while the suspect remains detained in the arresting State, and once the suspect reaches the detention centre of the ICC. Interim release in the arresting State is governed by Article 59(3) of the Rome Statute. According to this provision, the domestic court must decide whether 'given the gravity of the alleged crimes, there are urgent and exceptional circumstances to justify interim release'. The Pre-Trial Chamber of the ICC will make recommendations about interim release,[144] and the domestic court must take them into account. Nevertheless, the final decision remains with the domestic court. The minimal role played by the ICC, and the fact that a person granted interim release would remain in the arresting State, means that this type of interim release does not have a multi-actor dimension; the State handles it on its own.

Once the suspect is surrendered to the custody of the ICC in The Hague however, interim release takes on a distinctly multi-actor character. Simply put, if a suspect is to be released from custody pending trial, they must have somewhere to reside. The ICC itself cannot offer this as it has no territory of its own. Granting interim release where warranted is an important ICC function, but it is a function which requires the assistance of States. The following sections will discuss the obligations of two of the actors involved – the ICC and States Parties – with regards to interim release.

3.3.2 Obligations of the ICC

The obligations of the ICC with respect to protecting the right to liberty through interim release are found in Article 60 of the Rome Statute.

---

[142] Article 9(3) of the ICCPR, and Compilation of General Comments and General Recommendations Adopted by Human Rights Treaty Bodies, UN Doc. HRI/GEN/Rev.6, 12 May 2003, 130. For more see Clemens A. Muller, 'The Law of Interim Release in the Jurisprudence of the International Criminal Tribunals' (2008) 8 *International Criminal Law Review*, 589, 593–4.

[143] Khan, 'Article 60', 1474.

[144] Article 59(5) and (6).

Paragraph 1 of this provision obliges the ICC to satisfy itself that the suspect has been informed of their right to apply for interim release pending trial. If the suspect chooses to exercise this right, the ICC is obliged to hear the application and render a decision. There are three types of situation in which the ICC would be bound to grant an application for interim release, and these are listed in paragraphs 2-4 of Article 60.[145]

The first situation in which the ICC would be obliged to grant interim release is where the requirements for the issuance of an arrest warrant are no longer met. Article 60(2) provides as follows:

> A person subject to a warrant of arrest may apply for interim release pending trial. If the Pre-Trial Chamber is satisfied that the conditions set forth in Article 58, paragraph 1 are met, the person shall continue to be detained. If it is not so satisfied, the Pre-Trial Chamber shall release the person, with or without conditions

Article 58(1) lists the requirements for the issuance of an arrest warrant, which are:

- There are reasonable grounds to believe that the person has committed a crime within the jurisdiction of the Court (Article 58(1)(a)); and
- The arrest of the person appears necessary (Article 58(1)(b)):
  - To ensure the person's appearance at trial,
  - To ensure that the person does not obstruct or endanger the investigation or the court proceedings, or
  - Where applicable, to prevent the person from continuing with the commission of that crime or a related crime which is within the jurisdiction of the Court and which arises out of the same circumstances.

The way that Articles 60(2) and 58(1) are structured means that if any of the requirements of the latter provision are met, then the detention is justified and interim release will be denied. This is supported by ICC decisions.[146] Only if, at the time of the application, none of the factors under Article 58(1)(b) are satisfied, must interim release be granted. From the compulsory language in Article 60(2), and from elaboration

---

[145] This section will not go into detail regarding what substantive criteria a Chamber must look at when making an interim release decision on the facts. For a comprehensive study of these issues, see Zeegers, International Criminal Tribunals and Human Rights, from 246 onwards.
[146] Zeegers, International Criminal Tribunals and Human Rights, 247, footnote 291.

in ICC decisions, it is clear that the Chamber has no discretion in whether or not to grant release if the conditions are met.[147] Furthermore, the Chamber must review its decision on release or detention every 120 days.[148]

Article 60(4) contains the second situation in which interim release may be granted: where the suspect has been detained for an unreasonable time due to an inexcusable delay on the part of the Prosecutor. The purpose of this provision is to allow the Chamber to weigh respect for the rights of the suspect, in particular the right to liberty, against the public interest,[149] and is said to be in line with the ICCPR, ECHR, and ACHR requirement of being tried within a reasonable time.[150] Case law confirms that release on this basis can be permitted even if the detention is justified under Article 60(2),[151] although this provision lacks the compulsory nature of Article 60(2), as it only obliges the ICC to consider releasing the accused, leaving the discretion with the judges.

The wording of the Article 60(4) does not elaborate on what can be considered an 'unreasonable time' or an 'inexcusable delay'. The only guidance from practice is that the determination must be made based on the circumstances of the individual case, and not in the abstract.[152] Single Judge Jorda in *Lubanga* held that in examining the circumstances of a case, the case's complexity will be particularly important, determined in part by the amount of evidence and where the evidence is located.[153] Given that international criminal trials are nearly always complex by their very nature, one might assume that the period would need to be long indeed for a determination of unreasonableness to be made. Indeed, one commentator notes that 'in reviewing the overall period of detention,

---

[147] *Bemba*, 14 August 2009, §77; *Bemba*, 2 December 2009, §105; *The Prosecutor v. Thomas Lubanga Dyilo*, ICC-01/04-01/06-824, Judgment on the Appeal of Mr Thomas Lubanga Dyilo against the Decision of Pre-Trial Chamber I Entitled 'Décision sur la demande de mise en liberté provisoire de Thomas Lubanga Dyilo', 13 February 2007 (Appeals Chamber) (*Lubanga*, 13 February 2007), §134. For more decisions, see Zeegers, International Criminal Tribunals and Human Rights, 247.

[148] Article 60(3) of the Rome Statute and Rule 118(2) of the ICC RPE.

[149] *The Prosecutor v. Thomas Lubanga Dyilo*, ICC-01/04-01/06-924, Second Review of the 'Decision on the Application for Interim Release of Thomas Lubanga Dyilo', 11 June 2007 (Pre-Trial Chamber I), 7.

[150] Zeegers, International Criminal Tribunals and Human Rights, 273.

[151] *Lubanga*, 13 February 2007, §4.

[152] *The Prosecutor v. Thomas Lubanga Dyilo*, ICC-01/04-01/06-586-tEN, Decision on the Application for the Interim Release of Thomas Lubanga Dyilo, 18 October 2006 (Pre-Trial Chamber I) (*Lubanga*, 18 October 2006), 7; *Lubanga*, 13 February 2007, §122.

[153] *Lubanga*, 18 October 2006, 7.

the complexity of the cases has mostly been considered an almost absolute justification for the length of pre-trial proceedings'.[154] While one year was not enough to qualify as an unreasonable delay in the *Bemba* case,[155] it is important to note that there is not a bright-line rule on what is and is not reasonable.

Article 60(4) is limited in its applicability because the inexcusable delay must be attributable to the ICC prosecutor. In a 2014 decision, Pre-Trial Chamber II tried to sideline this requirement and used Article 60(4) to release four of the defendants charged with administration of justice offences in relation to the *Bemba* case (hereafter the *Bemba et al.* case).[156] Finding that the defendants would otherwise be detained for an unreasonable period, Single Judge Tarfusser held that Article 60(4) enshrined the paramount concern that pre-trial detention not be unreasonable – regardless of whether the delay is due to the Prosecutor[157] – and ordered their release. The Appeals Chamber overturned this decision, determining that the wording of Article 60(4) was unequivocal, and that prosecutorial fault was required.[158] This limitation to Article 60(4)'s applicability has been criticised, in particular on the basis that a person detained for an unreasonable period will care little which actor is at fault.[159] In response to this limitation there is now a third, judge-made, ground for granting interim release.

Article 60(3) imposes an obligation on the ICC to review its decision on interim release periodically (the 120-day rule is set out in the RPE). From a simple reading therefore, it does not appear to provide an additional ground for interim release. However, in a decision taken in May 2015, the Appeals Chamber gave Article 60(3) a much more substantial role. Interpreting Article 60(3) pursuant to Article 21(3), it was

---

[154] Zeegers, *International Criminal Tribunals and Human Rights*, 269.
[155] *Bemba*, 14 August 2009, §28.
[156] *Situation in the Central African Republic in the Case of the Prosecutor v. Jean-Pierre Bemba Gombo, Aimé Kilolo Musamba, Jean-Jaques Mangenda Kabongo, Fidèle Babala Wandu and Narcisse Arido*, ICC-01/05-01/13-703, Decision Ordering the Release of Aimé Kilolo Musamba, Jean-Jaques Mangenda Kabongo, Fidèle Babala Wandu and Narcisse Arido, 21 October 2014 (Pre-Trial Chamber II) (*Bemba et al.*, 21 October 2014).
[157] *Bemba et al.*, 21 October 2014, 5.
[158] *The Prosecutor v. Jean-Pierre Bemba Gombo, Aimé Kilolo Musamba, Jean-Jaques Mangenda Kabongo, Fidèle Babala Wandu and Narcisse Arido*, ICC-01/05-01/13-969, Judgment on the Appeals against Pre-Trial Chamber II's Decisions Regarding Interim Release in Relation to Aimé Kilolo Musamba, Jean-Jacques Mangenda, Fidèle Babala Wandu, and Narcisse Arido and Order for Reclassification, 29 May 2015 (Appeals Chamber) (*Bemba et al.*, 29 May 2015), §42.
[159] Khan, 'Article 60', 1482.

held to be the 'proper legal avenue to protect the right to liberty of a person, as well as the right to be tried within a reasonable period of time'.[160] According to the decision, the length of time an accused has spent in detention is one of the factors that needs to be considered when conducting the periodic review required by Article 60(3). A balance must be struck between the risks under Article 58(1)(b) and the duration of the detention, taking into account what caused the delay in proceedings and the circumstances of the case as a whole.[161] If on balance the period of detention has become unreasonable, interim release must be ordered.

Whenever interim release is granted, regardless of under which part of Article 60, the Chamber can choose to impose conditions. This is clearly indicated by the wording of paragraphs 2 and 4, and may be assumed in the case of paragraph 3, since there is no reason for interim release under the latter to be treated differently.[162] The types of conditions that can be imposed are found in Rule 119 RPE, and include travel restrictions and restrictions on contact with victims and witnesses.

An overarching question that affects interim release in general is whether the ICC is obliged to secure the cooperation of a State before a person can be released. It seems that the answer is yes. This means that the ICC must identify the State where the accused will be hosted while on interim release, and secure the consent of that State to act as host. This conclusion is not apparent from the Rome Statute protection framework, which contains only one provision on this issue. Regulation 51 of the Regulations of the Court provides that: 'For the purposes of a decision on interim release, the Pre-Trial Chamber shall seek observations from the host State and from the State to which the person seeks to be released.' Seeking observations is not the same thing as securing cooperation in a particular case. But there is support for the proposed interpretation of the ICC's obligations in the case law of the ICC.

In a decision in 2009 that refused interim release to Bemba, the Appeals Chamber stated that the ICC is

> dependent on State cooperation in relation to accepting a person who has been conditionally released as well as ensuring that the conditions

---

[160] *Bemba et al.*, 29 May 2015, §43. This approach to Article 60(3) was also applied by Trial Chamber VII in *The Prosecutor v. Jean-Pierre Bemba Gombo, Aimé Kilolo Musamba, Jean-Jaques Mangenda Kabongo, Fidèle Babala Wandu and Narcisse Arido*, ICC-01/05-01/13-2291, Decision on Mr Bemba's Application for Release, 12 June 2018 (Trial Chamber VII) (*Bemba et al.*, 12 June 2018), §16.

[161] *Bemba et al.*, 29 May 2015, §45.

[162] Such was the finding of the Appeals Chamber in *Bemba et al.*, 29 May 2015, §48.

imposed by the Court are enforced. Without such cooperation, any decision of the Court granting conditional release would be ineffective.[163]

On the basis of this reasoning, the Chamber held that an order to grant conditional interim release cannot be made unless a State is identified that is willing to host the accused and enforce any conditions attached to the release.[164] This overturned a Pre-Trial Chamber decision which had granted interim release to Bemba, but which had left the determination of conditions and the identification of the host State to a future hearing.[165] Instead, the Appeals Chamber determined that the decision to release and the imposition of conditions are to be taken in one unseverable decision.[166]

One can appreciate the logic that the Appeals Chamber was following: if interim release is only possible if conditions are imposed, then before the release is granted a State must be identified that is willing and able to enforce those conditions. However, the author proposes that the same logic can be achieved without the Appeals Chamber's degree of strictness. It should be possible to decide that interim release should be granted, and specify the conditions, and yet defer the decision on which State will host the accused until a later date. This would mean that the decision on whether or not to *grant* interim release is not dependent on State cooperation, but the *implementation* of the decision is. While one might argue that this does not much improve the situation facing an accused where cooperation is lacking, it does at least provide a declarative protection of the right to liberty. Better that the ICC declare that the accused is entitled to release, but have trouble implementing it, than to subjugate the right to liberty entirely to State cooperation by denying interim release where a host State cannot be found.

Trial Chamber VII went some way towards endorsing this approach in a decision taken in 2018.[167] On appealing his conviction for war crimes and crimes against humanity, Bemba was acquitted by the Appeals Chamber in June 2018.[168] Whereas a full acquittal on appeal would

---

[163] *Bemba*, 2 December 2009, §107.
[164] *Bemba*, 2 December 2009, §106.
[165] *Bemba*, 14 August 2009, 35–7. The Appeals Chamber not only dismissed the approach of the Pre-Trial Chamber as to identifying the host State and setting conditions, but also disagreed with the decision to grant interim release at all.
[166] *Bemba*, 2 December 2009, §105.
[167] *Bemba et al.*, 12 June 2018.
[168] *The Prosecutor v. Jean Pierre Bemba Gombo*, ICC-01/05-01/08-3636-Red, Judgment on the Appeal of Mr Jean-Pierre Bemba Gombo against Trial Chamber III's 'Judgment pursuant to Article 74 of the Statute', 8 June 2018 (Appeals Chamber).

normally result in immediate release from custody, proceedings in the *Bemba et al.* case were ongoing regarding the charges of witness interference. *Bemba et al.* ultimately resulted in a conviction at both Trial and Appeal levels, but at the time of the acquittal in the principal case, Bemba was still awaiting a sentencing decision from the Appeals Chamber. Trial Chamber VII confirmed that Article 60(2) and (3) continued to apply until proceedings against an accused were entirely concluded, even when the guilt of an accused had been confirmed on appeal and all that remained was the sentencing decision.[169] It was held that, in light of Article 60(2) and (3) and under the circumstances of the case, continued detention while awaiting sentencing was not justified.[170] In granting interim release, a number of conditions were imposed[171] (such as notification to the Court of overnight travel and changes of address), but it was not definitively determined where Bemba would be released to. The Chamber noted that Bemba had requested release to Belgium, that Belgium had expressed a willingness to host Bemba in the past, and that Belgium had signed an agreement with the Court on hosting individuals granted interim release. This was deemed sufficient, and the Chamber was 'satisfied that no further submissions on this point' were necessary at that time.[172]

The circumstances surrounding this 2018 decision differ from those surrounding the 2009 decision in which the Appeals Chamber set down the strict condition of needing to identify a host State before interim release was granted. In the 2009 case, the Pre-Trial Chamber that made the initial release determination gave no indication of which State may be prepared to act as host, and deferred this consideration to an entirely separate decision to be taken at a later time. In the 2018 decision, the plan for releasing Bemba to Belgium was more concrete. However, in not confirming Belgium's willingness at the time of the release decision, Trial Chamber VII's approach is less strict than the Appeals Chamber's approach, which may indicate a shift in favour of the interpretation of Article 60 proposed in the preceding paragraph. Indeed, there is no support for the Appeals Chamber's position in the drafting history, Rome Statute protection framework, or other relevant interpretation materials. As such, the author argues that in line with Article 21(3), the

---

[169] *Bemba et al.*, 12 June 2018, §11.
[170] *Bemba et al.*, 12 June 2018, §§18–24.
[171] *Bemba et al.*, 12 June 2018, §26.
[172] *Bemba et al.*, 12 June 2018, §25.

interpretation and application of the law that best protects human rights is the one to be preferred, even if this protection is just declaratory.

Article 60 allows for the possibility that an accused be granted interim release without conditions attached. In this case, the logic of the Appeals Chamber in the 2009 decision would not apply. This is true in theory, but the situation is very unlikely to arise in practice. It seems distinctly unlikely that an ICC accused, given their prominence and the gravity of the alleged crimes, would be released unconditionally. Even for accused charged with administration of justice offences, which are relatively minor compared to the core crimes, conditions have been attached for release.[173] It has been the practice of the Court that, at the very least, accused must provide details of the address at which they will be residing while on interim release.[174] This seemingly simple condition necessitates that the accused have made arrangements for where they will be released. In the *Bemba et al.* case, the addresses were provided to the Court before the accused were released.[175] With respect to one of the accused (Jean-Jacques Mangenda Kabongo), release was deferred after the other three defendants were released because arrangements with the UK had not been finalised (although the UK had been specified in the release decision as the designated host State).[176]

Before concluding the discussion on the ICC's obligations, it is necessary to inquire whether the interpretation of Article 60 passes the Article 21(3) test. It can be safely said that Article 60(2), (3), and (4) provide comprehensive protection for the right to liberty, in the sense that they provide for interim release in the different situations in which it might be warranted. Where matters become problematic in terms of human rights protection is the requirement that the ICC identify and secure the cooperation of a host State before an order for interim release can be implemented. This has been criticised for going down the 'wrong and dangerous'[177] path of making the right to liberty dependent on 'practical

---

[173] *The Prosecutor v. Jean-Pierre Bemba Gombo, Aimé Kilolo Musamba, Jean-Jaques Mangenda Kabongo, Fidèle Babala Wandu and Narcisse Arido*, ICC-01/05-01/13-1151, Decision Regarding Interim Release, 17 August 2015 (Trial Chamber VII).

[174] *Bemba et al.*, 21 October 2014, 6.

[175] Aimé Kilolo Musamba to Belgium, Jean-Jacques Mangenda Kabongo to the UK, Fidèle Babala Wandu to the DRC, and Narcisse Arido to France (*Bemba et al.*, 21 October 2014, 5-6).

[176] 'Aimé Kilolo Musamba, Narcisse Arido and Fidèle Babala Wandu released from ICC custody', ICC Press Release, 23 October 2014.

[177] Göran Sluiter 'Atrocity Crimes Litigation: Some Human Rights Concerns Occasioned by Selected 2009 Case Law' (2010) 8 *Northwestern Journal of International Human Rights*, 248, 265.

arrangements'.[178] Such views are justified given the reluctance ICC judges have noted on the part of States to host accused on interim release.[179] However undesirable this state of affairs, it is attributable to the limitation on the ICC's competence, and on the absence of corresponding obligations on States to host accused. As will be discussed in the following section, Article 21(3) cannot be used to remedy this deficiency, as it does not require States to undertake entirely new obligations to which they did not consent, including the hosting of accused on interim release on their territory.

3.3.3 Obligations of States

States are clearly indispensable for the protection of the right to liberty through the implementation of interim release. The question of great importance is therefore whether they are under an obligation to provide the assistance and cooperation required for interim release to be implemented. No relevant obligations are to be found beyond the Rome Statute protection framework, as human rights law does not require a State to take onto its territory and into its jurisdiction a person who would not otherwise be there. The present inquiry must therefore focus on the Rome Statute protection framework.

There is no provision within this framework that deals explicitly with this point. If such an obligation exists, it would be the result of an interpretation of the cooperation obligations in Part 9 of the Statute. The Single Judge in the Pre-Trial Chamber in the *Bemba* case made some ambiguous remarks on this question. After noting that the Court is dependent on State cooperation, she recalled the general obligation on States Parties to cooperate under Article 86 of the Rome Statute, and underlined that that provision applied to the whole Statute, including Article 60 on interim release.[180] One commentator offers support for the Single Judge's apparent position when making an argument on the meaning of the phrase 'investigation and

---

[178] Sergey Golubok, 'Pre-Conviction Detention before the International Criminal Court: Compliance or Fragmentation' (2010) 9 *Law & Practice of International Courts & Tribunals*, 295, 308.
[179] See for example, *The Prosecutor v. Jean-Pierre Bemba Gombo, Aimé Kilolo Musamba, Jean-Jaques Mangenda Kabongo, Fidèle Babala Wandu and Narcisse Arido*, ICC-01/05-01/13-588, Decision on 'Narcisse Arido's Request for Interim Release', 24 July 2014 (Pre-Trial Chamber II) (*Bemba et al.*, 24 July 2014), §27.
[180] *Bemba*, 14 August 2009, §§85 and 86.

prosecution of crimes'. It is in relation to these activities that the general cooperation obligation in Article 86 obliges States to assist the Court. The commentator argues that 'investigation and prosecution' should be given a broad meaning that includes interim release, as this is related to prosecution.[181]

The Appeals Chamber, when reviewing the Single Judge's decision, did not endorse this position. Instead, in the 2009 decision discussed in the previous section, the judges noted that granting interim release was dependent on identifying a 'willing State'.[182] Contrary to the comments of the Pre-Trial Chamber, this supports the idea that assistance must be provided voluntarily. Moreover, in further decisions, the language used by the Appeals Chamber when discussing possible host States is notable for terms such as 'availability', 'willingness', and 'ability',[183] none of which have a compulsory character. A further indication of the voluntary nature of State assistance is a report by the ICC to the Assembly of States Parties, in which measures to encourage State assistance in interim release are clearly discussed under the heading of 'Voluntary Agreements'.[184] Such reports are valuable as an additional source of practice, outside of judicial decisions, and illustrate how the ICC understands its obligations.

The argument that the term 'investigation and prosecution' can be said to cover interim release has merit, especially in light of Article 21(3). However, the ICC is not empowered – even by Article 21(3) – to use cooperation requests to create obligations for States to host accused on interim release. This interpretation was not envisaged by the Rome Statute, and does not find support in practice, the drafting history, or the Rome Statute protection framework more broadly. As explained in Chapter 2, Article 21(3) cannot be used as a means to oblige States to accept non-nationals on their territory, given the proximity of this issue to the core tenets of State sovereignty, and in the absence of explicit consent to this effect.

---

[181] Sluiter, 'Atrocity Crimes Litigation', 266.
[182] *Bemba*, 2 December 2009, §§104, 106
[183] *The Prosecutor v. Jean-Pierre Bemba Gombo*, ICC-01/05-01/08-1722, Judgment on the Appeal of Mr Jean-Pierre Bemba Gombo against the Decision of Trial Chamber III of 2 September 2011 Entitled 'Decision on the "Demande de mise en liberté de M. Jean-Pierre Bemba Gombo afin d'accomplir ses devoirs civiques en République Démocratique du Congo"', 9 September 2011 (Appeals Chamber), §38; *Bemba et al.*, 24 July 2014, §27.
[184] Assembly of States Parties (ASP), 'Report of the Court on Cooperation', ICC-ASP/12/35, 9 October 2013, 5.

3.3.4 Problems in Human Rights Protection

The granting and implementation of interim release is an important ICC function, but is one that requires the involvement and assistance of States. States, however, are under no legal obligation to provide this assistance. The result is a structural gap in protection: the actor with the *obligation* to protect the right to liberty lacks the *capacity* to do so (the ICC), and the actor with the *capacity* to protect the right to liberty lacks the *obligation* to do so (States).

This structural problem will only be relevant where the accused who is to be granted interim release cannot return to a State that is obliged to take them, for example, the State of nationality or permanent residence. In the *Bemba et al.* case, the four accused were granted interim release to countries that they were either a national of, or for which they had a visa or residence permit.[185] In future cases it is more than likely that interim release will be granted only on the condition that the accused *does not* return to their home country. This may be in an effort to prevent them from interfering with witnesses, of taking advantage of their network, or because they would not be safe. In these cases, it is necessary that a third State volunteer to host them. The potential problem with this arrangement is evident: how is the right to liberty to be adequately protected if no State agrees to host an accused on interim release?

In acknowledgment of this problem, the ICC has taken a proactive approach. Even though it was not foreseen by the Rome Statute protection framework, the ICC drafted a model agreement on interim release to be signed by States willing to act as hosts.[186] The agreement is designed to facilitate consultations between the ICC and States (in line with Regulation 51 of the Regulations of the Court), identify willing States, and streamline discussions on State cooperation.[187] Such an agreement was concluded in 2014 between the ICC and Belgium, and in 2018 between the ICC and Argentina.[188] The ICC is committed to concluding further agreements with other States.[189]

---

[185] *Bemba et al.*, 21 October 2014, 5–6.

[186] ASP, 'Report of the Court on Cooperation', §39.

[187] Anne-Aurore Bertrand and Natacha Schauder, 'Practical Cooperation Challenges Faced by the Registry of the International Criminal Court', in Olympia Bekou and Daley Birkett (eds.), *Cooperation and the International Criminal Court: Perspectives from Theory and Practice* (Brill, 2016), 170.

[188] Framework Agreement between the Argentine Republic and the International Criminal Court on Interim Release 2018, ICC-PRES/25-01-18.

[189] 'Belgium and ICC sign agreement on interim release', ICC Press Release, 10 April 2014.

Such agreements are a step in the right direction, but ultimately do not solve the structural problem facing interim release at the ICC. The agreement between the ICC and Argentina enabled Argentina to indicate its 'willingness' to accept individuals granted interim release,[190] but makes clear that the decision on whether to accept an individual will be taken on a case-by-case basis.[191] Argentina retains therefore the discretion to refuse to host a particular individual. The content of the agreement between the ICC and Belgium is confidential, but Pre-Trial Chamber II provided some crucial details about it in a decision concerning the interim release of one of the accused in the *Bemba et al.* case. The Agreement is described by the Chamber as *not* providing for an unconditional availability and willingness on the part of Belgium to accept accused, and certainly not as establishing an obligation on Belgium to do so.[192] Instead, the agreement regulates the procedure by which consultations are to take place, leaving the ultimate decision on whether to accept a particular individual in a particular instance to the State concerned.[193]

3.3.5 Conclusion

Extended periods of pre-trial detention appear to be the norm in international criminal justice. While in many cases detention is justified because of flight risk, potential interference with the investigation, and so on, careful consideration must be given in each instance as to whether the accused qualifies for interim release. The mechanism of interim release is an important safeguard for the right to liberty of accused, and is included in the Rome Statute protection framework in Article 60 of the Statute.

Granting interim release where merited is an important function of the ICC. However, the institutional nature of the ICC, and in particular its lack of territory into which an accused could be released, means that it is a function that the Court cannot carry out alone. A successful interim release system at the ICC therefore requires the involvement of multiple

---

[190] Article 2 of the Framework Agreement sets out the 'purpose of this agreement' as: 'The Argentine Republic hereby indicates to the Registrar of the Court ("Registrar") its willingness to accept person(s) granted Interim Release by a Chamber.'
[191] Article 4(2) of the Framework Agreement.
[192] *The Prosecutor v. Jean-Pierre Bemba Gombo, Aimé Kilolo Musamba, Jean-Jaques Mangenda Kabongo, Fidèle Babala Wandu and Narcisse Arido*, ICC-01/05-01/13-612, Decision on the First Review of Jean-Jacques Mangenda Kabongo's Detention Pursuant to Article 60(3) of the Statute, 5 August 2014 (Pre-Trial Chamber II), §32.
[193] 'Belgium and ICC sign agreement on interim release'.

actors. Unfortunately, the Rome Statute protection system does not oblige States to play a part in interim release. This state of affairs results in a structural problem, whereby the right to liberty of accused is left vulnerable to the willingness of States. Agreements on interim release between the ICC and States are a first step in remedying the protection gap, but in their current formulation still leave the Court reliant on voluntary cooperation.

3.4 Treatment in the Enforcement State

3.4.1 Introduction

With a guilty verdict pronounced, appeals exhausted, and sentence handed down, the punishment in the name of the international community can begin. The most common form that this punishment takes is a custodial sentence. The period of imprisonment can be up to thirty years, or a life sentence in very extreme cases.[194] Enforcing these sentences has been described as the backbone of the international criminal justice system.[195]

The ICC does have its own detention centre, but this is designed to hold accused during the trial and on a temporary basis thereafter. Instead, the predominant feature of the enforcement of sentences at the international level is that it is done in national prison facilities provided by States, and not at the ICC itself. So once a conviction is finalised, the individual will be transferred to a State Party and will serve their sentence in that State (hereafter the 'enforcement State'). The enforcement State carries out the day-to-day aspects of the sentence, while the ICC, as the actor that handed down the guilty verdict and custodial sentence, maintains a supervisory role.

There are a number of reasons why the drafters of the Rome Statute chose this approach to enforcement. One is that, by delegating enforcement to States, the drafters could avoid developing ICC prison rules;[196] another is that this way the costs of enforcement lie with the State.[197] As

---

[194] Article 77 of the Rome Statute.
[195] Claus Kreß and Göran Sluiter, 'Enforcement' in Antonio Cassese, Paola Gaeta, and John R. W. D. Jones (eds.), *The Rome Statute of the International Criminal Court: A Commentary* (Oxford University Press, 2002), 1752.
[196] Schabas, A Commentary on the Rome Statute, 1082.
[197] Rule 208 of the ICC RPE. The cost aspect is important: numbers may seem small at present, but the ICTY in its twenty years convicted ninety individuals with at least some more to come before the Residual Mechanism for International Criminal Tribunals

the title suggests, the focus of this section is on the period of time that the convicted person spends in a national prison, and not the time spent at the ICC detention facility. While the current practice of the ICC seems to be to host convicted persons for an extended period after their conviction,[198] the applicable legal regime in such cases has been dealt with extensively elsewhere.[199]

Faced with a long stretch in detention, a core concern for the detained person will be the treatment they receive during that period, and as such the right to protection from torture and inhuman and degrading treatment and punishment (hereafter 'inhuman treatment') will be the focus of this section. This right encompasses a number of concerns: Is the prison overcrowded? Is there sufficient food and water, good hygiene, and access to medical treatment? Is corporal punishment used? In addition to these considerations, an important element of the right to protection from inhuman treatment is protection from being removed to a State where an individual would be exposed to such treatment. The prohibition on removal aspect of this right is well established in the case law of international human rights bodies,[200] including the ECtHR[201] and the

---

closes (www.icty.org/en/cases/key-figures-cases, last accessed 2 May 2019). With housing one person in the ICC Detention Centre costing hundreds of euros a week, the financing would soon become untenable.

[198] Following his conviction for war crimes and crimes against humanity, Germain Katanga was sentenced to twelve years imprisonment in May 2014. Thomas Lubanga, convicted of war crimes, had his sentence of fourteen years confirmed by the Appeals Chamber in December 2014. And yet, it was not until December 2015 that the ICC designated the DRC as the enforcement State for both individuals, and transferred them there that same month ('Thomas Lubanga Dyilo and Germain Katanga transferred to the DRC to serve their sentences of imprisonment', ICC Press Release, 19 December 2015). In the interim, both spent an extended period of time in ICC detention, present on Dutch territory.

[199] For a comprehensive overview, see Abels, 'Prisoners of the International Community'.

[200] In literature and case law, the term 'non-refoulement' is often used in reference to both Article 33 of the Refugee Convention *and* the prohibition on removal under human rights law. So as to avoid confusion, the term non-refoulement has been avoided in this study. Instead, and in order to indicate that the focus of the analysis is on human rights law, the terms used include 'protection from removal' and 'protection in the State'. Instead of terms such as 'asylum application', the book refers to 'applications for protection'.

[201] One of the first instances of this was the *Soering* case (*Case of Soering* v. *The United Kingdom*, Application no. 14038/88, Judgment, 7 July 1989) before the ECtHR, in which the UK was prevented from sending an individual to the United States, as to do so would violate Article 3 ECHR by exposing him to a real risk of inhuman treatment. Other ECHR provisions have since been interpreted as containing similar prohibitions, including Articles 2 and 6 ECHR (see Maarten den Heijer, 'Whose Rights and Which Rights? The Continuing Story of Non-Refoulement under the European Convention on Human Rights' (2008) 10 *European Journal of Migration & Law*, 277).

Human Rights Committee,[202] and codified in Article 3 of the Convention Against Torture.[203]

The Rome Statute provisions establishing the system for the enforcement of sentences was one of the most delicately drafted in Part 10 of the Statute.[204] It seeks to balance the reality that sentences will be administered in a State, with the Court's overall responsibility for sentence enforcement;[205] and balance States' desire for autonomy with the need to ensure uniform human rights protection.[206] As is often the case with systems that are the product of careful compromise, the regime is at times specific and at times vague. Understanding how the right against inhuman treatment is protected through the obligations of the ICC and States Parties involves creative interpretation in order to flesh out the sometimes ambiguous provisions.

3.4.2 Obligations of the ICC

The ICC's obligations can be divided into two categories. The first relates to the prohibition on removing a convicted person to a State where they will be subjected to inhuman treatment. These are discussed first in this section since they are logically prior. The second category of obligations relates to those applicable once a convicted person is already in a State of enforcement.

3.4.2.1 Prohibition on Removal

When a sentence of imprisonment is handed down, it is the task of the ICC to designate an enforcement State. Article 103 of the Rome Statute gives the ICC discretion in doing so, and the task is carried out by the Presidency of the Court.[207] States that have expressed their willingness to

---

[202] *Ng v. Canada*, Communication No. 469/1991, 7 January 1994, §16.2; Human Rights Committee, 'General Comment 31', CCPR/C/21/Rev.1/Add.13, 26 May 2004, §12.
[203] Convention against Torture and Other Cruel, Inhuman or Degrading Treatment or Punishment 1984, Article 3 states: 'No State Party shall expel, return ("refouler") or extradite a person to another State where there are substantial grounds for believing that he would be in danger of being subjected to torture.'
[204] Hirad Abtahi and Steven Arrigg Koh, 'The Emerging Enforcement Practice of the International Criminal Court' (2013) 45 *Cornell International Law Journal*, 1, 12.
[205] Kimberley Prost, 'Chapter 14: Enforcement' in Roy Lee (ed), *The International Criminal Court, Elements of Crimes and Rules of Procedure and Evidence* (Transnational Publishers, 2001), 673.
[206] Michael Stiel and Carl-Friedrich Stuckenberg, 'Article 106', Case Matrix Network, 30 June 2016, §1243.
[207] Rule 199 of the RPE.

enforce sentences are included on a list, and will generally conclude an 'Enforcement of Sentences Agreement' with the Court (Enforcement Agreement). From this group of States, the Presidency will designate an enforcement State in a particular case.[208] It is then for the designated State to either accept or reject the designation.

Article 103(3) of the Rome Statute constitutes the key obligation on the ICC's part that protects convicted persons from removal to a situation of risk. This provision sets out the factors that are to guide the Presidency's discretion in designating an enforcement State. They include the convicted person's nationality, the convicted person's own preferences, and the principle of equitable distribution among States. Importantly, one of the factors guiding the Presidency's discretion is the 'application of widely accepted international treaty standards governing the treatment of prisoners'.[209] This term, while somewhat broad and vague, will undoubtedly include treaty provisions that require States to protect individuals from inhuman treatment while in detention (for example, Article 3 ECHR, Article 7 ICCPR, and Article 5 African Charter on Human and People's Rights (ACHPR)). The application of these standards by a potential enforcement State is therefore a factor that the Presidency should take into account.

Article 103 does not leave much space for interpretation, and its wording is unambiguous: it gives the ICC Presidency the discretion to choose an enforcement State, as long as, in exercising this discretion, the Presidency 'take(s) account' of certain considerations, including human rights. Despite being indicated by the wording of the Statute, such an application of the law would not, it is submitted, satisfy the Article 21(3) test. To safeguard the right to protection from removal to a situation of risk, it is necessary that there be legal constraints on the exercise of discretion, not just guidance. Otherwise the Presidency would be free to designate any State as long as it had 'taken account' of human rights, regardless of whether there is a real risk of inhuman treatment. The author therefore proposes that, in light of Article 21(3), Article 103 must be interpreted so as to create an obligation on the Presidency to refrain from designating an enforcement State where the convicted person would face a real risk of inhuman treatment. A necessary corollary of this is that the

---

[208] Article 103(1) of the Rome Statute.
[209] Article 103(3)(b) of the Rome Statute.

ICC is also obliged not to transfer a convicted person to a State of this type, nor to ask another actor to do so on its behalf.

3.4.2.2 Conditions of Imprisonment and Inhuman Treatment

Once an appropriate enforcement State has been designated by the Presidency, and that State has agreed to enforce the sentence, then the convicted person can be transferred to the enforcement State's custody. At this point, concern shifts away from protecting a convicted person from exposure to a risk of inhuman treatment, to protecting the person from conditions of imprisonment that would constitute inhuman treatment. As the individual is, by this point, no longer under the ICC's physical control, the Court's obligations relate to supervising the conduct of the enforcement State.

That the ICC has a supervisory role when it comes to the enforcement of sentences is clear from Article 106:

(1) The enforcement of a sentence of imprisonment shall be subject to the supervision of the Court and shall be consistent with widely accepted international treaty standards governing treatment of prisoners.
(2) The conditions of imprisonment shall be governed by the law of the State of enforcement and shall be consistent with widely accepted international treaty standards governing treatment of prisoners; in no case shall such conditions be more or less favourable than those available to prisoners convicted of similar offences in the State of enforcement.

However, what is not clear from the wording of the provision is the precise scope and nature of this supervisory role. In particular, two questions of importance are left unanswered: firstly, does the supervisory role require the ICC to monitor the conditions of imprisonment in a State of enforcement's detention facilities; and secondly, if there is such an obligation and the Court identifies that the enforcement State is failing to uphold the proper standards of treatment, what can the Court do to address this?

In terms of the first question, the very set up of Article 106 adds to the ambiguity. The ICC's supervisory role is mentioned only in the first subparagraph, and not in the second, and it is the second that specifically mentions conditions of detention. If subparagraphs (1) and (2) are read conjunctively, one could propose that the ICC is endowed with an overarching supervisory role, and the division in the article was done for the sake of readability. Alternatively, the two subparagraphs could be read disjunctively, in which case the ICC would have no supervisory role over the conditions of detention, which instead is left entirely to the enforcement State.

It is submitted that a conjunctive reading of the provision is the more plausible interpretation. Article 106(1) links the supervisory role of the ICC with the 'widely accepted international treaty standards governing treatment of prisoners'. As these treaty standards concern the *treatment* of prisoners, they are clearly linked to conditions of imprisonment. Therefore, even though the term 'conditions of imprisonment' is only used in Article 106(2), it must be envisaged that the Court will have some supervisory role in this respect. Support for this proposition can be found in the opinions of academic commentators[210] and in developments at the Special Court for Sierra Leone (SCSL). The Statute of SCSL, drafted two years after the Rome Conference, states that the conditions of imprisonment are governed by national law, but specifically makes them subject to the supervision of the Court.[211]

Still further support stems from the broader context in which Article 106 is located, namely other provisions of the Rome Statute protection framework. Both Rule 211 RPE and provisions in the Enforcement Agreements between States and the Court all provide the ICC with ways to collect information concerning sentence enforcement. According to Rule 211(a), the Presidency is obliged to make arrangements to ensure that a sentenced person's right to communicate confidentially and freely with the Court, as provided for in Article 106(3) of the Rome Statute, is respected. In this way, the convicted person can inform the Court of any problems. Rule 211(b) and (c) allow the

---

[210] Stiel and Stuckenberg, 'Article 106': 'enforcement ... must be understood to include not only the enforcement of the sentence as such but also the modalities of this enforcement, which is indicated by the reference to "standards governing the treatment of prisoners" in both paragraphs and further supported by Rule 211(1)(a)', §1244; Kreß and Sluiter provide a number of reasons why the term 'enforcement' in Article 106(1) should be read broadly, and thereby extend the supervisory power of the Court to conditions of imprisonment (Claus Kreß and Göran Sluiter, 'Imprisonment' in Antonio Cassese, Paola Gaeta, and John R. W. D. Jones (eds.), *The Rome Statute of the International Criminal Court: A Commentary* (Oxford University Press, 2002), 1805.

[211] Article 22 of the Statute of the Special Court for Sierra Leone 2002. Furthermore, this is mirrored in Article 3(2) of the Agreement between the Government of the United Kingdom of Great Britain and Northern Ireland and the Special Court for Sierra Leone on the Enforcement of Sentences of the Special Court for Sierra Leone 2007.

Presidency to request information from the enforcement State (or other reliable sources) and to designate an ICC judge or member of ICC staff to meet with the sentenced person without the national authorities present. In Enforcement Agreements concluded to date, States have agreed to permit regular inspections of their detention facilities by the Court, the International Committee of the Red Cross (ICRC), or the European Committee on the Prevention of Torture and Inhuman and Degrading Treatment and Punishment.[212] The existence of these inspection provisions strongly points towards an interpretation of Article 106 in which the ICC does supervise the conditions of enforcement, as otherwise information gathering would be without purpose.

The question which necessarily follows on from this is what course of action, if any, is the ICC empowered to take if it finds that an enforcement State is not upholding the necessary standards of treatment (as to what these standards of treatment are, this is discussed in Section 3.4.3 on the obligations of the enforcement State). This is the second question left open by the wording of Article 106.

One course of action open to the Court is contained in Article 104 of the Rome Statute, and indeed the very existence of this article is further support for a conjunctive reading of Article 106. In what has been termed the 'ultimate' exercise of supervision,[213] Article 104 permits the ICC to

---

[212] ICRC countries: Belgium (Article 7 of the Agreement between the International Criminal Court and the Government of the Kingdom of Belgium on the Enforcement of Sentences of the International Criminal Court 2010), Denmark (Article 7 Agreement between the Kingdom of Denmark and the International Criminal Court on the Enforcement of Sentences of the International Criminal Court 2012), Finland (Article 7 of the Agreement between the International Criminal Court and the Government of the Republic of Finland on the Enforcement of Sentences of the International Criminal Court 2011), Mali (Article 4(1)(b) of the Accord entre la Cour pénale internationale et le Gouvernement de la République du Mali concernant l'exécution des peines prononcées par la Cour 2012), Argentina (Article 4 of the Agreement between the Argentine Republic and the International Criminal Court on the Enforcement of Sentences of the International Criminal Court), Norway (Article 6 of the Agreement between the Kingdom of Norway and the International Criminal Court on the Enforcement of Sentences of the International Criminal Court 2016), and Serbia (Article 7 of the Agreement between the Republic of Serbia and the International Criminal Court on the Enforcement of Sentences of the International Criminal Court 2011); ICC: Austria (Article 7 of the Agreement between the International Criminal Court and the Federal Government of Austria on the Enforcement of Sentences of the International Criminal Court 2005); Torture Committee: UK (Article 6 of the Agreement between the Government of the United Kingdom of Great Britain and Northern Ireland and the International Criminal Court on the Enforcement of Sentences of the International Criminal Court 2007).

[213] Stiel and Stuckenberg, 'Article 106', §1244.

move a convicted person to a different enforcement State. While not a common practice, moving a prisoner to a different enforcement State is not unheard of in international criminal justice. After the ICTY convicted Radislav Krstić on genocide charges, he was transferred to the United Kingdom to serve his sentence. In 2010 he was attacked by three fellow inmates and severely injured.[214] While the decisions on the situation remain confidential, it would seem that the UK was deemed unable to secure Krstić's safety, resulting in his transfer back to The Hague. In 2014 the ICTY designated Poland as the enforcement State, where Krstić remains today.[215] In another case dealing with the UK, Charles Taylor applied to be moved from an English prison to a detention facility in Rwanda. In support of this application he cited threats to his safety, inhuman treatment resulting from his isolation, and his right to be closer to his family, who he claimed could not visit because of immigration constraints. In this case the SCSL did not consider it necessary for him to be moved, and dismissed his arguments.[216]

Limiting the ICC's options to the one contained in Article 104 would give the ICC an 'all-or-nothing' supervisory approach: either it must do nothing, or it must move the individual elsewhere.[217] The wording of Article 106 fails to indicate whether a less drastic course of action is available, such as obliging an enforcement State to make changes in the conditions of detention. In order to discern the availability of such an option, it is necessary to look beyond the wording of Article 106 itself and consider the drafting history of the provision, its broader context, and scholarly opinion.

From the drafting history of Article 106, it becomes clear that a distinction was intended between the ICC Presidency's supervision of the enforcement of the sentence *as such*, and the obligation to supervise the *modalities* (conditions) of enforcement.[218] The term 'enforcement of the sentence *as such*' refers to the fact that the sentence is served, not the way in which it is served. It concerns issues such as early release and pardon, but not the conditions in the prison. The ICC's supervision of these elements of enforcement is to be strict.[219] For example, if a State

---

[214] Denis Dzidic, 'Srebrenica genocide convict sues Britain over attack', Balkan Transitional Justice, 6 November 2014.
[215] 'Polish jail takes Bosnian war criminal', news.com.au, 22 March 2014.
[216] 'Ex-Liberia president Charles Taylor to stay in UK prison', BBC News, 25 March 2015.
[217] Stiel and Stuckenberg, 'Article 106', §1244.
[218] Kreß and Sluiter, 'Imprisonment', 1805–6.
[219] Kreß and Sluiter, 'Imprisonment', 1805–6.

breaches Article 110(1) of the Rome Statute by releasing a convicted person before the end of their sentence, the Presidency can make a finding that the enforcement State is in breach of its obligations. The State may be ordered to arrest the person and re-imprison them. Given that issues of inhuman treatment are affected by the modalities/conditions of imprisonment, issues surrounding the enforcement of sentences *as such* need not be further discussed.[220]

As to the Court's supervisory powers over the conditions of imprisonment, the drafting history shows that a proposal to grant the ICC powers over everyday aspects of prison life was clearly rejected. As expressed in one academic commentary on the provision, 'the genesis of Article 106 makes it crystal clear that the ICC should not be given the power to order the modification of a condition of imprisonment'.[221] Based on this, the door is closed on an interpretation of Article 106 that would grant the ICC such intrusive powers.

The same commentary also argues that this same 'genesis' of the article precludes the ICC even from making any formal findings on the compliance of the enforcement State with 'treaty standards governing the treatment of prisoners'.[222] The author would disagree with this conclusion, and instead favour the view of a different commentary that argues that just because the Court cannot order a change in the conditions of detention does not mean that it could not make a finding on compliance.[223] At the very least, the broader context of Article 106 shows that the ICC can indirectly make statements on conditions of detention by using the inspection regimes established by the Enforcement Agreements. An example of how this works is Article 6(2) of the Enforcement Agreement between the United Kingdom and the ICC, which stipulates that the ICC and the UK should consult on the findings of the inspection committee, and that the UK should report any changes it has made pursuant to the committee's suggestions. The ICC could use this consultation procedure as an avenue to communicate concerns about human rights protection. Outside of the consultation procedure, nothing in Article 106 would seem to preclude the ICC from issuing a statement on conditions of imprisonment. Even though the Court cannot order a change, a public finding, or the threat of a public finding, could encourage compliance. In light of this, where

---

[220] For more detail on enforcement as such, see Kreß and Sluiter, 'Imprisonment'.
[221] Kreß and Sluiter, 'Imprisonment', 1805.
[222] Kreß and Sluiter, 'Imprisonment', 1805–6.
[223] Stiel and Stuckenberg, 'Article 106', §1244.

multiple interpretations are possible, Article 21(3) points to the interpretation that would best protect human rights. In this case, that would be to permit the ICC to make a finding on an enforcement State's compliance with its obligations, whether by means of the consultation procedure or otherwise.

The supervisory options available to the ICC therefore range from the relatively 'light' approach of consulting with the enforcement State through the inspection and reporting procedures contained in the Enforcement Agreements, to the stronger approach of making a formal finding of non-compliance, to the 'firm' approach of moving a convicted person to another State.

All that remains is the Article 21(3) test: is the interpretation and application of Article 106 of the Rome Statute outlined in this section, in particular as to the contours of the ICC's supervisory role, in accordance with internationally recognised human rights? One alteration is needed for this to be the case. The wording of the Statute is not unequivocally phrased in terms of an obligation for the ICC, but rather gives the ICC powers. If the supervision of conditions of enforcement were a discretionary matter, protection from inhuman treatment would not be sufficiently strong. The ICC should therefore have an obligation to exercise these powers: an obligation to supervise and an obligation to take action when conditions of treatment fall below the required standard.

The fact that the ICC is unable to order a change in the conditions of detention in an enforcement State does not mean that the interpretation fails to accord with Article 21(3). It may have ultimately provided greater protection to convicted persons if this had been the case, but Article 21(3) does not require this. The duty to interpret and apply the Rome Statute protection framework in accordance with human rights does not extend to imposing entirely new obligations on States to which they did not consent when signing the Statute. And an obligation to comply with orders to change conditions of enforcement would constitute an entirely new obligation. Article 106 was one of the most delicately drafted in Part 10 of the Statute,[224] with respective areas of competence being carefully carved out. The supervisory obligations that the ICC does have allow it to take a range of actions when confronted with a non-compliant enforcement State, and this together with the obligations binding on States, detailed in Section 3.4.3, is enough to comply with Article 21(3).

---

[224] Abtahi and Koh, 'Emerging Enforcement Practice of the ICC', 12.

3.4.3 Obligations of States

The obligations of a State of enforcement will only be relevant when a convicted person is located in a national prison facility. As such, this section will first explain how a State becomes an enforcement State, and after this will set out the State's obligations to protect a convicted person from inhuman treatment.

To be considered as a potential enforcement State, a State must first express its willingness to accept sentenced persons. This is a voluntary action on the part of the State, as nothing in the Rome Statute protection framework or elsewhere obliges a State to act as an enforcement State for the ICC.[225] Once a State expresses this willingness, it is included on a list of potential enforcement States kept by the Registrar.[226] From this list, and taking into account the factors in Article 103(3) of the Rome Statute, the Presidency designates a State to be the enforcer of the sentence in a particular case.[227] The designated State is then free to accept or refuse this designation;[228] in case of a refusal the Presidency will designate another State.[229] This has been called a system of double consent: consent to be included on the list of potential enforcement States, and consent to accept an individual in a particular instance.[230]

When a State puts itself forward as a potential enforcement State, it is common practice for that State to conclude an Enforcement Agreement with the Court, with the aim of providing further detail and clarification on its duties and obligations.[231] This is not a prerequisite to hosting a sentenced person, but such an agreement is invariably entered into before an individual is accepted by a State.[232] Enforcement Agreements allow for enhanced flexibility, making States more likely to accept

---

[225] Kreß and Sluiter, 'Imprisonment', 1787.
[226] Rule 200(1) of the RPE. The State is also free to withdraw from the list at any time, Rule 200(4) of the RPE.
[227] Article 103(1)(a).
[228] Article 103(1)(c).
[229] Rule 205 of the RPE.
[230] Róisín Mulgrew, 'The International Movement of Prisoners' (2011) 22 *Criminal Law Forum*, 103, 127.
[231] Such agreements are provided for in Rule 200(5) of the RPE, and are entered into between the Presidency and the State as per Regulation 114 of the Regulations of the Court.
[232] In the case of the DRC acting as the enforcement State for Katanga and Lubanga, there was no pre-existing framework enforcement agreement; however, an ad hoc agreement was put in place for hosting them in particular ('Lubanga and Katanga transferred to the DRC to serve their sentences').

sentenced persons,[233] albeit with the safeguard that the agreements must be consistent with the Rome Statute.[234] By 2018, eleven States had signed Enforcement Agreements with the ICC, including Austria, Belgium, and Mali. The Enforcement Agreements have been largely based on the model Enforcement Agreement, without significant departures.[235]

Once the procedure of double consent is completed and the convicted person is accepted and imprisoned in an enforcement State facility, it is at this point that the State acquires obligations. Under the Rome Statute protection framework, the State must ensure firstly that the convicted person is treated in accordance with 'widely accepted international treaty standards governing treatment of prisoners', and secondly that the convicted person is not treated any more or less favourably than other individuals convicted in that State of similar offences. These obligations are found in Article 106(2) of the Rome Statute.

Conditions of detention are to be governed by domestic law, but the State of enforcement is required to respect a certain floor in the level of protection, below which standards cannot drop. What constitutes this 'floor' turns on the meaning of the words 'widely accepted international treaty standards governing treatment of prisoners'.[236]

The use of the term 'treaty standards' in Article 106(2) excludes soft law instruments. This position is supported by Article 106(2)'s drafting history, which indicates that States were not willing to accept the very detailed and ambitious standards that soft law instruments contain.[237] Examples of such instruments include the Basic Principles for the Treatment of Prisoners[238] and the Body of Principles for the Protection of All Persons under Any Form of Detention or Imprisonment.[239] However, while these instruments are not directly applicable, it is not true that the principles they contain are entirely irrelevant; they are

---

[233] Gerhard Stijards, 'Enforcement', in Otto Triffterer (ed), *Commentary on the Rome Statute of the International Criminal Court: Observers' Notes, Article by Article* (Nomos, 1999), 1166.
[234] Rule 200(5) of the RPE.
[235] Abtahi and Koh, 'Emerging Enforcement Practice of the ICC', 8.
[236] With the drafting of the Rome Statute a deliberate departure was made from the sentence enforcement practice of the ICTY. In setting out the standards applicable to imprisonment, the ICTY Trial Chamber in the *Erdemović* sentencing judgment included not only universal human rights treaties, but also regional treaties and soft law instruments (Kreß and Sluiter, 'Imprisonment', 1779).
[237] Kreß and Sluiter, 'Imprisonment', 1802; Stiel and Stuckenberg, 'Article 106', §1245.
[238] General Assembly Resolution 45/111, A/45/49 (1990), 14 December 1990.
[239] General Assembly Resolution 43/173, A/43/49 (1988), 9 December 1988.

relevant to the extent that they guide the interpretation of provisions in universal treaties such as the ICCPR,[240] which are in turn covered by Article 106(2). For example, the Human Rights Committee calls on States to apply the rules contained in the Standard Minimum Rules for the Treatment of Prisoners (among others) in their compliance with the ICCPR.[241] The importance of these principles is further indicated by the fact that a number of Enforcement Agreements between States and the ICC 'recall' these bodies of rules.[242] In respect of the standard of treatment it must ensure for convicted persons, Finland has chosen to omit the word 'treaty' from its Enforcement Agreement with the Court, referring instead to 'international standards'.[243] In a similar vein, the UK has chosen the wording 'international human rights standards'.[244]

The use of the term 'widely accepted' in Article 106(2) excludes regional treaties to the extent that these differ from universal treaties. If the ECtHR has given a provision of the ECHR a particularly broad meaning, one can see how this might not qualify as a 'widely accepted' standard. While the text of Article 106(2) itself does not provide a way of discerning what would be considered widely accepted and what would not, one commentary suggests that if from a significant number of

[240] Kreß and Sluiter, 'Imprisonment', 1802; Schabas, A Commentary on the Rome Statute, 1082.
[241] Human Rights Committee, 'General Comment 21', HRI/GEN/1/Rev.1, 27 May 2008, §§5 and 13; *Mukong v. Cameroon*, Communication No. 458/1991, 21 July 1994, §9.3.
[242] For example see the third preambular paragraph of the Agreement between the International Criminal Court and the Government of the Kingdom of Belgium on the Enforcement of Sentences of the International Criminal Court 2010: 'RECALLING the widely accepted standards of international law governing the treatment of prisoners, including the Standard Minimum Rules for the Treatment of Prisoners approved by ECOSOC resolutions 663 C (XXIV) of 31 July 1957 and 2067 (LXII) of 13 May 1977, the Body of Principles for the Protection of all Persons under any Form of Detention or Imprisonment adopted by General Assembly resolution 43/173 of 9 December 1988, and the Basic Principles for the Treatment of Prisoners adopted by General Assembly resolution 45/111 of 14 December 1990.'
[243] Article 6(1) of the Agreement between the International Criminal Court and the Government of the Republic of Finland on the Enforcement of Sentences of the International Criminal Court 2011: 'The conditions of imprisonment shall be governed by the law of Finland and shall be consistent with widely accepted international standards governing treatment of prisoners; in no case shall such conditions be more or less favourable than those available to prisoners convicted of similar offences in Finland.'
[244] Article 5 of the Agreement between the Government of the United Kingdom of Great Britain and Northern Ireland and the International Criminal Court on the Enforcement of Sentences of the International Criminal Court 2007: 'The conditions of imprisonment shall be equivalent to those applicable to prisoners serving sentences under the law of the United Kingdom and shall be in accordance with relevant international human rights standards governing the treatment of prisoners.'

regional human rights treaties a common standard can be derived, then this may qualify as 'widely accepted'.[245]

An interpretation of Article 106(2) that excludes soft law and some regional law may narrow the standard of protection that enforcement States are obliged to provide for ICC convicted persons, but the Article 21(3) test is still satisfied. This is particularly so since the standard of 'widely accepted international treaty standards' in Article 106 is arguably broader than the phrase 'internationally recognised human rights' in Article 21(3).[246]

The second part of Article 106(2) makes the provision more far reaching than simply providing a minimum threshold of treatment for ICC convicted persons. States are obliged to ensure that conditions for ICC prisoners are 'no more or less favourable than those available to prisoners convicted of similar offences in the State of enforcement'. One effect of this is that if ICC prisoners must be afforded a certain level of treatment, and they cannot be treated more favourably than domestic convicted persons, then it seems that all prisoners in an enforcement State must be treated in accordance with widely accepted treaty standards, and not just the ICC prisoners. Another effect is that if the enforcement State has obligations beyond the Rome Statute protection framework that require a higher standard of treatment, this must be extended to ICC convicted as well as domestic convicted. The potential of this provision is therefore very great. If enforcement States with poor prison conditions are obliged to raise standards across the board, this would counteract the practice common in countries such as Rwanda, where special prison facilities have been built to ensure that international prisoners are housed in accordance with human rights, but where these facilities are not available to domestic prisoners.[247] While Article 106(2) seems to be clear in its meaning, academic commentators have registered a degree of scepticism as to whether the provision will indeed be applied this way. Instead, it has been suggested that States will interpret this obligation as requiring that they not treat ICC prisoners any worse than their domestic counterparts.[248] It will be interesting to see how practice around this provision develops.

---

[245] Kreß and Sluiter, 'Imprisonment', 1803.
[246] Kreß and Sluiter, 'Imprisonment', 1803.
[247] Barbora Holá and Joris van Wijk, 'Life after Conviction at International Criminal Tribunals: An Empirical Overview' (2014) 12 *Journal of International Criminal Justice*, 109, 114.
[248] Damien Scalia, 'Enforcement' in Paul De Hert, Jean Flamme, Mathias Holvoet, and Olivia Struyven (eds.), *Code of International Criminal Law and Procedure, Annotated* (Larcier, 2013), 486.

The final set of enforcement State obligations to consider are those which have their source beyond the Rome Statute protection framework. ICC accused serving custodial sentences on enforcement State territory and subject to enforcement State law clearly fall within that State's jurisdiction under human rights law. As such, the State will have obligations according to its human rights law commitments, independently from its commitments under the Rome Statute. In most situations, this will not alter a convicted person's situation, as the obligations of the State within and beyond the Rome Statute protection framework will be the same. However, if for example the enforcement State is a member of a regional treaty with stricter inhuman treatment protection, this will entitle the convicted person to a higher degree of protection than that offered under the Rome Statute protection framework.

3.4.4 Problems in Human Rights Protection

As ever with situations at the ICC involving multiple actors, many potential challenges for human rights protection can be pre-empted through a detailed understanding of the obligations involved. This is the case at this stage in relation to the ICC and the enforcement State. The delimitation of tasks and obligations between these two actors is clear: the enforcement State must ensure that a convicted person is afforded a certain standard of treatment when detained, and the ICC must monitor the enforcement State. In terms of the nature, scope, and allocation of obligations therefore, this situation presents no problems with human rights protection as between the ICC and States Parties.

3.4.5 Conclusion

As was the case with arrest and surrender, the provisions relating to treatment of convicted persons in the enforcement State contain a number of elements that are open to interpretation, and which can be read in different ways. Recourse to the drafting history, broader Rome Statute protection framework context, and academic opinion are important tools for interpretation, as is Article 21(3). As was also the case with arrest and surrender, this complexity has its advantages. The respective obligations of the ICC and enforcement States, once interpreted, are clear in the delimitation of competences: the ICC must ensure that convicted persons are not sent to a State where they would be at risk of inhuman treatment, and once the person is transferred to an enforcement State the

Court must monitor their situation and act if necessary; the enforcement State is tasked with ensuring the day-to-day protection of convicted persons. As between these two actors, a clear understanding of their respective roles prevents the emergence of the problems often found in situations of multi-actor human rights protection at the ICC.

However, the ICC and States Parties are not the only actors involved in the enforcement of sentences: the ICC's host State also has a role to play. The role of the host State in protecting the rights of convicted persons will be discussed in Part II, where it will be shown that the clarity we see in the relationship between the ICC and States Parties in the enforcement of sentences is not mirrored in the relationship between the ICC and its host State.

3.5 Acquittal and Release

3.5.1 Introduction

It would be dubious justice indeed if every person on trial at the ICC were convicted. Acquittals can be seen as supporting the legitimacy of international criminal justice, rather than undermining it, as it demonstrates a refusal on the part of the judges to convict where the standard of proof is not met, regardless of the political consequences. Even the International Military Tribunal at Nuremberg, with the accusations of victor's justice and political bias, acquitted three of the defendants.

Arriving at the decision to acquit is a task that the ICC carries out independently, in the same way as convicting an accused would be. Rendering judgment is a function that has been entrusted by the States Parties to the ICC alone. As such, the involvement of multiple actors only occurs in the events following an acquittal decision. Upon being found not guilty, the former accused person must be released from custody. Sometimes the individual will return home, as was often the case with persons acquitted by the ICTY. Vlatko Kupreškić was reportedly welcomed back to Croatia with fireworks, a band playing patriotic songs, and thousands of well-wishers.[249] At other times, the former accused is not guaranteed such a warm welcome. Concerns about security in Rwanda led to acquitted persons needing protection from the ICTR long after their trials concluded. Andre Ntagerura spent more

---

[249] Kevin Jon Heller, 'What Happens to the Acquitted?' (2008) 21 *Leiden Journal of International Law*, 663, 665.

than ten years in a Tribunal safe house waiting for a safe country to agree to accept him.[250]

It is this second group of acquitted individuals, those who cannot return to their home countries, with which this section is concerned. Faced with security concerns, at-risk acquitted persons will be primarily concerned with ensuring their protection from death or inhuman treatment. Vis-à-vis the ICC, this will manifest as a concern that the Court not order an acquitted person to be removed to a State where there is a risk of death or inhuman treatment; vis-à-vis the States Parties, this will manifest as a concern that a safe State be found that is willing to allow the acquitted person to reside on its territory, and that once there, will not subject them to ill treatment. There is a stark contrast between the number of provisions in the Rome Statute protection framework dealing with post-conviction, and the number dealing with post-acquittal. Discussion of the obligations within this framework is therefore brief as compared to the discussion in Section 3.4.

3.5.2   Obligations of the ICC

The ICC's obligations to protect acquitted persons from removal to a situation of risk can be traced to one provision. Following an acquittal, Rule 185 RPE obliges the Court to make such arrangements as it considers appropriate for the transfer of acquitted persons to a receiving State. The receiving State can be one that is obliged to receive the acquitted person, a State that has agreed to receive the person, or a State that has sought the acquitted person's extradition. A State that is obliged to receive a person is, for example, the State of nationality. In arranging the transfer, Rule 185 requires that the views of the acquitted person be taken into account. A decision of the Appeals Chamber indicates that the views of the individual should be interpreted so as to include the person's views regarding their security situation.[251]

---

[250] 'Acquitted of Rwanda genocide, now left in legal limbo', Daily Mail, 18 December 2014. It should be noted that not all ICTR acquitted have been unsuccessful: Jean Mpamabara, acquitted of genocide charges by the ICTR in 2007, was permitted by France to join his family on Mayotte, a small French island in the Indian Ocean; Bagambiki, also acquitted by the ICTR, now lives in Belgium. (Heller, 'What Happens to the Acquitted?', 669).

[251] *The Prosecutor v. Mathieu Ngudjolo Chui*, ICC-01/04-02/12-74-Red, Decision on Mr Ngudjolo's Request to Order the Victims and Witnesses Unit to Execute and the Host State to Comply with the Acquittal Judgment of 18 December 2012 Issued by Trial Chamber II of the International Criminal Court, 12 June 2013 (Appeals Chamber), §13.

From a reading of the text of Rule 185 alone, it would seem that the ICC can order the person's transfer to any State willing or obliged to receive them, as long as the views of the acquitted person have been at least considered. The views and practice on this point are very limited, but they do not support this simple reading of Rule 185. In a letter by the Dutch Minister of Justice to the Dutch Parliament, elaborating on the Netherlands' position vis-à-vis ICC connected asylum claims (considered in detail in Part II), Rule 185 was cited as grounds for preventing the ICC from transferring an acquitted person to an unsafe country.[252] The practice of the ICTR with respect to acquitted persons was protective. On a number of occasions individuals were kept in safe houses for years at the Tribunal's expense, rather than being returned to face harm in Rwanda. It is difficult to justify why the approach of the ICTR and the ICC should differ so substantially.

Finally, such an interpretation of Rule 185 would inevitably fail the Article 21(3) test. The ICC's obligations pursuant to this rule must be interpreted and applied consistently with human rights law. The only permissible interpretation of Rule 185 is one that obliges the ICC to make arrangements for an acquitted person's transfer to a *safe* State, not to any State that is willing. The ICC would otherwise be implicated in violating a fundamental human rights law norm: the prohibition on removal to a situation of risk of death or inhuman treatment.

3.5.3 Obligations of States

The potential role of States Parties in this situation is to provide assistance to the ICC by agreeing to host at-risk acquitted individuals. The question is therefore whether States Parties are under an obligation to do this. There is nothing specific on this point in the Rome Statute protection framework. The only possible basis for such an obligation is Article 93(1)(l) of the Statute, requiring States to cooperate with the ICC in providing 'any other type of assistance ... with a view to facilitating the investigation and prosecution of crimes within the jurisdiction of the Court'. A broad interpretation of this provision would allow the ICC to use the cooperation regime in the Rome Statute to oblige a State to accept an acquitted person on its territory.

---

[252] Letter from the Minister of Justice to the Speaker of the Lower House of Parliament, The Hague, July 2002, 28 098 (R 1704) (Letter from Justice Minister to Parliament), 9.

Arguments against this interpretation were presented in Chapter 2; however, more arguments can be offered here. The first is based on the wording of Article 93(1) itself. The provision permits the ICC to request cooperation 'in relation to investigations or prosecutions'. Based on the plain meaning of the words 'investigation' and 'prosecution', it is difficult to see how protecting acquitted persons fits within this provision. By definition, a person's involvement with an investigation and prosecution has concluded once an acquittal has been rendered. Acquittals at first instance may merit different treatment; if an appeal has been lodged, then the prosecution is in some ways ongoing. The same cannot be said for acquittals on appeal.

Another argument is based on practice, both of the ICC and of other international criminal tribunals. In terms of ICC practice, the case of Mathieu Ngudjolo Chui is instructive. Ngudjolo was the first accused to be acquitted by the ICC, and following this acquittal he raised concerns about being returned to his native DRC. Having acted as a witness in his own defence during his trial, he claimed that his testimony – implicating the DRC government leadership in atrocities in the country – would place him at risk if he returned there.[253] This case will be explored in great detail in Chapter 6, and for now it suffices to note that no attempt was made by the ICC to compel any State to host Ngudjolo after his acquittal. Instead, this was considered to be a diplomatic and political issue. In terms of ICTR practice, the judges of that Tribunal have been explicit on this point. At the Trial Chamber level it was held that a State's obligation to cooperate on relocating acquitted persons extended to consulting with the Tribunal only; the State was not required to grant residence or extend special treatment to the acquitted individual.[254] This was confirmed by the Appeals Chamber, which stated that 'there is no legal duty under Article 28 of the Statute for States to cooperate in the relocation of acquitted persons'. Article 28 of the ICTR Statute is the general cooperation provision, and is phrased in an almost identical way to Article 93 of the Rome Statute.

[253] *The Prosecutor* v. *Mathieu Ngudjolo Chui*, ICC-01/04-02/12-15-tENG, Urgent Defence Application for the International Relocation of Mathieu Ngudjolo Outwith the African Continent and His Presentation to the Authorities of One of the States Parties to the International Criminal Court for the Purposes of Expediting His Asylum Application, 21 December 2012 (Appeals Chamber) (*Ngudjolo*, 21 December 2012), §§27–9.
[254] *The Prosecutor* v. *André Ntagerura*, Case No. ICTR-99-46-A28, Decision on the Motion by an Acquitted Person for Cooperation from Canada, Article 28 of the Statute, 15 May 2008 (Trial Chamber III), §4.

The Article 21(3) test does not alter this interpretation of State Party obligations. Article 21(3) does not require States to accept non-nationals on their territory without their consent, which is what an obligation to host acquitted individuals would constitute. Only if a State Party should volunteer to host an acquitted person, and that person then travels to the State's territory, would that State then acquire obligations with respect to that person under human rights law (stemming from sources beyond the Rome Statute protection framework). These obligations would prevent the State Party from treating the individual in a way that violated their right to life and right to protection from inhuman treatment. This would include a prohibition on transferring the acquitted person to an unsafe State, but would not oblige the State Party to accept the acquitted person in the first place.

3.5.4 Problems in Human Rights Protection

The structural problem that arises from the involvement of multiple actors in interim release is also present in the situation of acquittal and release. The absence of an obligation on the part of States to host acquitted persons impedes the ICC's ability to comply with its obligation to protect acquitted persons from being sent to a State where they would be at risk. The ICC cannot protect individuals if States do not assist it by agreeing to host them. The issues that result from this structural problem can be seen in the experience of the ICTR. A number of acquitted individuals cannot return to Rwanda, and so the ICTR provides them with protection in a safe house near the Tribunal until a host State is found. This process can take years, and for many acquitted, the situation was still not resolved at the time that the Tribunal closed in late 2015. The task of protecting the acquitted that remain in the safe house has now passed to the UN International Residual Mechanism for Criminal Tribunals.

Following Ngudjolo's acquittal, the possibility arose that he too would face a long-term safe house situation, at least pending his appeal. After his acquittal at first instance, the ICC informed the Dutch authorities that, because a UN travel ban was in place against him, it would take time for preparations to be made for Ngudjolo's departure from the Netherlands. As the ICC could not detain him in the meantime,[255] the ICC requested

---

[255] The ICC's obligation to release a person immediately after an acquittal is quite strict. Article 81(3)(c) of the Rome Statute is unequivocal in the obligation it imposes on the ICC to release acquitted persons from its custody immediately. Where the acquittal is

that Ngudjolo be permitted to reside in the Netherlands temporarily. The Dutch authorities rejected this idea, but the ICC and the Netherlands reached a compromise by which Ngudjolo would reside in an 'ICC designated area', namely a room in a hotel at Schiphol Airport. Ngudjolo would wait there while arrangements were made for his stay in a safe country (at this point in time the ICC still considered that he would be at risk if returned to the DRC). The hotel in question has two sections, one on the terminal side of the airport, and one on the land side of the airport. An administrative error led to the room reservation being made on the land side, whereas the agreement specified that Ngudjolo must remain on the terminal side, as then he would be in the international area of the airport. Unwilling to allow Ngudjolo to remain on the land side of the hotel, moves were made to remove him from the country, at which point he communicated to the Netherlands a request for protection under human rights and refugee law (more on this in Chapter 6).[256] Had this administrative error with the hotel booking not occurred, Ngudjolo could have spent a considerable time in the hotel room if no State had come forward to host him pending his appeal; the time between his initial acquittal and his acquittal on appeal was over two years. He would then have been in a situation analogous to the ICTR acquitted in the Tanzania safe house: found not guilty but still subject to limitations on his liberty.[257]

Ultimately, the events in the Ngudjolo case unfolded differently. In practice, the Netherlands took on the role of filling the gap in protection caused by the structural issue, thereby preventing a situation in which

rendered at first instance and is subject to appeal, the possibility to maintain detention is subject to the high threshold of 'exceptional circumstances'. When the Prosecution challenged Trial Chamber II's order that Ngudjolo be immediately released following the acquittal at first instance, the Appeals Chamber followed a strict approach and held that the possibility that the accused would abscond was not sufficient to outweigh the 'fundamental right to liberty of the person' (*Prosecutor v. Mathieu Ngudjolo Chui*, ICC-01/04-02/12-12, Decision on the Request of the Prosecutor of 19 December 2012 for Suspensive Effect, 20 December 2012 (Appeals Chamber), §§22–4).

[256] Details on this series of events can be found in ECLI:NL:RVS:2013:2050, Council of State, 12 November 2013, §1.

[257] The author stops short of saying that this would have constituted an actual violation of the right to liberty per se. In the case of the ICTR acquitted, it was often the case that they had declined protection in an African country, preferring to be relocated to Europe or North America. They did therefore have the option to leave if they chose (*In Re André Ntagerura*, Case No. ICTR-99-46-A28, Decision on Motion to Appeal the President's Decision of 31 March 2008 and the Decision of Trial Chamber III of 15 May 2008, 18 November 2008 (Appeals Chamber), §18). In Ngudjolo's case, it would have depended on how facts had developed had he been confined to the hotel room.

Ngudjolo was left unprotected. However, this is not an entirely desirable solution, as will be elaborated on in Chapter 6, as a number of implementation problems arise which may themselves compromise human rights protection. After the Ngudjolo situation, the ICC took steps to address the structural gap in protection by drafting a framework agreement for the release of accused persons. An agreement of this type was signed between the ICC and Argentina in 2018, and sets out the relevant procedures for the release of ICC accused – including following an acquittal – and their status in Argentina. As with framework agreements for the hosting of accused granted interim release, this is a positive development; however, as is also the case with interim release agreements, there is no obligation on the signing State to accept a released person in any given instance. As such, while the procedure for releasing persons to a State such as Argentina may be simpler, and their status and rights when there clearer, it does not change the legal situation or eliminate the potential problems for human rights protection.

3.5.5 Conclusion

The story of acquitted persons at the ICC is still in its infancy. Time will tell whether the problems that plagued all the actors involved in the Ngudjolo case will be repeated following future acquittals. Much will depend on how the different forms of State involvement present at this stage are handled. The absence of an obligation on the part of States Parties to assist the ICC in hosting acquitted persons creates a structural problem resulting in a gap in protection. This gap was filled in Ngudjolo's case thanks to the involvement of the Netherlands in its role as ICC host State. As was the case for the situation of treatment in the enforcement State, the actors involved in the situation of acquittal and release are not limited to States Parties and the ICC; the ICC's host State is also very much involved. However, as will be discussed in Chapter 6, there are important implementation problems associated with relying on the Netherlands to fill the protection gap. As the ICC goes forward with its work, it will be necessary to search for an alternative solution to the structural problem identified in this section.

3.6 Conclusion

From the time that an individual comes under the suspicion of ICC investigators, to the moment when that individual is convicted or acquitted by the Court, there are a number of situations where the protection of their human rights falls to the cooperation of multiple actors. Some of the situations addressed in this chapter demonstrate how, with careful consideration, a legal framework can be constructed that effectively structures this cooperation. While complex, the way that obligations and roles are distributed between the ICC and States Parties in situations of interrogation, arrest and surrender, and treatment of prisoners in an enforcement State shows how the involvement of multiple actors in human rights protection can be managed. The challenge in these situations is understanding how the legal framework operates, but once the complexity is mapped out, this same framework provides most of the answers for ensuring the smooth protection of human rights in a multi-actor environment.

The other situations addressed in this chapter are much less complex in terms of how the legal framework works, but highlight the problems that the multi-actor nature of human rights protection can cause when legal provision is lacking. The obligations that exist for the ICC and States Parties in the situations of interim release and acquittal and release are straightforward – particularly for States, as the obligations are extremely limited. The ICC has the obligation to secure the release of individuals (either temporarily or permanently) and to ensure that the place they are released to is a place where they will be safe. But a lack of corresponding obligations on States to accept released persons creates structural problems for protection that will likely burden the Court for the foreseeable future. While it will not always be the case that the ICC will find itself unable to secure voluntary assistance from States – indeed, the Court has successfully managed to secure interim release for defendants through the voluntary scheme – the potential for problems will remain unless the legal framework is changed. The agreements made with States for interim release and release more generally are a step in the right direction, but do not alter the fundamentals of the situation.

As the discussion moves on in the following chapter to consider the protection of witnesses, the issues that have arisen in this chapter are largely repeated. A complex legal framework, while challenging to unpick and understand, is often a sign that the multi-actor nature of human rights protection has been considered and managed. A lack of obligations, on the other hand, is often a sign of a structural gap in protection. The discussion of witnesses in the next chapter will show how, in that context, greater creativity has been employed by the ICC in an effort to overcome the challenges that multi-actor human rights protection presents.

4

Witnesses

The success of the ICC will rise or fall on its ability to secure testimony from witnesses. Eye witness accounts of what happened, who was there, and who was in control are crucial to all criminal trials. The ICC Prosecutor's case against Kenyan president Uhuru Kenyatta was plagued by problems concerning witnesses: some refused to testify because of fears for their safety, others admitted to having been bribed to provide false testimony. This contributed first to an adjournment of the case,[258] and finally to the termination of the proceedings.[259]

An element crucial to getting witnesses before the Court is keeping them safe from the negative repercussions of testifying. Witness protection is therefore an essential function of the ICC. Some types of witness protection can be carried out by the ICC independently. These are principally 'in-courtroom' measures, such as the use of pseudonyms, voice and image distortion, and closed sessions. The ICC has control over the proceedings in the courtroom, and can provide these protective measures by, for example, ordering the parties to deal with information confidentially and by controlling the information that the Court conveys to the public. Through these measures the identity of a witness can be kept secret from the public but disclosed to the other parties to the proceedings.

The level and type of protection required will depend on the witness and their particular circumstances. For some witnesses, in-courtroom measures are sufficient; for others, the risk they face is more severe, and additional measures are necessary to guarantee their safety. Such cases will require 'out-of-courtroom' measures, designed to protect witnesses before they arrive at the ICC and after they leave it. Out-of-courtroom measures can involve protecting witnesses in their homes, moving them to a different location, or even relocating them to a different country. The

---

[258] 'Kenyatta case: Trial adjourned until 7 October 2014', ICC Press Release, 31 March 2014.
[259] 'Kenyatta case: Trial Chamber V(B) terminates the proceedings', ICC Press Release, 13 March 2015.

risk that these measures seek to address cannot be managed exclusively from the premises of the Court, but rather protection must be implemented on the territory of a State; as such, the protection of witnesses through 'out-of-courtroom' measures necessarily involves multiple actors. Where the ICC seeks to protect witnesses in their home State, the ICC must rely on the home State to provide the necessary assistance; where the risk to the witness is such that they cannot be protected in their home State, but instead must be relocated elsewhere, the ICC relies on States Parties to host them.

By its nature, witness protection is confidential and lacking in transparency. While the legal basis of the obligations can be traced to provisions in the applicable law, detail on their exact nature, and what precisely an actor is required to do, can be lacking. To a large extent one can understand this need for secrecy. The more information there is in the public domain about how witness protection at the ICC works, the easier it will be for the location of protected witnesses to be discovered. For example, if the ICC made public which countries have agreed to host relocated witnesses, then an ill-intentioned search for those witnesses could be narrowed down. This would leave witnesses vulnerable. As a result of the lack of information in the public domain, the discussion in this chapter of the obligations of the ICC and States concerning witness protection has required a degree of speculation.

The first situation considered in Section 4.1 is the out-of-courtroom protection of witnesses who remain in their home State. As this is the first discussion of ICC and State obligations regarding witnesses, it will include a description of the general framework of obligations, which in fact applies to all situations involving witnesses. The second situation in this chapter concerns witnesses who cannot remain in their home State, but who must be relocated abroad.

4.1 Witnesses Located in the Situation State

4.1.1 Introduction

Where witnesses can be protected while remaining in their own country, and possibly their own home, this is to be preferred over more disruptive measures.[260] The interference caused to a witness's life by their giving evidence in an ICC trial should be kept to a minimum. What is more, if

---

[260] 'Summary Report on the Seminar on Protection of Victims and Witnesses Appearing before the International Criminal Court', 24 November 2010 (2010 Summary Report), §17.

a witness can be protected within their own country, this is much more cost efficient, an ever-present concern for the ICC. Indeed, most witnesses are protected while remaining in their home country. While not always the case, for many witnesses their home country is the country where the alleged crimes took place and which is the subject of the ICC investigation. This State is referred to as the 'situation State'.

When a witness remains in the situation State, a concern of great importance will be their safety from harm, both physical and psychological. Threats to a witness's safety can stem from a number of sources. For example, one of the rival factions in the situation State may dislike the fact that the witness has testified in an ICC trial and may retaliate. Alternatively, prior to a witness giving testimony, interested parties may seek to prevent them from doing so, in order to weaken the prosecution or defence case. Such actions are generally accompanied by a threat of use of force, either against the witness or the witness's family. The right to life and to protection from torture and inhuman and degrading treatment are the rights that best address these risks, and as such will be the focus of this section.

There are a number of out-of-courtroom measures that the ICC and the situation State can work together to employ. Examples include safe houses, increased police patrols, close protection for government officials, enhanced surveillance of witnesses' homes, and investigations by national authorities. In the Central African Republic (CAR), the Office of the Prosecutor (OTP) and the Victims and Witnesses Unit (VWU) jointly set up a neighbourhood-watch style programme, consisting of local civilian guards patrolling areas where there is a high density of witnesses.[261] More extensive measures have seen the ICC request that a State protect an entire zone, camp, or passageway.[262]

While each of these measures is important and relevant, not all can be covered in this section. This is principally due to the availability of information in the public domain, which is greater for some measures than for others. For witnesses that are at liberty, two protective measures will be discussed: the Initial Response System, and internal resettlement. For witnesses that are detained – for example because they have been

---

[261] Markus Eikel, 'External Support and Internal Coordination: The ICC and the Protection of Witnesses', in Carsten Stahn (ed.), *The Law and Practice of the International Criminal Court* (Oxford University Press, 2015), 1126.

[262] 'Summary Report on the Round Table on the Protection of Victims and Witnesses Appearing before the International Criminal Court', 29–30 January 2009 (2009 Summary Report), 2.

convicted of a criminal offence by a domestic court – protective measures inside a prison will be discussed. For each actor, this section will first set out the generally applicable, overarching obligations to protect the rights of witnesses, and will then discuss the obligations with respect to these three types of measures. This is followed by an inquiry into the possible human rights protection problems that may result from the multi-actor nature of the situation.

4.1.2 Obligations of the ICC

4.1.2.1 Overarching Obligations

The central provision in the Rome Statute protection framework concerning the ICC's obligation to protect witnesses is Article 68(1) of the Rome Statute. This imposes an overarching obligation on the Court to 'take appropriate measures to protect the safety, physical and psychological well-being, dignity and privacy of victims and witnesses'. Article 68(1) is reinforced by Rule 86 RPE, which stipulates that all organs of the Court must take account of witnesses' needs in accordance with Article 68 when performing their functions.

Beyond this principal obligation in Article 68(1), the Rome Statute protection framework contains a great many provisions on witness protection. Some are addressed to the Court as a whole, while some are addressed to particular organs, such as Chambers, the Registry, the VWU, and the Prosecution.[263] This fragmentation of protection obligations across the different parts of the Court has led to some conflict between the different organs, and a great deal of confusion over which organ has responsibility for what and when.[264] Addressing these issues is not part of this study, which addresses the involvement of multiple actors in human rights protection rather than the involvement of multiple organs of the same actor. As such, the ICC will be treated as a single actor to which all of the obligations in the Rome Statute protection framework attach, regardless of the organ they pertain to.

A question that is central to the ICC's obligations, and which affects all of the Court's obligations in relation to witnesses, concerns the types of risk that the ICC is obliged to protect against under Article 68(1). Is the ICC obliged to protect a witness from all risks to their safety, or only

---

[263] Markus Eikel, 'Witness Protection Measures at the International Criminal Court: Legal Framework and Emerging Practice' (2012) 23 *Criminal Law Forum*, 97, 101–11.
[264] Eikel, 'Witness Protection Measures', 118.

those linked to their involvement with the Court? If a witness is threatened by the supporters of an ICC accused that they testified against, this is clearly a situation in which the ICC should be involved. But where a witness is threatened because a neighbour alleges that they stole money, is the ICC obliged to intervene?

This particular issue arose in the case of the detained Congolese witnesses, which is dealt with in detail in Chapter 7. In that case, Trial Chamber II interpreted the ICC's obligation under Article 68(1) as only applying to risks associated with a witness's involvement with the ICC. The Chamber distinguished between three types of risk: (1) risk incurred on account of cooperation with the Court, (2) risk arising from the broader human rights situation in the situation State, and (3) risk of treatment that would amount to persecution such as would found an asylum claim under the Refugee Convention. It was acknowledged by the Chamber that while the general human rights situation in a country would influence a witness's risk assessment, the three types of risk should not be conflated. The Chamber held that the ICC's witness protection role is restricted to the first type of risk: protective measures need only be provided against risks incurred because of cooperation with the Court, and not against the risk of human rights violations generally.[265]

On a purely textual reading, Article 68(1) does not favour one way or the other. However, support can be found for the Trial Chamber's approach when the Rome Statute protection framework is looked at more broadly: Rules 17 and 87 RPE do link protective measures with 'risk on account of testimony'. From other ICC decisions and academic commentary, one can collect more arguments in favour of a limited view of Article 68(1). The ICC has made clear that it is not a human rights court, and is not a court of last resort on human rights issues.[266] It has been argued that the ICC would be departing from its core mandate if it took a broad approach to the scope of witness protection, and would be directly or indirectly interfering with domestic proceedings.[267]

---

[265] *Katanga/Ngudjolo*, 9 June 2011, §§59–62.
[266] *The Prosecutor v Germain Katanga*, ICC-01/04-01/07-3405-tENG, Decision on the Application for the Interim Release of Detained Witnesses DRC-D02-P-0236, DRC-D02-P-0228 and DRC-D02-P-0350, 1 October 2013 (Trial Chamber II) (*Katanga*, 1 October 2013), §26.
[267] Joris van Wijk and Marjolein Cupido, 'Testifying behind Bars: Detained ICC Witnesses and Human Rights Protection', in Carsten Stahn (ed.), *The Law and Practice of the International Criminal Court* (Oxford University Press, 2015), 1100.

There are, however, also arguments in favour of a broad interpretation of the risks covered by Article 68(1). For one, there is an element of double standards that emerges if the Court follows the Trial Chamber's decision. Before a witness testifies, it is almost certainly the case that all necessary measures will be taken to secure their safety and so ensure that they can give their evidence at trial, even if the risk is unrelated to their testimony. But once their witness function is complete, the types of risk they are to be protected from are reduced.

A further argument is pragmatic, as one can question whether the Trial Chamber's distinction between the three types of risk is feasible. Indeed, in a decision later that same month, the same Trial Chamber stated that: 'in practice it will be impossible to determine whether any attempt to harm the witnesses will be linked to their testimony'.[268] Trying to draw the proposed distinction raises thorny issues of causation. The VWU has stated, by way of example, that if the threat to a witness's safety is linked to domestic violence that is unconnected to the person's status as a witness, the VWU would not take action.[269] But how can the reasons behind domestic violence be determined?[270] Perhaps acting as a witness caused the victim to be away from home for an extended period, and this contributed to the violence. Another example is the risk that individuals face from crime. Being an ICC witness could be one of the reasons that an individual was made a target for armed robbery, but another reason was their wealth. To assume that the reasons for actions can be separated into three neat categories may be detrimental to the protection of the witness.

It is this last point which leads the author to conclude that a narrow reading of Article 68(1) would not accord with the Article 21(3) test. A narrow reading leaves an ever-present risk of arbitrariness in the determination of whether the risk facing a witness is due to their association with the ICC. Especially where decisions need to be made quickly, it is possible that information pertaining to the distinction may be not immediately available. For this reason, if Article 68(1) is to be interpreted and applied in accordance with human rights, the net of protection must

---

[268] *The Prosecutor v Germain Katanga and Mathieu Ngudjolo Chui*, ICC-01/04-01/07-3033, Decision on the Security Situation of Three Detained Witnesses in Relation to Their Testimony before the Court (Art. 68 of the Statute) and Order to Request Cooperation from the Democratic Republic of the Congo to Provide Assistance in Ensuring Their Protection in Accordance with Article 93(1)(j) of the Statute, 22 June 2011 (Trial Chamber II) (*Katanga/Ngudjolo*, 22 June 2011), §38.

[269] 2009 Summary Report, 2.

[270] This is a particularly important question in the domestic violence context, given the culture of silence and stigma that discourages victims from disclosing their experience.

be cast broadly. It should cover all risks that are not patently unconnected to the individual's testimony, and the threshold for unconnectedness should be set high.

Having set out this general basis for the ICC's obligations, we can now turn to the more particular obligations that arise with respect to protecting witnesses through the Initial Response System, internal resettlement, and protective measures in prison.

4.1.2.2 Particular Obligations: The Initial Response System (IRS)

The IRS is essentially a twenty-four-hour emergency hotline that can be used by individuals located within a defined geographical area to seek assistance should their security be threatened. A call to this hotline activates a network of local partners who can then extract the individual to a safe location. In other words, if a witness is afraid of being imminently targeted, or is in fact targeted, they can call the hotline and help will be sent to remove them from the dangerous situation. Once they are safe, a risk assessment is carried out by the VWU to see what further protective measures might be needed.[271] Such programmes have been maintained in the DRC, CAR, Kenya, and Cote d'Ivoire situations.[272] An IRS was also set up in Mali, although in the beginning there was reported to be little need for it,[273] and the one in Uganda was discontinued when the threat level decreased.[274]

The only reference to the IRS in the Rome Statute protection framework is in Regulation 93 of the Regulations of the Registry, which refers to 'Local Protection Measures':

---

[271] Human Rights Watch, 'Courting History: The Landmark International Criminal Court's First Years' (July 2008) (HRW Courting History report), 152–3; Eikel, 'Witness Protection Measures', 120; Silvana Arbia, 'The International Criminal Court: Witness and Victim Protection and Support, Legal Aid and Family Visits' (2010) 36 *Commonwealth Law Bulletin*, 519, 522.

[272] Assembly of States Parties, 'Report on Activities and Programme Performance of the International Criminal Court for the Year 2013', ICC-ASP/13/19, 8–17 December 2014 (2013 Report on Activities), §171.

[273] Assembly of States Parties, 'Report on Activities and Programme Performance of the International Criminal Court for the Year 2014', ICC-ASP/14/8, 18–26 November 2015 (2014 Report on Activities), §261.

[274] Assembly of States Parties, 'Report of the Court on the Kampala Field Office: Activities, Challenges and Review of Staffing Levels; and on Memoranda of Understanding with Situation Countries', ICC-ASP/9/11, 6–10 December 2010 (Report of Kampala Field Office), §8.

1. The Registry shall implement measures for the protection of witnesses, victims who appear before the Court and persons at risk on the territory of the State of their residence.
2. The Registry shall, where appropriate, be responsible for establishing and maintaining an *immediate response system* as a local security measure for witnesses, victims who appear before the Court and persons at risk. The system shall operate round-the-clock for the purposes of extricating and bringing to safety those witnesses, victims who appear before the Court and persons at risk who fall within its purview.

(Over time the name of the system has evolved from 'immediate' to 'initial'.[275] No explicit justification is given, but perhaps it is reflective of the fact that the IRS is the first point of contact for a witness at risk.)

The wording of both paragraphs of Regulation 93 is compulsory. The ICC 'shall' put in place local protection measures. This obliges the ICC to establish and maintain IRSs in situation States where needed. Beyond the brief explanation of what an IRS involves, Regulation 93 provides little detail on how the system is supposed to operate in practice. For further elaboration on the obligations of the ICC, it is necessary to look at information from other sources, mainly from ICC reports and academic commentators. From these sources it can be discerned that the ICC's obligation to maintain an IRS requires the training of local partners, regular contact with these partners and the local authorities, and frequent testing of the responsiveness of the IRS in question.[276] In terms of staffing an IRS, this appears to be done in collaboration with the situation State. While details on staffing are lacking, it appears that the ICC provides the management personnel, and the situation State provides the individuals who respond to the calls.[277] Paying for these staff, as well as financing the IRS in general, is also part of the ICC's obligation, as evidenced by the inclusion of the IRS in the ICC's budget.[278]

---

[275] By 2013, this change had been made (§171 of 2013 Report on Activities) and was maintained in the list of abbreviations for the proposed budget for 2016 (Assembly of States Parties, 'Proposed Programme Budget for 2016 of the International Criminal Court', ICC-ASP/14/10, 18–26 November 2015 (2016 Proposed Budget)).

[276] Report of Kampala Field Office, §10.

[277] I extrapolate from the fact that HRW Courting History report says that the people doing the extraction are local partners and that those running the IRS are ICC staff. Also that the identities of witnesses in the IRS are withheld from these local partners, supposedly by the ICC staff members. (HRW Courting History report, 152–3).

[278] Assembly of States Parties, 'Proposed Programme Budget for 2008 of the International Criminal Court', ICC-ASP/6/8, 30 November–14 December 2007 (2008 Proposed Budget), §356; see also Eikel, 'Witness Protection Measures', 121.

Once a witness activates the IRS and is extracted to a safe place, the VWU must then carry out a new risk assessment to determine what protection measures are necessary going forward.[279] If the risk assessment reveals that the witness is at such a degree of risk that they must be transferred to another location, then the ICC may internally resettle them or relocate them abroad.

4.1.2.3 Particular Obligations: Internal Resettlement

If a witness cannot remain in their own home and community, the next least disruptive measure is for them to move to another region within the situation State. This is referred to as 'internal resettlement' (as opposed to 'relocation', which will be used to refer to when a witness is moved abroad). There are two types of internal resettlement: resettlement through the International Criminal Court Protection Programme (ICCPP) and assisted move. The degree of ICC assistance differs between the two, and the choice between them depends on the level of risk that the witness faces.

The ICCPP is designed to offer protection to ICC witnesses who are most at risk. Through the ICCPP, witnesses can be internally resettled or relocated to a third State. The obligation on the ICC to establish and maintain the ICCPP is set out in Regulation 96(1) of the Regulations of the Registry: 'The Registry shall take all necessary measures to maintain a protection programme for witnesses, victims who appear before the Court and persons at risk.' Once again, the language of this provision is compulsory, thereby establishing an obligation on the Court.

Information on the ICCPP has been compiled from ICC sources, reports on the ICC, and academic commentators. This section sets out the available details on the factors for inclusion in the ICCPP and some of the tasks conducted by the ICC in this context. The precise procedures and measures connected with the programme are confidential.[280]

Regulation 96(3) contains two sets of factors to be taken into account when deciding whether to include witnesses in the ICCPP. For the first set the provision refers back to the factors listed in Article 68(1): age, gender, health, and the nature of the crime. The second set of factors are listed in Regulation 96(3) itself, and are: (a) the involvement of the person before the Court; (b) whether the person and/or their close relatives are endangered because of their involvement with the Court; and (c) whether

---

[279] Eikel, 'Witness Protection Measures', 120; and HRW Courting History report, 152–3.
[280] Regulation 96(7) of the Regulations of Registry.

the person agrees to enter the programme. In addition, a decision of Trial Chamber I tells us that there must be a 'high likelihood that the witness will be harmed or killed unless action is taken'.[281]

The assessment process for inclusion in the ICCPP can take up to three months, during which time interim measures may be used, such as temporary resettlement or relocation.[282] The need for a witness's continued involvement in the programme is reassessed every twelve months,[283] and can be concluded when the protection is no longer warranted or the person breaches the terms of the confidentiality agreement.[284] This agreement requires the witness to keep details of the ICCPP secret, and avoid communication with family and friends except through VWU staff.[285] Once the witness and their family are resettled, the VWU will monitor them for as long as necessary. This may be on a long-term basis, depending on the security situation and threat level.

Running the ICCPP is resource intensive for the ICC. Participants are subject to psychological assessments,[286] and medical, psychosocial, and educational support.[287] The aim of this support is for the participants to become self-sufficient in their new location, which the Court can assist with by finding witnesses jobs and accommodation.[288] The intensive nature of internal resettlement through the ICCPP, in particular the costs involved, means that alternatives will be used where the risk is not as acute. The alternative to resettlement through the ICCPP is resettlement under assisted move.

According to Regulation 95 of the Regulations of the Registry, assisted move may be used where 'a person at risk cannot be managed in the geographical area where the person is staying and said person has initiated a move to another area'. Where this move is necessary for that person's security, the Registry may provide 'limited financial or logistical support' for the move, but the move shall remain the decision and

---

[281] *The Prosecutor v. Thomas Lubanga Dyilo*, ICC-01/04-01/06-1311-Anx2, Annex 2, Decision on Disclosure Issues, Responsibilities for Protective Measures and Other Procedural Matters, 24 April 2008 (Trial Chamber I), §43.
[282] HRW Courting History report, 154.
[283] Regulation 96(6) of the Regulations of Registry.
[284] Regulation 96*bis* of the Regulations of Registry.
[285] HRW Courting History report, 154.
[286] 2013 Report on Activities, §172.
[287] Assembly of States Parties, 'Report on Activities and Programme Performance of the International Criminal Court for the Year 2012', ICC-ASP/12/9, 20–28 November 2013 (2012 Report on Activities), §158.
[288] HRW Courting History report, 154.

responsibility of that person (Regulation 95(2)). The more limited involvement of the ICC stems from the lower level of risk faced by the witness. Namely, the witness will not have been exposed to an imminent, life-threatening incident.[289] As with resettlement through the ICCPP, the ICC provides assistance with a view to helping the witness settle in their new location and eventually become self-sufficient.

Unlike the wording of Regulation 96 concerning the ICCPP, the wording of Regulation 95 on assisted move gives the ICC discretion on whether to provide the assistance: 'the Registry *may* assist'. This is the only element of the IRS and internal resettlement obligations that is problematic for the Article 21(3) test. It is proposed that, while the ICC is not obliged to provide assistance to a witness in moving to another part of the situation State, the Court is obliged to consider and decide upon the witness's application. Regulation 95 therefore does not grant unfettered discretion.

4.1.2.4 Particular Obligations: Protective Measures in Detention

Detained witnesses can make a very valuable contribution to an ICC trial, especially if they are insider witnesses whose imprisonment is linked to the crimes for which the ICC accused is being tried. However, as they are detained, most of the usual protective measures such as an IRS or internal resettlement are unavailable. The fact of detention places the witnesses entirely within the control of the State, making the ICC's role necessarily more limited.

There is no specific provision in the Rome Statute protection framework that deals with protecting detained witnesses in the situation State, but the practice of the ICC confirms the existence of an obligation to this effect arising under Article 68(1) of the Statute. In the detained Congolese witnesses case (detailed in Chapter 7), the ICC determined that its protection obligations under this provision were fulfilled by the fact that it secured from the DRC a number of assurances as to how the detained witnesses would be protected while in prison. These assurances included that:

(a) the witnesses would be detained in a secure prison facility and protected from the aggression of other inmates
(b) the guards who would be guarding the witnesses were trained according to international standards and selected in consultation between the VWU and the DRC authorities

---

[289] Eikel, 'External Support and Internal Coordination', 1126.

(c) the VWU would maintain regular and direct contact with the guards in order to anticipate any change in the security situation of the witnesses
(d) the VWU would regularly visit the detained witnesses to assess their security situation
(e) the VWU would monitor any legal proceedings against the detained witnesses.[290]

According to the ICC's interpretation of Article 68(1), in the case in question securing these assurances from the detaining State qualified as protective measures sufficient to fulfil the ICC's obligation to protect witnesses. Whether this interpretation satisfies the Article 21(3) test depends on the corollary obligations of the situation State.

4.1.3   Obligations of States

4.1.3.1   Overarching Obligations

Part 9 of the Rome Statute contains a number of provisions that oblige States to assist the Court in protecting witnesses. These apply to all States Parties to the ICC, non-States Parties that have made a declaration granting the ICC jurisdiction under Article 12(3), and non-States Parties that have been referred to the ICC by the UN Security Council. As with Section 4.1.2, this section will set out the obligations of a general nature, and the following section will discuss the IRS, internal resettlement measures, and measures to protect detained witnesses.

Article 86 of the Rome Statute contains an overarching obligation: 'States Parties shall, in accordance with the provisions of this Statute, cooperate fully with the Court in its investigation and prosecution of crimes within the jurisdiction of the Court.' Article 87 provides that the ICC 'shall have the authority to make requests to States Parties for cooperation'. If a State fails to comply with a request for cooperation, the ICC may make a finding of non-compliance under Article 87(7) and refer the matter to the Assembly of States Parties (ASP).[291] Taken together, these provisions make clear that a request for cooperation

---

[290] *The Prosecutor* v. *Katanga and Ngudjolo*, ICC-01/04-01/07, Decision on the Security Situation of Witnesses DRC-D02-P-0236, DRC-D02-P-0228, and DRC-D02-P-0350, 24 August 2011 (Trial Chamber II) (*Katanga/Ngudjolo*, 24 August 2011), §13.

[291] Or where the situation was referred to the ICC by the UN Security Council, the non-compliance is referred to the Security Council also.

issued by the ICC creates a binding obligation on the State Party whose assistance is requested.

In relation to witnesses, Part 9 contains more specific provisions. Article 93(1)(j) provides that States Parties shall comply with requests by the ICC to provide assistance in the protection of witnesses; Article 87(4) provides that 'In relation to any request for assistance presented under this Part, the Court may take such measures, including measures related to the protection of information, as may be necessary to ensure the safety or physical or psychological well-being of ... potential witnesses and their families.'

There is then, a clear obligation on States under Part 9 to comply with ICC requests relating to the protection of witnesses. The content of these requests, and therefore the particular measures that the ICC can require States to take, is not specified in Part 9. Discussion on this point is left to the individual sections, both immediately to follow and elsewhere in this book.

4.1.3.2 Particular Obligations: The Initial Response System, Internal Resettlement, and Protective Measures in Detention

Turning to the particular obligations of the situation State in the protection of witnesses, the Rome Statute protection framework does not contain provisions equivalent to Regulations 93, 95, and 96 of the Regulations of the Registry that are aimed at States rather than at the ICC. The obligations of the situation State within this framework, as regards an IRS and internal resettlement, derive from cooperation requests made by the ICC under Part 9 of the Statute. It is possible that alongside cooperation requests there are agreements between the ICC and the State, setting out the respective tasks of each actor;[292] where this is the case, these agreements could also be a source of obligations. Concerning protective measures in detention, Part 9 also plays a role, although this is less clear-cut.

A concrete discussion of the obligations of the situation State suffers from a lack of available information. Based on different sources, in this section the author describes in limited detail the role played by the State

---

[292] In a decision during the *Lubanga* case, Pre-Trial Chamber I ordered the Registrar to 'treat as a matter of urgency the negotiation of cooperation agreements and *ad hoc* arrangements on matters related to the protection of witnesses' (*The Prosecutor v Thomas Lubanga Dyilo*, ICC-01/04-01/06-447, Decision on a General Framework Concerning Protective Measures for Prosecution and Defence Witnesses, 19 September 2006 (Pre-Trial Chamber I) (*Lubanga*, 19 September 2006), 5.

with respect to the IRS and internal resettlement. It is not suggested that every action carried by a State is done pursuant to a specific obligation; that is not supported by the sources. It is possible that the situation State is cooperating with the Court on a more informal, voluntary basis. However, if it considered it necessary and appropriate, the cooperation provisions in Part 9 do empower the ICC to create obligations for the situation State.

In terms of the IRS, it seems that the situation State's principal role is to cooperate with the ICC in arranging local partners to carry out the extractions. Who exactly makes up this staff appears to differ between situation countries. In Uganda, the police force was trained to assist with the IRS.[293] In other places, the staff are made up of local personnel from the security sector, or individuals with previous security sector experience.[294] Much will depend on the realities in the situation State, such as whether State infrastructures – like a police force – have survived the conflict and unrest.

As to the situation State's role with regards to internal resettlement, these will likely differ in the long and short term. In the short term, the role is probably to support the ICC in its efforts to internally resettle witnesses or to support the assisted moves. This could be by, for example, providing information on the availability of property for safe houses or new homes, or even in providing accommodation to the witnesses. In the long term, the situation State could cooperate with the Court in setting up a national witness programme and take over many (or all) of the witness protection tasks from the ICC.[295]

In addition to the IRS and internal resettlement, there is a plethora of other ways that the situation State can assist and work with the ICC in protecting witnesses. For example, the State could provide information that forms the basis for the witness risk assessments. This was common at the ICTR, where Rwandan intelligence reports formed the basis for internal relocation decisions on the part of the ICTR witnesses unit.[296] This could be purely voluntary, or it could be an obligation on the State if a cooperation request is issued to that effect.

For measures protecting detained witnesses inside prison facilities, the question is whether the situation State is obliged to honour the assurances that it makes to the ICC, of the type given by the DRC in the

---

[293] Report of Kampala Field Office, §10.
[294] Chris Mahony, 'The Justice Sector Afterthought: Witness Protection in Africa', Institute for Security Studies, 2010, 41.
[295] *Lubanga*, 19 September 2006, 5.
[296] Mahony, 'Justice Sector Afterthought', 73.

detained Congolese witnesses case. It is not entirely clear whether the assurances are binding undertakings or non-binding diplomatic assurances. In the detained Congolese witnesses case, the ICC did not go as far as to say that the assurances created legal obligations for the DRC, but they were said to carry 'great weight'.[297] It was deemed essential that the assurances were made within the general framework for cooperation under Part 9 of the Rome Statute, which is based on mutual trust and good faith.[298] They were said to 'commit' the DRC to both the ICC and the ASP.[299] It is here that the Article 21(3) test becomes important. If the assurances are not binding, the author proposes that this would not be an interpretation of Article 68(1) that is consistent with human rights, as it leaves the witnesses vulnerable to the whims of the State. Instead, if Part 9 can be used by the ICC to create obligations for States, it is proposed that a State can create obligations for itself under the same Part. As such, the assurances given by the DRC should be seen as creating legal obligations.

Beyond the obligations that a situation State might have under the Rome Statute protection framework, the State will have obligations to protect both detained and non-detained witnesses that derive from sources outside this framework, principally under international human rights law. As stated by the UN High Commissioner for Human Rights: 'the protection of the life, physical and psychological integrity, privacy and reputation of those who agree to testify before courts is more generally required under relevant ICCPR provisions protecting the right to life, prohibiting torture and inhuman or degrading treatment, etc.'[300] These obligations arise regardless of the individual's status as an ICC witness, from the simple fact that the witness is located on the State's territory and subject to its jurisdiction. The right to life and to be protected from inhuman treatment are found in a number of human rights provisions, such as Articles 6 and 7 ICCPR, Articles 2 and 3 ECHR, and Articles 4 and 5 ACHPR.

4.1.4 Problems in Human Rights Protection

Implementation problems are the primary issue affecting the protection of ICC witnesses' rights in the situation State. These are intimately

---

[297] *Katanga/Ngudjolo*, 22 June 2011, §40.
[298] *Katanga/Ngudjolo*, 22 June 2011, §40.
[299] *Katanga/Ngudjolo*, 22 June 2011, §40.
[300] Human Rights Council, 'Annual Report of the United Nations High Commissioner for Human Rights and Reports of the Office of the High Commissioner and the Secretary-General; Right to Truth', A/HRC/12/19, 21 August 2009, §34.

connected to the multi-actor nature of this protection, and can be distinguished into three types: (1) dependence on unstable and/or uncooperative States; (2) lack of transparency and clarity as to the precise nature of obligations; and (3) competition between a State's obligations within and beyond the Rome Statute protection framework.

Situation States are often rendered unstable by years of conflict and political turmoil, meaning that they can be unsafe for both witnesses and ICC protection teams. A 2013 report recounted how the IRS in CAR had to be scaled down because of a deterioration in the security situation following the conflict and the change in government.[301] In the *Lubanga* case, the Pre-Trial Chamber noted that a deterioration in the security situation in some parts of the DRC meant that the range of measures available to protect witnesses was limited.[302] The ICC depends on the situation State to have control over its territory, as this control is important to creating an environment in which witnesses can be properly protected.

Aside from general political instability, ICC witness protection structures are vulnerable to obstacles created by uncooperative governments. In the words of the ICC Prosecutor with regards to the Kenya situation:

> The Office's independent and impartial investigations and prosecutions in the Kenya situation have been methodically undermined by a relentless campaign that has targeted individuals who are perceived to be Prosecution witnesses, with threats or offers of bribes, to dissuade them from testifying or persuade witnesses to recant their prior testimony.[303]

While the Prosecutor did not go so far as to explicitly accuse the Kenyan government of witness interference, the high level of organisation and the financing of the campaign points in that direction.[304] That being said, violence has taken place on both sides, with defence witnesses also being

---

[301] 2013 Report on Activities, §171.
[302] *Lubanga*, 19 September 2006, 4.
[303] 'Statement of the Prosecutor of the International Criminal Court, Fatou Bensouda regarding the unsealing of arrest warrants in the Kenya situation', ICC Press Release, 10 September 2015. See also *The Prosecutor v. Wiliam Samoei Ruto and Joshua Arap Sang*, ICC-01/09-01/11-446, Prosecution Motion Regarding the Scope of Witness Preparation, 13 August 2012 (Trial Chamber V), §17.
[304] *The Prosecutor v. Paul Gicheru and Philip Kipkoech Bett*, ICC-01/09-01/15-1-Red, Decision on the 'Prosecution's Application under Article 58(1) of the Rome Statute', 10 March 2015 (Pre-Trial Chamber II) (*Gicheru and Bett*, 10 March 2015); see also: 'Reporters, witnesses silenced 'one by one' with ICC link deadly in Kenya', AlJazeera America, 24 August 2015.

targeted.[305] Even where a government is cooperative, the next election might bring a change in attitude towards the ICC, which is problematic given the long-term nature of witness protection. In these circumstances, the fact that the ICC must rely on the cooperation and assistance of the situation State in order to implement its own protection obligations is a major weakness in its ability to protect witnesses.

One could describe these problems as political, which is in many ways true. If the ICC cannot implement its obligations because of instability or lack of cooperation, this leaves witnesses vulnerable. Possibly it could mean that a trial cannot proceed. Where cooperation is the issue, the Rome Statute allows the ICC to make a finding of non-compliance, with the option of referring the matter to the ASP (or where the situation was referred by the UN Security Council, to the Security Council).[306] In addition, the ICC could bring criminal charges of witness intimidation and interference under Article 70 of the Rome Statute, as it has done in the *Bemba et al.* case[307] and the Kenya situation.[308] Where instability is the issue, there is no quick fix.

The second type of implementation problem arising in witness protection is linked to the ambiguity surrounding the actors' obligations. Generally speaking, the present book's aim in discussing obligations is to provide clarity on the question of which actor must perform which task. However, for the protection of witnesses in the situation State, there is still much that remains unknown. The confidential nature of witness protection measures, while understandable and necessary, renders it difficult to know how the generally worded provisions of the Rome Statute protection framework operate in practice.

It is possible that this ambiguity exists for outside observers only, and that between the ICC and the situation State the respective roles, tasks,

---

[305] 'Kenyan 'ICC defence witness' in Ruto's trial killed', BBC News, 6 January 2015. The ICC Prosecutor has vehemently denied any ICC involvement, 'Statement of the Office of the Prosecutor regarding the reported abduction and murder of Mr Meshak Yebei', ICC Press Release, 9 January 2015.
[306] Article 87(7) of the Rome Statute.
[307] 'Bemba, Kilolo et al. trial opens at the International Criminal Court', ICC Press Release, 29 September 2015; *The Prosecutor v. Jean-Pierre Bemba, Aimé Kilolo Musamba, Jean-Jacques Mangenda Kabongo, Fidèle Babala Wandu and Narcisse Arido*, ICC-01/05-01/13-1-Red2-tENG, Warrant of Arrest for Jean-Pierre Bemba, Aimé Kilolo Musamba, Jean-Jacques Mangenda Kabongo, Fidèle Babala Wandu and Narcisse Arido, 20 November 2013 (Pre-Trial Chamber II).
[308] 'Situation in Kenya: ICC judges unseal an arrest warrant against Paul Gicheru and Philip Kipkoerch Bett', ICC Press Release, 10 September 2015; *Gicheru and Bett*, 10 March 2015.

and obligations have been clearly arranged (confidentially). However, in the interests of covering all potential issues with human rights protection, it is necessary to contemplate situations where this is not the case. If the actors are not clear on their role in witness protection, obligations may not be properly implemented, placing the rights of the witness at risk. The Rome Statute protection framework provides a tool to help prevent this potential problem. Rule 16(4) RPE allows the Registrar to make agreements for the 'provision of support services on the territory of a State' for witnesses at risk. Such an agreement could explicitly set out the actors' respective obligations and tasks. A model agreement of this type could be produced by the ICC and modified to fit the particular circumstances of the situation State and the witness protection needs. Pre-Trial Chamber I has promoted the use of such agreements,[309] acknowledging their value in protecting witnesses.

The third problem concerns the interaction between the situation State's obligations within the Rome Statute protection framework, and beyond it. Under the witness protection regime within the framework, the situation State must comply with cooperation requests from the ICC. As far as the author has been able to ascertain, with respect to an IRS and internal resettlement, the role of the situation State is a supportive one. For example, it might provide the staff for an IRS and accommodation for internal resettlement. The ICC takes the lead in these measures, and the State provides assistance. Beyond the Rome Statute protection framework, human rights law creates positive obligations for States that may require a more proactive approach to protection. In other words, under human rights law it is the State that must take the lead in protection measures.

This distinction is relevant because of the ICC's approach of only protecting witnesses from risks that are connected to their involvement with the Court. In situations where it is not clear whether the risk is indeed connected to the Court or not, it is possible that both the situation State and the ICC each assume that the other actor should take the lead in protection. If the result of this is that neither takes the lead, this leaves the witness vulnerable.

4.1.5 Conclusion

Witnesses remaining in their homes, or if that is not possible, at least within their home country, is the ICC's preferred form of witness

---

[309] *Lubanga*, 19 September 2006, 5.

protection. It minimises disruption to witnesses' lives and reduces costs for the ICC. Making this happen is an important ICC function, and one in which the situation State is also involved. Establishing and maintaining witness protection measures such as the Initial Response System and internal resettlement is required of the ICC by the Rome Statute protection framework. Through cooperation requests issued by the Court, States are required to assist the ICC with those protection measures. Together, these form the obligations through which the two actors protect ICC witnesses on the territory of a situation State.

The highly confidential nature of witness protection at the ICC has meant that this section must inevitably be left somewhat incomplete. Particularly with respect to the situation State, there is little information available about the specific nature of obligations beyond the general provisions in Part 9 of the Rome Statute. Consequently, when identifying possible problems associated with the multi-actor nature of the situation, some speculation was required. The potential deficiencies in the protection of witnesses can be linked to implementation problems. There is no absence of legal provision, but rather circumstances could arise that would prevent their full implementation. This leaves witnesses vulnerable.

Section 4.1 has considered the protection of witnesses in the situation State, on the assumption that the majority of witnesses testifying in a case would be nationals or residents of the situation State. However, there will be witnesses who are nationals or residents of a third State, and so require protection in that third State. If that third State is a party to the Rome Statute, obligations to protect the witness will flow from Part 9 of the Statute, and the content of the obligations will be tailored to the specific situation. For example, if only one witness lives in a given third State, establishing a full IRS will not be necessary. If that third State is not a party to the Rome Statute, then absent a specific agreement between the ICC and the State, the witness will rely on the protections the third State affords them pursuant to obligations arising beyond the Rome Statute protection framework. In terms of potential problems for human rights protection that arise in such situations, these would not differ significantly from those set out in Section 4.1.4.

Not all witnesses can be protected within the situation State (or a third State in which they live) even if they are moved to a different part of the country, such is the danger they face on account of their testimony. This leads to the more dramatic way of protecting ICC witnesses: relocating them to another country entirely.

4.2 Relocating Witnesses to a Third State

4.2.1 Introduction

Where the threat to a witness is so severe that it cannot be managed within the situation State, even by internal resettlement, the remaining option is to move the witness abroad. Reports abounded in relation to the Kenya situation, with stories of witnesses being moved to Europe and given lifelong protection, even completely new identities.[310] This individual type of relocation is the most commonly practised, but relocation can also take place on a large collective scale. As the ICC Prosecutor prepared to announce the first arrest warrants in the Darfur situation, the Court simultaneously evacuated 150 refugees from eastern Chad to a more secure location at a new camp.[311]

Relocation abroad is relatively unusual compared to the use of protective measures within the situation State. In 2016 the ICC foresaw that only 23 witnesses would be relocated abroad.[312] This is a reflection of the fact that relocation is a 'serious measure' of last resort, which can have a 'dramatic impact' on the life of the witness.[313] Removing the witness from their normal surroundings and family ties can have a significant psychological effect.[314] To minimise this, the ICC strives to relocate witnesses to a region with similar cultural, linguistic, and geographic characteristics.[315] Relocation is also undesirable because it may actually highlight an individual's involvement with the ICC, making it harder for them to return home at a later point. For these reasons, relocation must involve careful and long-term planning for the safety and well-being of the witness.[316]

---

[310] '80 Kenyan ICC witnesses in safe houses abroad', Mwakilishi, 23 January 2013; 'Ocampo witnesses now sent to Europe', Property Kenya, 10 March 2011.

[311] There is no indication of where this new camp was (Schabas, A Commentary on the Rome Statute, 825). For more on this, see Assembly of States Parties, 'Report on Programme Performance of the International Crminal Court for the Year 2007, Addendum', ICC-ASP /7/8/Add.1, 14–22 November 2008, §9 and 2008 Proposed Budget, §42.

[312] 2016 Proposed Budget, §191.

[313] *The Prosecutor v Germain Katanga and Mathieu Ngudjolo Chui*, ICC-01/04-01/07-776, Judgment on the Appeal of the Prosecutor against the 'Decision on Evidentiary Scope of the Confirmation Hearing, Preventive Relocation and Disclosure under Article 67(2) of the Statute and Rule 77 of the Rules' of Pre-Trial Chamber I, 26 November 2008 (Appeals Chamber) (*Katanga/Ngudjolo*, 26 November 2008), §§66 and 67.

[314] The VWU discourages relocation because of the psychological harm: 2010 Summary Report, §17.

[315] 2010 Summary Report, §26.

[316] *Katanga/Ngudjolo*, 26 November 2008, §§66 and 67.

In order to protect a witness through relocation abroad, it is necessary that the ICC has the cooperation and assistance of States willing to host these witnesses and allow them to make new lives on their territory. These States will be termed 'relocation States'. Because the protection of witnesses through relocation abroad cannot be done without the assistance of States, this is a situation in which multiple actors are involved in the protection of human rights. However, this situation differs from that where a witness is protected within the situation State: whereas the situation State is obliged to assist the ICC pursuant to Part 9 of the Rome Statute, for relocation abroad the Court must rely on the voluntary assistance of States.

Just as for a witness who remains in their home country, when a witness is relocated abroad the primary concern will be threats to their physical safety, and as such the discussion will focus on the right to life and to protection from inhuman treatment. The discussion in this section will also include the prohibition on removal aspect of protection from inhuman treatment and the right to life. This will be relevant once the witness has already been relocated, as it prevents the relocation State from returning them to a country where they would be at risk. The discussion of obligations in the following section is done in relation to these two rights and covers the ICC and the relocation State in turn.

Detained witnesses, while often crucial to ICC trials, are not considered in this section. Unless they were reaching the end of their sentences, it is very unlikely that the situation State, which is also the detaining State, would be willing to release a witness from custody and allow them to be relocated to a third State to live in freedom.

4.2.2   Obligations of the ICC

The obligations of the ICC can be discussed under two categories: those that relate to protecting a witness from inhuman treatment before they arrive in the relocation State, and those that relate to protecting the witness after. Regarding pre-arrival, the obligations involve including a witness in the ICCPP and finding a relocation State to which they can be transferred. Regarding after arrival, the obligations are aimed at ensuring the witness's well-being once they are settled in the relocation State.

Protecting a witness through relocation abroad is done within the ICCPP. The source of the ICC's obligations is the same as that discussed in relation to the ICCPP and internal resettlement: Article 68(1) imposes an overarching duty to protect witnesses, and Regulation 96(1) requires that the ICC set up a witness protection programme. Article 68(1) states that the ICC must take 'all appropriate measures' to protect witnesses, and what these measures are will depend on the circumstances. In the context of relocating witnesses abroad, an essential task that the ICC must undertake is to seek the cooperation of States Parties and request that they act as relocation States. When searching for a relocation State, it goes without saying that this must be a State which does not itself present a threat to the witness's safety.

The way in which the ICC goes about requesting assistance from States is through diplomatic channels. This can be done in an ad hoc way, without any formal arrangements between the two actors, but the Rome Statute protection framework also provides for a more structured approach by means of relocation agreements. The ICC has the power, pursuant to Rule 16(4) RPE, to 'negotiate agreements on relocation and provision of support services on the territory of a State to witnesses'. This provision is not phrased as an obligation, but rather leaves the choice on whether to conclude such an agreement to the discretion of the Registry. Relocation agreements are framework agreements between the ICC and a potential relocation State that indicate a willingness on the part of a State to host witnesses, and which streamline the relocation process. For instance, instead of the ICC dealing with a range of government agencies, a relocation agreement allocates the task to just one. This significantly speeds up the process of identifying a relocation State.[317] Importantly, however, while relocation agreements ease the communication process, as currently formulated they do not require States to accept a particular witness in any given instance (more on this in Section 4.2.4).

Once the ICC secures a State's cooperation, the witness can be transferred to that State. It is then possible to discuss the obligations of the ICC to protect witnesses after their relocation. The ICC's obligation under Article 68(1) to protect a witness from inhuman treatment and threats to their life, and to protect other rights affected by their involvement with the Court, does not end when the witness arrives in the relocation State. Rather, the ICC has stated that the VWU must monitor relocated

---

[317] International Bar Association, 'Witnesses before the International Criminal Court: An International Bar Association International Criminal Court Programme Report on the ICC's Efforts and Challenges to Protect, Support and Ensure the Rights of Witnesses' (July 2013) (IBA report), 36. Information concerning relocation agreements is discerned from secondary sources, as the text of the agreements themselves are confidential.

witnesses for as long as necessary.[318] If this monitoring revealed threats to a witness that were not being addressed by the relocation State, the author proposes that included in the term 'all appropriate measures' in Article 68(1) is an obligation on the Court to contact the relocation State and attempt to prevent violations of a witness's rights. The intervention by the ICC could be done, for instance, through mediation or appropriate forms of pressure, including issuing a cooperation request.[319]

There is one type of measure, aimed at protecting a witness once they arrive in the relocation State, that the ICC can take pre-emptively using the relocation agreements. In addition to streamlining the relocation process, relocation agreements regulate the conditions of stay of a protected person and the respective obligations of the Court and the State.[320] In this sense they play an important function in providing detail to the otherwise very general obligations in the Rome Statute. When drafting relocation agreements, the Court could seek to prevent certain types of problems. For example, it is proposed that one of the 'appropriate measures' referred to in Article 68(1) is the inclusion of protection from removal provisions in relocation agreements. This is designed to preclude the relocation State from removing the witness and their family to a country where they would be at risk, such as the country from which they were relocated in the first place.

One way for the ICC to do this would be to include a provision in the relocation agreement explicitly stating that the witness cannot be removed to a situation of risk. However, the drafting and signing of these agreements requires a cooperative and conducive atmosphere, which may be hampered by such a provision if the relocation State resents the implication it entails. There is a subtler option, inspired by the agreements on enforcement of sentences. These agreements between the ICC and States set out the terms under which a State enforces a sentence handed down by the Court. They always contain a provision on the transfer of the convicted person on completion of sentence. If the enforcement State does not permit a released person to remain on its

---

[318] '[T]he situation of relocated witnesses can be monitored by the Court as long as is needed' (2010 Summary Report, §§6–9).

[319] When discussing the obligations of the relocation State, it will be argued that the ICC cannot use a cooperation request issued under Part 9 of the Rome Statute to compel a State to act as a relocation State. However, once the State has agreed to this role, the ICC could issue a cooperation request if the actions of the State were placing a witness at risk.

[320] ECLI:NL:RBDHA:2013:BZ7942, District Court of The Hague, 8 March 2013 (The Hague District Court, 8 March 2013), §3.

territory, as is often the case, it may transfer them elsewhere. Such a transfer must be done 'in accordance with the law of' the enforcement State. It has been argued elsewhere in this book that such phrases in the Rome Statute protection framework should be interpreted as including both the State's domestic law obligations and its international law obligations. These would include the prohibition on removal, given its customary law nature. When concluding relocation agreements, the ICC could push for the inclusion of a similar provision, stating that the witness cannot be removed except in accordance with the law of the relocation State.

Part of this section has concerned actions that the ICC is *obliged* to take: it is obliged to seek the cooperation of potential relocation States, and it is obliged to monitor witnesses after their transfer to those States and step in where necessary. However, this section has also discussed actions that the ICC *may* take: it may conclude relocation agreements, and it may include in these agreements provisions seeking to pre-empt certain problems. These actions are, according to the Rome Statute protection framework, discretionary. However, they play an important role in protecting witnesses. The existence of agreements helps to relocate a witness quickly, limiting their exposure to risk in the situation State. Tailoring the agreements in the way suggested would help prevent exposure to risk once the relocation has happened. For this reason, the author proposes that these options should not be interpreted as entirely discretionary. If Article 86 and Rule 16(4) are to be interpreted and applied consistently with human rights law, as the Article 21(3) test requires, there must be a degree of compulsion to these actions. It would not be appropriate to make the conclusion of agreements compulsory, as the ICC is dependent on States to agree to them voluntarily. However, the provisions should be interpreted as obliging the ICC to use its best efforts to conclude relocation agreements, and its best effort to ensure that, in terms of substance, they provide as much protection to witnesses as possible.

4.2.3   Obligations of States

The obligations of the relocation State must also be distinguished into two stages, but in this case between those applicable before the State agrees to be a relocation State, and those applicable once the witness arrives. This distinction is largely similar to the one made in the context of enforcement States in Chapter 3: States are not under an obligation to be an enforcement State, but once they agree to be and accept the convicted person, a number of obligations become applicable. The same is true here: States are not obliged to be relocation States, but where they agree to be so, it comes with obligations.

4.2.3.1 Obligations before Agreeing to Be a Relocation State

There is an important difference between situation States and relocation States. For situation States, the witness is already present on the territory and is often a national or resident. For relocation States, the witness is outside the territory and has yet to enter it. As was the case for the stages of interim release and acquitted persons, there is nothing in the Rome Statute protection framework that deals explicitly with whether States are obliged to act as relocation States for at-risk witnesses. Potential sources for such an obligation are found in Part 9 of the Rome Statute, namely Article 86, which creates a general obligation for States Parties to cooperate with the ICC, and Article 93(1)(j), which requires States to cooperate with requests relating to the protection of witnesses.

These provisions could be interpreted in such a way as to allow the ICC to issue a binding cooperation request to a State, whereby the Court obliges a State to accept a witness on its territory. In support of such an interpretation is the wording of the provisions themselves. They empower the ICC to ask for cooperation from States 'in relation to investigations or prosecutions'.[321] Relocating witnesses is an intrinsic part of investigations and prosecutions in so far as neither of these would be possible without witnesses, and so witnesses must be adequately protected.

Opposing this interpretation of Article 86 and Article 93(1)(j) are two arguments (in addition to those put forward in Chapter 2) which are, in the author's opinion, convincing. The first argument is based on practice. Where ICC reports refer to witness relocation, it is clear that it is considered to be a voluntary measure.[322] This is supported by the practice of some States Parties, whose national legislation implementing the Rome Statute, including Part 9, explicitly leaves the decision on whether to admit a witness to the national authorities.[323] At the ad hoc tribunals,

---

[321] Article 93(1) of the Rome Statute.
[322] Assembly of States Parties, 'Report of the Court on Cooperation', ICC-ASP/14/27, 18–26 November 2015 (2015 Report on Activities), §41.
[323] In Canada, the Minister of Citizenship and Immigration must give consent for the admittance of an ICC witness into the country. In the UK, admittance of a witness depends on a court decision. See Valerie Oosterveld, Mike Perry and John McManus, 'Cooperation of States with the International Criminal Court, The Twenty-Fifth Memorial Issue: The Eve of

relocation was also done on a voluntary basis. In the context of relocating an acquitted person, the ICTR considered that a State's obligation to cooperate on such matters extended to consulting with the Tribunal only; the State was not required to grant residence or extend special treatment to the acquitted individual.[324] This was the same when it came to relocating witnesses.[325] The ICTR's approach reflects the idea that being free to control who enters its territory is an important element of State sovereignty. The second argument looks to academic opinion, which favours the view that, in the long term, an approach based on requests and not orders will provide a more sustainable way of protecting witnesses through relocation.[326]

A corollary of the proposed interpretation is that States are under no obligation to conclude relocation agreements with the Court. Indeed, in the practice so far, relocation agreements have been drafted in such a way that even if a State does conclude one with the Court, it does not create an obligation to accept a witness in any given instance. Instead, relocation will only take place if the State has accepted a proposal from the ICC regarding a specific witness.[327]

The proposed interpretation of Articles 86 and 93(1)(j) means that States are under no obligation to act as a relocation State for an at-risk witness, and the ICC may not use those provisions to create obligations to that effect. The remaining question is whether this interpretation satisfies the Article 21(3) test. Article 21(3) has its limits in what it can require from the interpretation and application of the Rome Statute protection framework. One such limit is that it cannot require the creation of entirely new obligations for the States Parties, which is what a broad reading of Articles

---

the International Criminal Court: Preparations and Commentary – How the World Will Relate to the Court' (2001–2002) 25 *Fordham International Law Journal*, 767, 814–16.

[324] *The Prosecutor v. André Ntagerura*, Case No. ICTR-99-46-A28, Decision on the Motion by an Acquitted Person for Cooperation from Canada, Article 28 of the Statute, 15 May 2008 (Trial Chamber III), §4.

[325] For an interesting case on this, see the case law surrounding refugee witnesses at the ICTR. A number of defence witnesses were living unlawfully in Kenya. The defence counsel argued that if Kenya deported them back to Rwanda, they would disappear and so not be available to testify. To remedy this, the defence asked the ICTR to order Kenya to grant the witnesses refugee status. The ICTR held that it did not have the power to compel a State to grant such status, but it did ask the Registrar to seek the cooperation of Kenya in ensuring that the witnesses would be available for trial. See Mohamed Othman, 'The "Protection" of Refugee Witnesses by the International Criminal Tribunal for Rwanda' (2002) 14 *International Journal of Refugee Law*, 495.

[326] Othman, 'The "Protection" of Refugee Witnesses by the ICTR', 502–3.

[327] IBA report, 36.

86 and 93(1)(j) would entail. As such, while the outcome is not optimal from a protection point of view, the Article 21(3) test is met.

4.2.3.2 Obligations after Agreeing to Be a Relocation State

Once a State volunteers to host a relocated witness, it is then possible to speak of legal obligations for the State. The obligations relevant for this discussion are those that require the State to protect the witness's right to life and to keep the witness safe from inhuman treatment, including by not expelling the witness to another State where they would be at risk.

A discussion of the obligations arising under the Rome Statute protection framework begins with Part 9 of the Rome Statute. Once the State has agreed to act as a relocation State and has accepted a witness, Articles 86 and 93(1)(j) can properly be used to issue cooperation requests in relation to that witness. For example, the ICC may request that a State refrain from certain behaviour with respect to a witness, or provide increased protection to a witness. Because of the compulsory nature of these requests, the relocation State is obliged to comply. In addition to this, a relocation State may have obligations arising from a relocation agreement if one was signed, although given their confidential nature, this is hard to know for sure. It is possible that these agreements do not contain new obligations, but rather add detail to existing obligations or refer to obligations the State has beyond the Rome Statute protection framework.

Given that relocated witnesses are undeniably within the territory and jurisdiction of the relocation State, they are entitled to protection beyond the Rome Statute protection framework. Provisions including Articles 6 and 7 ICCPR, Articles 2 and 3 ECHR, and Articles 4 and 5 ACHPR (depending on the region) all provide for the right to life and for the prohibition on inhuman treatment. Intrinsic in these rights is protection from exposure to risk in another State. As such, where relocation agreements make reference to the law of the relocation State, the line between obligations within and beyond the Rome Statute protection framework will become somewhat blurred; in effect, the State's obligations beyond the ICC protection framework will be incorporated within it. However, even if the relocation agreements make no such reference, the human rights law obligations of the relocation State will apply to ICC witnesses.

4.2.4 *Problems in Human Rights Protection*

The discussion of the obligations of the ICC and the relocation State highlights a significant structural problem in the ICCPP relocation regime. There is a task that requires the involvement of multiple actors – witness protection through relocation – but the actor with the obligation to carry it out (the ICC) lacks the capacity to do so, and the actor with the capacity to carry it out (the relocation State) lacks the obligation to do so.

The lack of obligations on the part of potential relocation States to host at-risk witnesses makes the ICC entirely dependent on the voluntary assistance of States. This can create a gap in protection where a witness faces the possibility that no State will be willing to host them. Given the level of threat against them, without a relocation State witnesses will be exposed to harm. Even if the witness is withdrawn from ICC proceedings, this will not always neutralise the risk the witness faces. For instance, it may be known in the witness's community that they have been in intensive contact with ICC staff, even if they have not yet testified. In the words of one commentator: 'Out of all the protective tools available to the Court, the ICCPP serves as a prime example to show how the limitations of external support significantly weaken the Court's protection capabilities.'[328]

The ICC's current approach to dealing with this structural problem utilises four related measures. Each is designed to encourage States Parties to provide voluntary assistance in relocating witnesses, albeit in different ways. They will be discussed in turn, with a comment on their advantages and disadvantages.

Relocation agreements have been mentioned already, and are at the forefront of the ICC's efforts to encourage States to volunteer as relocation States. The Court regularly calls on States to conclude relocation agreements if they have not already done so.[329] Increasing the number of agreements is an ongoing aim for the ICC, with one of its strategic goals for 2013–2017 being to 'encourage States to conclude further voluntary agreements with the court on ... relocation of witnesses'.[330]

Concluding relocation agreements and using these as the basis for relocating witnesses is an alternative to relocating witnesses on an ad hoc basis. The clearest advantage of this is that, in signing such an agreement, the State demonstrates its willingness to act as a relocation State. This means that when the ICC has a witness in need of relocation, there is a pool of States which it can contact, and it can rely on the expedited procedures provided for in these agreements to relocate the witness

[328] Eikel, 'External Support and Internal Coordination', 1123.
[329] 2012 Report on Activities, §172; 2013 Report on Activities, §188; 2015 Report on Activities, §42.
[330] 2016 Proposed Budget, 193.

quickly. This can be key, especially when there is an urgent need for protection. If there is an existing group of willing States, this reduces the chance that no relocation State can be found for a witness.

There are further advantages to using relocation agreements over ad hoc arrangements. First, in terms of the quality of life of the witness and their family, relying on ad hoc arrangements can leave them in a state of constant anxiety over their uncertain situation. Second, in terms of financial costs, ad hoc solutions entail increased management costs for the Court. For example, witnesses who are in an uncertain situation will not be able to integrate into their new society and find a job, their health care costs will be higher as they will not be covered by domestic insurance policies, and children will need to be educated in private international schools until a permanent situation is found.[331] Because witnesses relocated pursuant to a relocation agreement are in a more certain situation, these additional costs will be less, meaning that the costs of relocating witnesses pursuant to an agreement is 45–75 per cent lower than without an agreement.[332]

Despite these clear advantages, signing a relocation agreement and indicating to the ICC a willingness to accept at-risk witnesses appears to be a significant commitment for States. One of the disadvantages of relocation agreements is the reluctance of States to conclude them. In 2009, 210 *notes verbales* were sent to States Parties requesting cooperation on relocation, and the ICC only received thirty-one responses, the majority of which did not result in agreements being signed.[333] As the activities of the ICC continue to expand, this will grow increasingly problematic. A report presented by the Court to the Assembly of States Parties highlighted an urgent need for new agreements to be concluded.[334] A greater number of agreements would also better protect witnesses, as there will be more places they could potentially be, making them harder to find.[335]

There are further limits on how well relocation agreements can fill the structural gap in protection created by the multi-actor nature of witness relocation. As currently drafted, relocation agreements are only framework agreements, couched in general terms; they do not impose an obligation on States to accept a witness in any given instance. This allows

---

[331] 2015 Report on Activities, §41.
[332] 2015 Report on Activities, §41.
[333] Eikel, 'External Support and Internal Coordination', 1125.
[334] 2015 Report on Activities, §42.
[335] IBA report, 36.

for a situation whereby some States sign relocation agreements but never accept a witness.[336] Once again relocation agreements are comparable to enforcement agreements, which require the separate consent of a State to the hosting of each convicted person. There is a justified reluctance to write these agreements in such a way as to create an obligation on States to accept an individual, as it might well make States even more reluctant to sign them.[337]

While the signing of relocation agreements is certainly positive, their lack of specific obligations means that they are of less assistance in protecting the types of witness who are hardest to relocate in the first place. States will generally not raise an objection to receiving a witness who was a peaceful farmer or school teacher. They are less likely to welcome witnesses who are themselves accused of participation in criminal activity, especially in war crimes or crimes against humanity. Consider a former child soldier or a low-to-mid-ranking soldier. And yet it is these types of insider witnesses who are often key in ICC prosecutions, and who also have a right to protection. In relation to individuals such as these, Western States have been accused of employing a double standard, with the suggestion that in at least one case a potential suspect was given training in a European military academy, and yet protection was refused to prosecution witnesses.[338]

A further disadvantage of relying on relocation agreements to overcome structural problems in witness protection is that they are ill equipped to deal with emergency situations. While relocating witnesses pursuant to a relocation agreement is faster than without, the process can still take months. At the beginning of 2011, the ICC was faced with an urgent and unforeseen situation, and requested States Parties to temporarily accept witnesses on their territory. Nine requests of this type were made, none of which received a positive reply.[339] In February 2016, an ICC prosecutor accidentally released the names of a number of protected witnesses in the *Gbagbo and Blé Goudé* trial.[340] This mistake could have placed these witnesses in imminent danger, and possibly it was necessary to relocate them (information is naturally very limited).

---

[336] IBA report, 36.
[337] IBA report, 36.
[338] Mahony, 'Justice Sector Afterthought', 54.
[339] Assembly of States Parties, 'Report of the Bureau on Cooperation', ICC-ASP/12/36, 20–28 November 2013 (2013 Report on Cooperation), §45
[340] 'Gbagbo Trial: ICC 'mistakenly' discloses names of witnesses', Africa News, 6 February 2016.

These types of events, although hopefully rare, illustrate that relocation might be necessary on very short notice, and the current system struggles to cope. It is essential that the ICC be able to urgently evacuate a witness to a safe country when a life-threatening situation arises, and where it cannot, there is a serious risk to that witness.[341]

The ICC acknowledges the shortcomings of relying on relocation agreements alone, and so continues to look for further solutions to be taken alongside these agreements.[342] States may be unwilling to conclude a relocation agreement because hosting a witness is, either politically or economically, too onerous. To enable States to provide voluntary assistance short of acting as a relocation State, the ICC has devised three alternative ways in which States can assist the ICC with its witness protection functions. The first is to contribute to the 'Special Fund for Relocations'; the second is to sponsor a particular witness; and the third is to act as a platform State.

The Special Fund for Relocations was set up to make hosting relocated witnesses more attractive. In the classic relocation model, the relocation State financially contributes to the relocation. It is not clear what the particular distribution between the ICC and the relocation State is, in terms of financing housing, schooling, healthcare etc., but it is clear that the State must bear at least part of the burden. While this works for some States, particularly developed States, it may not be as viable for developing countries. If the ICC wants to encourage States with similar linguistic, cultural, and geographic attributes to volunteer as relocation States, then the question of financing is important. To that end, the Special Fund distinguishes between relocation States and donor States. A State that lacks resources but is willing to host a witness can do so, while a State that is unable to host a witness but can afford to do so can contribute to the Fund. Money is then sent to the relocation State to provide for the witness's welfare and sustainability,[343] allowing that State to host the witness in a cost-neutral arrangement.[344]

The second type of voluntary measure for addressing structural gaps in protection also involves the Special Fund: specific sponsorship.[345] A State

---

[341] 2013 Report on Cooperation, §§45–6.
[342] 2015 Report on Activities, §41.
[343] 2010 Summary Report, §32.
[344] Arbia, 'The ICC: Witness and Victim Protection and Support', 523; Emma Irving, 'Protecting Witnesses at the International Criminal Court from Refoulement' (2014) 12 *Journal of International Criminal Justice*, 1141, 1150.
[345] Arbia, 'The ICC: Witness and Victim Protection and Support', 523; 2010 Summary Report, §32.

that is contributing to the Special Fund can choose to direct the money to a specific State or witness. For example, when the United Kingdom gave £200,000 to the Fund in 2010, the money was specially earmarked for relocating persons at risk in the Kenya situation.[346] This flexibility is aimed at promoting contributions to the fund.

The advantage of the Special Fund is clear: it enables States that are willing to host witnesses to do so without the financial burden, and it allows States to provide assistance without actually having to host. However, the idea of the Special Fund has not been without criticism. When the idea was developed, representatives from Belgium opposed the idea on the basis that relocation States would be discouraged from taking over responsibility for the witness. The fear was that relocation States would not be committed to effectively integrating the person into their society because there is no financial consequence of not doing so. As an alternative, the Belgian representatives suggested that Special Fund relocations be restricted to pre-established time frames, after which the relocation State would take over responsibility for the costs.[347] It does not seem from the information available that this approach was adopted, nor is there information on whether Belgium's fears have been substantiated in practice.

The third type of voluntary measure available to States is to agree to act as a 'platform State'. In this capacity a State would issue a witness with an emergency visa and host them on a temporary basis. This would be appropriate in situations where a witness needs relocating urgently and it is essential to extract them from their current situation immediately. Having bought some time, a permanent solution could then be found. While this approach would provide flexibility in difficult situations, it does have an important drawback about which States have expressed concern: the possibility of the witness applying for protection/asylum in the platform State.[348]

The measures outlined in this section, in combination, go far in addressing the structural problems that affect human rights protection in the relocation of witnesses abroad. If States respond positively, and contribute in one or more of the available ways, these measures may be enough to prevent the structural problems from detrimentally impacting witnesses in need of protection. However, the voluntary nature of these

---

[346] 'ICC welcomes UK contribution for relocating at-risk persons in Kenya', ICC Weekly Update, 30 November 2010.
[347] 2010 Summary Report, §34.
[348] IBA report, 36.

schemes means that the structural problems are by no means solved, and a degree of vulnerability remains for witnesses in need of relocation abroad, particularly those witnesses whom States are reluctant to welcome into their territory.

4.2.5 Conclusion

Relocating a witness to another State is a drastic measure that the ICC does not consider lightly. The degree of disruption it can cause to a witness's life should be avoided if possible. Where relocation is the only option, the ICC faces challenges. If a witness is to be relocated, they must be relocated onto the territory of a State, meaning that the ICC is dependent on State assistance. Unlike when a witness is protected in the situation State, relocation States are under no obligation to assist the Court. This creates a structural problem: if no State volunteers to host a witness, a gap in protection will exist and the witness's rights will be at risk.

There are a number of ways in which the structural problems of witness relocation have been addressed by the Court. Relocation agreements are the most prominent way in which the ICC has sought to encourage voluntary assistance from States, but they are not very numerous and offer an incomplete solution. To complement relocation agreements, measures such as the Special Fund have been put in place. While these are all moves in the right direction, their voluntary nature means that some vulnerability for witnesses remains.

4.3 Conclusion

Depending on the degree of risk, the ICC has a range of measures it can employ for the protection of witnesses. These range from in-courtroom measures such as distorted speech and pseudonyms, to out-of-courtroom measures such as the IRS and relocation. Only the latter measures involve multiple actors, as the ICC must enlist the cooperation of States on whose territory the witness is located. Two types of situations were considered in this chapter: those where the witness remains in their home State (referred to as the situation State) and those where the witness is relocated to a third State (referred to as the relocation State).

The protection of witnesses in the situation State is addressed by several provisions of the Rome Statute protection framework, which contains obligations for both the ICC and situation States. These range from overarching provisions that apply to the protection of witnesses generally, to specific obligations such as the requirement that the ICC establish and maintain IRS programmes. There is, therefore, not a lack of legal provision for this situation, and if tasks are clearly allocated, problems can be avoided.

A particularly complex aspect of the multi-actor protection of witnesses in situation States is connected to how the operationalisation of these obligations changes from one situation State to another. In some countries, State infrastructure may have remained intact despite the conflict, and so witness protection schemes can utilise national resources such as the police. In other situations, such State infrastructure may be non-existent, or too closely aligned with one of the parties appearing before the Court, in which case witness protection must operate differently. The particularities of how witness protection tasks are allocated between the situation State and the ICC follows a case-by-case model and is kept confidential by the Court. That being said, the potential implementation problems for human rights protection in this situation are similar regardless of the State in question. The challenges of State cooperation, political instability, and on-the-ground security issues are ever present. There is one implementation problem that is particularly closely linked to the multi-actor nature of the situation, and this relates to the way in which Article 68(1) of the Rome Statute was interpreted by the ICC. By narrowing the range of risks against which the ICC is obliged to protect witnesses, the line establishing where the responsibility of the ICC ends and that of the State begins is difficult to ascertain in borderline cases. In such cases, witnesses may go unprotected if the ICC and the situation State both consider that the lead role in protection falls to the other actor.

In cases where the only way to ensure a witness's safety (and that of their family) is to relocate them to a third State, the legal framework is less detailed. While the ICC retains both its overarching and specific protection obligations, there is no corresponding obligation on relocation States to cooperate with the Court. This differs from the situation State, which does have obligations to this effect. If a State agrees to act as a relocation State voluntarily, and accepts a witness on its territory, then a range of obligations come into effect. However, neither the Rome Statute protection framework nor general international law contains an obligation on States to agree to become relocation States. This structural problem of multi-actor human rights protection was also present in the situations of interim release and acquittal and release addressed in the previous chapter. While there is an absence of legal obligation, the ICC has been very creative and proactive in seeking ways to overcome the structural gap in protection. There are a range of ways in which States can assist the Court in the relocation of witnesses that fall short of agreeing to act as a relocation State, and yet which are designed to make accepting witnesses more appealing. A complex web of partial solutions has therefore been developed to address the particular challenge that multi-actor human rights protection poses to witness protection.

It is unclear, in terms of numbers, how many witnesses have been (or might be in future) affected by the implementation and structural challenges identified in this chapter. The protection of ICC witnesses is kept confidential, and justifiably so. That being said, the problems we see in witness protection has led some witnesses to seek protection from a different actor. Rather than relying on the ICC and the situation or relocation State, some witnesses have involved the Netherlands in their protection by submitting asylum claims when they arrive at the seat of the Court in The Hague. These situations, which add another layer to the multi-actor nature of the situation, are addressed in Chapter 7. Before proceeding to discuss the involvement of the ICC host State in witness protection however, it is necessary to first consider general questions regarding the host State's human rights law obligations (Chapter 5), and examine situations where the host State is involved in protecting accused, convicted, and acquitted (Chapter 6).

PART II

Multi-Actor Human Rights Protection
The ICC and Its Host State

5

The Human Rights Obligations of the ICC Host State

The Netherlands, as the ICC's host State, plays a crucial role in the functioning of the ICC. Not only does it provide the physical space for the ICC's premises, it is also intricately involved in the everyday activities of the Court. The transport of witnesses to and from the point of entry into the Netherlands is carried out by the Dutch authorities; the transport of accused between the ICC Detention Centre and the Court is also carried out by the Dutch authorities. If an enforcement State cannot be found for a convicted individual, there is provision for the Netherlands to temporarily step in. Without the Netherlands' practical support, the operations of the Court would be severely impacted.

As a result of this, a number of multi-actor situations arise where the Netherlands and the ICC are both involved in protecting the human rights of witnesses, as well as accused, convicted, and acquitted persons. In order to fully understand how human rights are protected in multi-actor situations, it is therefore necessary to consider how the obligations of these two actors interact and overlap. Before considering these multi-actor situations in detail in Chapters 6 and 7, the present chapter will identify the sources of the host State's obligations, both within and beyond the Rome Statute protection framework. As with Chapters 1 and 2, the discussion in this chapter is centred around the obligations of the Netherlands with respect to human rights protection, and does not purport to be an exhaustive examination of all obligations applicable to the situations discussed.

The Netherlands is not only the ICC's host State, it is also an ICC State Party. As such, the Netherlands is subject to the same obligations as other States Parties, in addition to those that attach to it in its host State capacity. As State Party obligations have already been discussed, the focus of this chapter will be the host State-specific obligations.

5.1 Within the Rome Statute Protection Framework

As the ICC's host State, the Netherlands has a special legal relationship with the Court. With this special relationship come particular legal obligations. An important source of obligations is the Headquarters Agreement between the Netherlands and the ICC, a bilateral treaty that sets out the respective tasks and competences of the two actors. For a number of obligations arising under this agreement the human rights protection dimension is clear. For example, Article 47(2) requires the Netherlands to continue the interim release of accused who return to the seat of the Court after spending time on interim release in a different State. Other obligations arising under the Headquarters Agreement provide for the protection of human rights more indirectly, and instead form a link in the chain of human rights protection in multi-actor situations. For example, when a witness travels to the ICC in order to provide testimony, they might be relocated to a third State once their testimony is complete. Part of the Netherlands' obligations under the Headquarters Agreement is to transport witnesses from the airport to the ICC on arrival, and from the ICC to the airport on departure.[349] Transporting the witness to the airport is an important link in the chain that leads to their relocation to a safe State, and therefore to the protection of their human rights. Other sources of host State obligations with a human rights dimension include the Rome Statute itself and the ICC Implementation Act (the domestic legislation that implemented the Rome Statute and Headquarters Agreement); however, the obligations arising beyond the Rome Statute protection framework are of greater significance to the situations that will be addressed in the subsequent chapters.

5.2 Beyond the Rome Statute Protection Framework

When the Netherlands performs its obligations under the Rome Statute protection framework, whether pursuant to the Rome Statute, Headquarters Agreement, or other protection framework documents, it does not do so in a vacuum. Rather, its actions may activate other obligations that the Netherlands has under international law beyond the Rome Statute protection framework. For example, when the Dutch authorities comply with the obligation vis-à-vis the ICC to transport a witness to the airport, the

---

[349] Article 45 of the Headquarters Agreement between the International Criminal Court and the Host State 2002 (Headquarters Agreement).

Netherlands must also comply with its obligation vis-à-vis the transported witness under human rights law.

In contrast to the previous section, the relevant obligations beyond the Rome Statute protection framework are specifically phrased in human rights terms, and are found in the Netherlands' human rights law treaty commitments. The most pertinent set of human rights obligations for the Netherlands are those contained in the ECHR, as this is the instrument most invoked in domestic proceedings.[350]

Generally speaking, all individuals present on the territory of the Netherlands will be entitled to protection under the ECHR. This follows from the basic jurisdictional clause in Article 1 of the Convention, and is often reaffirmed by the ECtHR.[351] However, complications arise as a result of the relationship between the ICC and its host State. The essence of this complication relates to jurisdiction, and can be illustrated as follows. Witnesses and accused who come to the ICC necessarily enter the territory of the Netherlands, in the sense that they are physically present there. However, because those individuals came to the Netherlands under the auspices of the ICC, the link between territory and jurisdiction can be interrupted. In other words, under certain circumstances, the Netherlands may lack jurisdiction over individuals located on the premises of the ICC, because these premises have a special status.

This interruption between territory and jurisdiction will affect those individuals who are restricted to the premises of the ICC itself – namely because they are detained there – but not those who can move around the Netherlands freely. The majority of witnesses who come to the ICC to give evidence will be accommodated away from the premises of the ICC itself, in an apartment or a hotel. They come to the Court voluntarily, and are free to wander around The Hague at leisure, perhaps even visit other cities. These circumstances mean that, although they entered the country under the auspices of the ICC, they are very much within the jurisdiction of the Netherlands in the normal way, and the Dutch authorities have accepted as much.[352] The Dutch authorities have also

---

[350] Janneke Gerards and Joseph Fleuren, 'The Netherlands', in Janneke Gerards and Joseph Fleuren (eds.), *Implementation of the European Convention on Human Rights and of the Judgments of the ECtHR in National Case Law: A Comparative Analysis* (Intersentia, 2014), 217.

[351] See for example *Behrami and Behrami v. France; Saramati v. France, Germany and Norway*, Application no. 71412/01, Admissibility Decision, 2 May 2007, §69.

[352] Letter from Justice Minister to Parliament, 8.

accepted that individuals who are in the process of being transported from the ICC premises to the point of departure from the Netherlands are within Dutch jurisdiction.[353] More on these two situations in subsequent chapters.

The case is different for those who are detained on the premises of the ICC itself, either because they are a suspect or because they are a detained witness. The term 'premises' includes the Court's detention facility. The ICC premises have a special nature, given to them by the Headquarters Agreement: the premises are inviolable,[354] the law of the Netherlands only applies to them to the extent that it is consistent with the rules of the Court,[355] only ICC staff can carry weapons on the premises of the Court,[356] the Court has privileges and immunities,[357] and so on. With respect to the detention of individuals at the seat of the Court, Section 88 of the Implementation Act states that Dutch law does not apply to the deprivation of liberty at the Court.

As a result of this special arrangement, the general rule according to the ECtHR is that a State hosting an international criminal tribunal does not have jurisdiction over individuals located on the premises of these tribunals. One could say that jurisdiction is *suspended* over that portion of territory, making this an exception to the principle of territoriality (whereby jurisdiction is deemed to be primarily linked to territory).[358] In the *Longa* case, the ECtHR specifically reiterated this exception in the context of the ICC.[359] The case concerned detained witnesses located in the ICC Detention Centre. The four witnesses were detained in the DRC on a number of charges, and had travelled to the ICC to give testimony. As they were detained in the DRC, they remained detained while at the seat of the Court. Once their testimony was complete, and claiming to

---

[353] In a letter written by the Dutch Minister of Justice to the Dutch Parliament, it is stated that the Netherlands would be obliged to interrupt the transport if it appeared that to remove the person would violate human rights law (Letter from Justice Minister to Parliament, 6). Furthermore, according to the domestic legislation implementing the Headquarters Agreement, a person who is being transported falls under Dutch authority (Section 85 of International Criminal Court (Implementation) Act 2002 (ICC Implementation Act)).

[354] Article 6 of the Headquarters Agreement.
[355] Article 8(3) of the Headquarters Agreement.
[356] Article 8(5) of the Headquarters Agreement.
[357] Article 5 of the Headquarters Agreement.
[358] *Galić* v. *The Netherlands,* Application no 22617/07, Decision on Admissibility, 9 June 2009 (*Galić,* 9 June 2009) §42.
[359] *Djokaba Lambi Longa* v. *The Netherlands,* Application no. 33917/12, Decision, 9 October 2012 (*Longa,* 9 October 2012).

fear for their safety if returned to the DRC, the witnesses applied for asylum in the Netherlands. The legal issues this claim gave rise to were complicated, and are addressed in detail in Chapter 7. For now, it suffices to say that while these legal issues were being resolved, the witnesses remained detained at the ICC Detention Centre for an extended period of time. In an attempt to end this detention, one witness brought a claim before the ECtHR against the Netherlands, claiming a violation of his right to liberty. The question for the ECtHR was whether the witness was within the Netherlands' jurisdiction.

The ECtHR held that 'the fact that the applicant is deprived of his liberty on Netherlands soil does not itself suffice to bring questions touching on the lawfulness of his detention within Dutch "jurisdiction"' under Article 1 ECHR.[360] In support of this, the ECtHR cited other examples of exceptions to the territoriality principle, including NATO Status of Forces Agreements and the Scottish court set up in The Hague to try the suspects in the Lockerbie bombing.[361] The ECtHR also recalled one of its previous cases, concerning two defendants on trial at the ICTY. These defendants made a number of complaints on the basis of Article 6 ECHR (fair trial), arguing that since the ICTY was located on Dutch territory, and since the Netherlands had signed a Headquarters Agreement with the ICTY, the violations of their fair trial rights were attributable to the Netherlands.[362] The ECtHR held the case to be inadmissible: 'the Court cannot find the sole fact that the ICTY has its seat and premises in The Hague sufficient ground to attribute the matters complained of to the Kingdom of the Netherlands.'[363] While the ICTY case concerned attribution rather than jurisdiction, the reasoning of the ECtHR is the same: it is not sufficient that the international court was simply present on Dutch territory.

If the *Longa* case reiterated the exception to the territoriality principle, then there is what one might call an 'exception to the exception' resulting from a decision of a Dutch domestic court. The same situation of detained witnesses that gave rise to the *Longa* decision also gave rise to a number of other decisions. Before a Dutch court, the witnesses argued that they could not be returned to the DRC because of safety concerns, and so pursuant to Article 3 of the ECHR, the Netherlands was precluded from removing

[360] *Longa*, 9 October 2012, §73.
[361] *Galić*, 9 June 2009, §44.
[362] *Galić*, 9 June 2009, §40.
[363] *Galić*, 9 June 2009, §46.

them. The Dutch government argued that it had no jurisdiction under the ECHR, as the witnesses were on ICC premises, and so it could not admit the witnesses to a procedure that would determine their entitlement to protection under Article 3. Unlike in *Longa*, the Dutch State argument was rejected by the domestic court.[364] It held that, because a domestic procedure on protection would not interfere with the ICC's functions, and because the witnesses had nowhere else to turn for protection, there were sufficient grounds to establish jurisdiction.

While this case predates *Longa*, it was arguably not overruled by the ECtHR decision. *Longa* dealt specifically with Article 5 ECHR – the right to liberty – and did not purport to make statements of a general nature. The Dutch court decision establishing the 'exception to the exception' concerned Article 3 ECHR, not Article 5. Furthermore, the decision was not appealed by the Dutch government at the time, and has not been challenged since, which implies an acceptance of it. The substantive chapters will show that this 'exception to the exception' will not *always* permit a prohibition on removal claim to be made from ICC premises, but for some individuals it will prove an important decision.

The *Longa* case represents the state of the law on the question of the Netherlands' jurisdiction vis-à-vis the right to liberty of individuals held on the ICC premises. The discussion of obligations in the substantive chapters is done according to that decision. That being said, it will be argued in Chapter 8 that the decision is flawed. It will be shown that the *Longa* decision leaves significant problems for the adequacy of human rights protection, and an alternative way of approaching host State obligations will be put forward.

5.3 Conclusion

Assistance from the Netherlands is essential to the everyday functioning of the ICC, and often the Netherlands plays a small but key role in the protection of human rights in multi-actor situations. Transporting witnesses to the airport so they can travel to their new home in a relocation State is an example of this. At other times though, the role of the Netherlands in multi-actor human rights protection will be more substantial. As the following two chapters will show, where accused and

---

[364] ECLI:NL:RBSGR:2011:BU9492, The Hague District Court (sitting in Amsterdam), 28 December 2011 (The Hague District Court, 28 December 2011).

witnesses choose to invoke obligations of the Netherlands beyond the Rome Statute protection framework, this can lead to significant involvement by the ICC host State in protecting human rights. Setting out the general sources of these obligations is therefore important to laying the foundation for understanding this additional complication to multi-actor human rights protection.

6

Accused, Convicted, and Acquitted

This chapter revisits situations that were addressed under Part I, and adds an additional layer of complexity to them. Human rights protection during interim release, enforcement of sentence, and acquittal and release involves, in addition to the ICC and States Parties, also the ICC host State. Chapter 3 set out the role that States Parties play in these situations, including how they become involved and what their obligations are. The present chapter explores the role that the ICC host State plays.

The involvement of the ICC host State in these situations stems from the fact that, at some point during each of these situations, the accused, acquitted, or convicted person finds themselves on the host State's territory: an application for interim release is made once the accused has been arrested and surrendered to the Court; for a convicted person to serve their sentence in an enforcement State, they must first be transported there from the seat of the Court; when an acquitted person is released, they are released from the Court's detention centre or from other premises of the Court. As this chapter will demonstrate, the presence of these individuals on the territory of the host State has the potential to engage the Netherlands' obligations to protect human rights, both under the Rome Statute protection framework and beyond it.

By virtue of the fact that these situations have already been addressed in Part I, the discussion in this chapter is necessarily briefer. The respective introductory sections will shortly revisit the right at stake in the situation, the ICC's obligations, and the obligations of States Parties, in order to supply the relevant context. This is followed by a description of the obligations of the ICC host State, and a discussion of the problems that the multi-actor nature of the situation may cause.

6.1 Interim Release

Every accused that arrives at the seat of the ICC must be considered for interim release, the purpose of which is to safeguard the right to liberty by ensuring that accused are detained only where necessary to prevent flight, interference with the investigation, or the continuation of crimes.[365] The Rome Statute protection framework imposes comprehensive obligations on the ICC to safeguard this right, with the different paragraphs of Article 60 of the Rome Statute covering the different scenarios where interim release may be warranted. However, whilst the ICC has the obligation to protect the right to liberty through the granting of interim release, it lacks the factual capacity to do so. As the ICC has no territory of its own, it cannot host accused granted interim release. As such, the ICC relies on States Parties to agree to host accused. As discussed in Chapter 3, nothing in the Rome Statute protection framework or beyond imposes an obligation on States Parties to agree to host accused on interim release, creating structural problems for the protection of the right to liberty of accused in this situation.

The host State's obligations with respect to interim release are somewhat limited. Like States Parties, the Netherlands is under no obligation to host accused granted interim release while awaiting trial, either pursuant to a provision within the Rome Statute protection framework or beyond it. The same arguments that apply to States Parties apply to the host State also. The only host State specific provision on this point is Article 47(1) of the Headquarters Agreement, which obliges the Netherlands to 'facilitate the transfer of persons granted interim release into a State *other than the host State*' (emphasis added).

There is one situation where an obligation arises under the Rome Statute protection framework for the Netherlands to host an individual on interim release: when an accused who has already been granted interim release, and was hosted by another country while on release, returns to the Netherlands to continue with the trial proceedings. Pursuant to the Headquarters Agreement, Article 47(2) requires the Netherlands to 'facilitate the re-entry into the host State of persons granted interim release and their short-term stay in the host State for any purpose related to proceedings before the Court'. The existence of this obligation is important, as it means that the accused does not have to return to ICC custody in order to be present for the ICC proceedings; if it was judged safe to grant the accused interim release while the trial was pending, it would be an interference with their right to liberty if they were per se required to return to custody in order to stand trial. From the information available, the four accused granted interim release in the

---

[365] Article 58(1) of the Rome Statute.

Bemba witness interference case (*Bemba et al.*) do not seem to have been rearrested when they arrived back in The Hague for their ICC trial. One must therefore assume that, for the duration of their trial, they resided at liberty somewhere on the territory of the Netherlands.[366]

Turning to the Netherlands' obligations beyond the Rome Statute protection framework, it has been suggested that the Netherlands has a residual obligation, under the ECHR, to host ICC accused who are entitled to interim release but for whom no host State can be found.[367] This line of argumentation rests on the fact that, even though ICC accused are held in the ICC Detention Centre, they are still present on the territory of the Netherlands. As the Netherlands must respect and ensure the human rights of individuals located on its territory, it must therefore ensure that ICC accused are not unjustifiably deprived of their liberty (as per Article 5 ECHR). Such an obligation could involve the Netherlands hosting an accused if no other solution is found.

In light of the ECtHR decision in the *Longa* case,[368] this line of argumentation can be quickly countered. As discussed in Chapter 5, the ECtHR determined that the fact that the ICC was located on the territory of the Netherlands was not sufficient to grant Dutch authorities jurisdiction over the individuals present on those premises, at least as far as Article 5 ECHR was concerned. The ICC premises have a special status, and constitute an exception to the territoriality of jurisdiction principle. As such, no obligation arises for the Netherlands from beyond the Rome Statute protection framework that requires it to host accused granted interim release.

In looking at the obligations of the Netherlands as ICC host State, it is clear that involving the Netherlands in the protection of accused entitled to interim release does not provide a solution to the structural gap in protection. The obligation in Article 47(2) of the Headquarters Agreement is limited to hosting accused who are returning from interim release elsewhere and is restricted to a short-term basis – only as necessary for the accused's involvement in proceedings before the ICC. As a result, the original structural problem of finding a place for interim release remains.

---

[366] A relevant press release mentions that Bemba is in custody, but does not say whether the four other defendants returned to custody after their return to The Hague ('Bemba, Kilolo et al. trial opens at International Criminal Court').

[367] Göran Sluiter, 'International Criminal Tribunals and Their Relation to States' in André Nollkaemper, Ilias Plakokefalos, and Jessica Schechinger (eds.), *The Practice of Shared Responsibility in International Law* (Cambridge University Press, 2017), 226.

[368] *Longa*, 9 October 2012.

6.2 Removal to the Enforcement State

6.2.1 Introduction

The drafters of the Rome Statute intended that custodial sentences resulting from an ICC conviction be served, not in an ICC administered detention centre, but in national prisons. States Parties can volunteer to enforce sentences, and when they do, they must provide human rights protections to the individuals they imprison. In particular, discussion in relation to the enforcement of sentences has focused on the right to protection from torture and inhuman and degrading treatment and punishment (hereinafter 'inhuman treatment'). The ICC maintains a supervisory role over the enforcement of sentences by States, and depending on the context, this supervision will be more or less strict. While the structure of the enforcement system is quite complex, the distribution of obligations between the ICC and States Parties is clear, with each actor having a delineated set of tasks that presents no obvious structural or implementation problems.

Matters are more complex when the ICC host State is added to the picture. At the moment an individual is convicted by the ICC, they will (almost always) be physically present at the seat of the Court, meaning that they are present on the territory of the Netherlands. Once an enforcement State is identified, the convicted person must be transported to that enforcement State, a task that falls to the Dutch authorities. This involvement of the ICC host State in the enforcement of sentences engages obligations of the Netherlands both under the Rome Statute protection framework and beyond it. As these two sets of obligations are intertwined, they are considered together.

6.2.2 Obligations of the Host State

When it comes to the ICC host State, the distinction made in Section 3.4 between obligations relating to the conditions of detention and obligations relating to the prohibition on removal to a situation of risk is once again relevant. There are three possible scenarios where the host State may have obligations to protect a person convicted by the ICC from inhuman treatment in connection with the enforcement of their sentence, and all of them arise while the person is still on Dutch territory post-conviction. The first scenario involves conditions of detention, and the last two involve the prohibition on removal.

The first scenario concerns the situation where the ICC is not able to find an enforcement State to host a particular convicted person. Given the system of double consent, this is a possibility, and arrangements were made in the Rome Statute for such an eventuality. Article 103(4) stipulates that when no State is designated as the enforcement State by the Court, the sentence shall be served in a domestic prison facility made available by the host State. This is designed to be a short-term solution, and the ICC must continue to search for a willing enforcement State.[369] Unlike with other enforcement States, in these circumstances the ICC covers the costs of the convicted person's stay in a Dutch prison.[370] When acting in its role as residual enforcer of sentences, the obligations of the Netherlands will derive from Article 106(2) of the Rome Statute in the same way as for any other enforcement State: the conditions of detention will be governed by Dutch law but subject to minimum human rights standards which the Netherlands must uphold. As is also the case with other enforcement States, the Netherlands will have obligations beyond the Rome Statute protection framework deriving from its international human rights obligations, in this case the ECHR.

In the ICC's practice to date, the Netherlands has not been called upon to fulfil its role as residual enforcer of sentences. As such, fears that enforcement in the host State will become the norm because then the Court bears the costs seem ungrounded.[371] Instead, the practice has been that while arrangements are made with potential enforcement States, the convicted persons have remained in the ICC Detention Centre, sometimes for extended periods. This scenario does not appear to have been intended,[372] but has been common practice.

The second scenario concerns the situation where the ICC designates an enforcement State, but the convicted person believes that they would be at risk of inhuman treatment in the designated State. While still in the ICC Detention Centre awaiting transfer, the convicted person could transmit

---

[369] Article 49(3) of the Headquarters Agreement.
[370] Article 103(4) of the Rome Statute.
[371] Trevor Pascal Chimimba, 'Establishing an Enforcement Regime', in Roy Lee (ed.), *The International Criminal Court: The Making of the Rome Statute – Issues, Negotiations, Results* (Kluwer Law International, 1999), 351.
[372] Article 50 of the Headquarters Agreement indicates that convicted persons were only meant to remain in the ICC Detention Centre if the time remaining on their sentence was less than six months: 'If, after conviction and final sentence, or after reduction of a sentence in accordance with article 110 of the Statute, the time remaining to be served under the sentence of the Court is less than six months, the Court shall consider whether the sentence may be enforced in the detention centre of the Court.'

ACCUSED, CONVICTED, AND ACQUITTED   151

an application for protection from removal to the Dutch authorities. The relevant obligation of the Netherlands in this situation is found beyond the Rome Statute protection framework, namely in Article 3 ECHR, which contains the right to protection from inhuman treatment. Through the case law of the ECtHR, prohibition on removal is now an intrinsic part of this provision.[373] In order for the Netherlands to be obliged to consider a claim for protection from removal under Article 3, it must first be ascertained whether there is jurisdiction over the convicted person. This is by no means straightforward, given that the individual is located on ICC premises. As discussed in Chapter 5, the ICC premises have a special status, and to an extent the jurisdiction of the Netherlands under human rights law over individuals on those premises is suspended.

There is some practice concerning asylum claims and claims for protection from removal from individuals located in the ICC Detention Centre that can be of assistance here. The existing practice concerns witnesses, and although the author disagrees that this precedent applies equally to convicted persons, the point needs to be addressed. The situation of the witnesses was discussed in Chapter 5 and will be analysed in detail in Chapter 7; for now it suffices to say that the relevant case involved four detained witnesses held at the ICC Detention Centre for the purpose of giving testimony, at the conclusion of which they were to be returned to the custody of the DRC.[374] Claiming to fear for their safety if returned, the witnesses requested protection in the Netherlands. The Dutch authorities argued that as they were on ICC premises, Dutch jurisdiction was not engaged, and so the Netherlands owed them no obligations under human rights law (or refugee law). This was rejected by The Hague District Court, which held that Dutch asylum and human rights law did in fact apply to the witnesses, despite the fact that they were confined in the ICC Detention Centre.[375] The Netherlands therefore did have jurisdiction and was obliged to hear the applications for protection and make a determination on the merits.

The case is interesting for many reasons, not least because of the contrast it makes with the *Longa* case.[376] As discussed in Chapter 5, this decision of

---

[373] There is a long line of cases to this effect, including *Soering v. United Kingdom*; *Cruz Varas and Others v. Sweden*, Application no. 15576/89, Judgment, 20 March 1991, §§69–70; *Vilvarajah and Others v. United Kingdom*, Application Nos. 13163/87, 13164/87, 13165/87, 13447/87, 13448/87, Judgment, 30 October 1991; *Chahal v. United Kingdom*, Application no. 22414/93, Judgment, 15 November 1996.

[374] For an overview of the procedural history, see *Katanga/Ngudjolo*, 9 June 2011.

[375] The Hague District Court, 28 December 2011.

[376] *Longa*, 9 October 2012.

The Hague District Court concerning Article 3 ECHR predates *Longa*, was not challenged by the Dutch authorities, and was not overturned by *Longa* (which concerned Article 5 ECHR specifically, not Article 3). This is the case that was described in Chapter 5 as the 'exception to the exception'.

At first glance it would seem illogical to argue that the Netherlands does have jurisdiction – for the purposes of Article 3 – over witnesses detained on ICC premises, but not over convicted persons detained on those same premises. But in fact the reasoning of The Hague District Court in the detained Congolese witnesses case cannot be wholesale applied to convicted persons. The case essentially rested on two considerations. The first was that to apply Dutch human rights and asylum law to the detained witnesses did not interfere with the functioning of the ICC; they had already given their testimony and their involvement with the Court was at an end.[377] This is not the case with convicted persons. To apply human rights law to them, and to potentially grant their application for protection, would interfere with the ICC's functioning because sentence enforcement is an important part of the criminal justice process. The convicted person is still very much involved with, and a concern of, the Court. The second consideration in the detained Congolese witnesses case was that the witnesses had nowhere else to turn.[378] The ICC, as it lacks territory, could not provide the necessary protection, and their home State was the one they were seeking protection from. By contrast, for convicted persons the ICC can provide protection. If necessary, a different enforcement State could be designated. If no suitable State is immediately available, the individual can remain at the ICC Detention Centre until one is found. Looking more closely at the reasoning of the District Court therefore, it is not a given that the outcome of the case would have been the same for a convicted person. Instead, if this factual pattern had come before a Dutch court, the author posits that the court would have extended the *Longa* decision and decided that no jurisdiction exists while the convicted person remains on ICC premises.

Finally there is the third scenario. As in the second scenario, this involves the ICC designating an enforcement State that the convicted person finds problematic for safety reasons. However, instead of submitting the asylum claim from the premises of the Court, the individual waits until they are being transported by the Dutch authorities to a point of departure for transfer to the enforcement State. Pursuant to the

---

[377] The Hague District Court, 28 December 2011, §9.
[378] The Hague District Court, 28 December 2011, §9.8.

Headquarters Agreement between the ICC and the Netherlands, the task of transporting convicted persons falls to the Netherlands.[379]

This scenario is distinguishable from the second for an important reason: the convicted person is not on ICC premises, but is under the authority of the Netherlands as they are transported to the point of departure.[380] This brings the individual within Dutch jurisdiction. Support for this can be found in a letter written by the Dutch Minister of Justice to the Dutch Parliament, in which it is stated that the Netherlands would be obliged to interrupt the transport if it appeared that to remove the person would violate human rights law.[381] In the case of an acquitted person requesting protection under essentially the same circumstances, the Netherlands did not contest the existence of jurisdiction (the *Ngudjolo* case is explored in detail in Section 6.3). Under these circumstances, there are no grounds for assuming that the situation of a convicted person would be treated differently from an acquitted person. In terms of outcome, even where protection is granted, it seems unlikely that the convicted person would remain in the Netherlands. Article 3 ECHR prohibits the removal of a person to a State where they would be at risk of inhuman treatment, but not to a safe third State. In all likelihood, in such a situation the ICC would designate a different, unproblematic enforcement State, and the convicted person could be transferred there.

6.2.3 Problems in Human Rights Protection

In the scenario where the Netherlands acts as the residual enforcer of sentences for the ICC (the first scenario in Section 6.2.2), the Netherlands is in the same position, and subject to the same obligations, as other States Parties who act as enforcement States. Just as there are no issues arising from the multi-actor nature of human rights protection in that situation, so too does the first scenario not raise any concerns. The second scenario need not be examined further, as it is concluded in Section 6.2.2 that the Netherlands has no jurisdiction under those circumstances, and given that the convicted person can simply wait for the third scenario to make their application for protection.

The third scenario would arise where the ICC designates a State of enforcement that the convicted individual considers problematic from

---

[379] Article 44 of the Headquarters Agreement.
[380] Section 85 ICC Implementation Act.
[381] Letter from Justice Minister to Parliament, 6.

a safety point of view. While this situation is highly unlikely given the obligations of the ICC in this regard, it is not inconceivable. In these circumstances, the Netherlands would take on a safety-net role thanks to its obligations beyond the Rome Statute protection framework under the ECHR. However, the implementation of these obligations is not without challenges.

The third scenario suffers from an implementation problem, but not the one often present in situations involving multiple actors, namely a lack of clarity as to which actor must act. It is clear enough that the ICC is the primary duty bearer: the task of designating the enforcement State is reserved to the ICC, and it is the ICC that issues the request to the Netherlands to carry out the transfer of a convicted person to that State. The Netherlands therefore takes on a secondary role, stepping in if and when the ICC designates an inappropriate enforcement State.

However, from the general attitude of the Netherlands towards such situations, gleamed from the different cases covered in this study, one can foresee a degree of reluctance on the part of the Netherlands to perform this safety-net role. Instead, the author considers it possible that the Dutch authorities will defer largely, if not entirely, to the ICC. The Netherlands may consider that since the ICC also has an obligation not to expose the individual to risk of harm, the Netherlands can rely on the ICC's determination of the convicted person's security situation. In a 2002 letter to the Dutch parliament discussing the possibility of convicted persons applying for asylum/protection during their transfer to the airport, the Minister of Justice indicated that deference to the ICC would be the government's approach. Even while acknowledging that during the transfer the Netherlands will have a non-refoulement obligation, the minister stated the following:

> It is ... inconceivable that such a risk of refoulement exists pending the proceedings before the ICC or after those proceedings ... the proceedings before the ICC provide all the guarantees required by the human rights conventions. In particular, the possibility that suspects will be subjected there to actions prohibited by Article 3 of the ECHR can be ruled out.[382]

While the Minister for Justice will in the great majority of instances be right, this clearly points to a reluctance on the part of the Netherlands to fully implement its own human rights obligations by conducting its own independent risk assessment. If a situation were to arise where intervention

---

[382] Letter from Justice Minister to Parliament, 6–7.

by the Netherlands was truly necessary, this outsourcing of the risk assessment to the ICC would be problematic.

A further problem is that the Netherlands may argue that even if the convicted person would be entitled to protection, the Netherlands' international obligations towards the ICC to conduct the transfer and to not interfere in ICC proceedings prevail over its obligations under human rights law. It is true that a human rights court such as the ECtHR would reject this notion wholeheartedly, but given the non-hierarchical nature of international law, there is indeed nothing that would compel a State to choose one set of obligations over the other. In either case it must violate an international obligation, and it falls to the State to determine which one.

6.2.4 Conclusion

Each of the scenarios explored in this section is fairly unlikely to arise in practice. The growing number of agreements between the ICC and States on the enforcement of sentences indicate that, despite the double consent system, the ICC is unlikely to face a situation where no State is willing to host a convicted person. The third scenario would only arise if the ICC failed to comply with its own obligation to refrain from removing a convicted person to a State where they would be at risk of harm, also (and hopefully) unlikely. However, if the ICC did designate an unsafe State as the enforcement State, it would fall to the Netherlands to prevent the transfer, pursuant to its obligations under the ECHR. Those obligations are engaged as soon as a convicted person leaves the ICC Detention Centre and enters a vehicle belonging to the Dutch authorities. These obligations though may not be readily implemented by the Netherlands. The attitude of the Dutch authorities in different situations, and in the statements described in this section, hint at the possibility of an implementation problem that would lead the Netherlands to neglect its safety-net role. This reluctance is particularly apparent in relation to acquittal and release, where the Netherlands' approach to the *Ngudjolo* case is highly relevant.

6.3 Acquittal and Release

6.3.1 Introduction

Following an acquittal, the former accused person is to be immediately released from custody; however, this may not be an entirely straightforward endeavour. In some instances, the acquitted individual may not be able to return to their State of nationality because to do so would put them at risk of harm. In this case the individual must find another State willing to accept them. As discussed in Chapter 3, while the ICC has an obligation not to arrange the transfer of an acquitted person to an unsafe State, States Parties have no obligation to accept at-risk acquitted persons who cannot return home. This creates a structural problem for the protection of the rights to life and to protection from inhuman treatment of acquitted persons. Given that acquitted persons find themselves on the territory of the ICC host State at the time that the acquittal is handed down, this section explores the obligations of the Netherlands to protect human rights in this situation.

6.3.2 Obligations of the Host State

The Netherlands could protect an acquitted person from removal to a situation of risk by permitting them to remain on Dutch territory. In its capacity as an ICC State Party, the Netherlands is in the same situation as any other State Party, and not subject to an obligation to host acquitted persons; the question addressed in this section is whether such an obligation exists for the Netherlands in its capacity as host State, whether this be under the Rome Statute protection framework or beyond it.

The Rome Statute protection framework does not contain a provision that directly deals with this issue, but it has been addressed in the legal frameworks of other international criminal tribunals. In the Headquarters Agreement between the Netherlands and the Special Tribunal for Lebanon (STL), it clearly states that acquitted persons cannot be released into the host State without the latter's consent.[383] In the Headquarters Agreement between Tanzania and the International Residual Mechanism for Criminal Tribunals (IRMCT), it is stated that a person released after an acquittal cannot remain permanently on Tanzanian territory without the latter's consent.[384] The fact that these agreements do deal with the issue directly, and the ICC Headquarters Agreement does not, could be seen in two ways. On the one hand, it could indicate that the situation at the ICC was intended to be different from

---

[383] Article 43(3) of the Agreement between the Kingdom of the Netherlands and the United Nations concerning the Headquarters of the Special Tribunal for Lebanon 2007.

[384] Article 39 of the Agreement between the United Nations and the United Republic of Tanzania concerning the Headquarters of the International Residual Mechanism for Criminal Tribunals 2013.

these other tribunals; on the other hand, it could indicate that the other agreements reflect the general state of affairs, and in the ICC agreement it was not deemed necessary to be explicit.

An argument has been made in favour of the former conclusion, based on an analogy with Article 103(4) of the Rome Statute. This article requires that the ICC host State enforce a sentence of imprisonment on its territory in situations where the Court is unable to find an enforcement State. The argument by analogy suggests that the host State has a similar residual role of hosting an acquitted person when no other safe State is found (albeit at liberty in this instance). Sluiter provides some arguments in favour of this position, citing the ECtHR case of *Waite and Kennedy* as authority for the proposition that the host States of international organisations have a residual responsibility for human rights violations committed by international organisations on their territory.[385] In other words, if a person's protection from removal to a place of risk is jeopardised because they have nowhere safe to reside, the Netherlands has a responsibility to act. Sluiter suggests that this is simply the price that the Netherlands must pay for being the legal capital of the world.[386]

The author disagrees with this argument in the context of the Rome Statute protection framework. It is not appropriate to create obligations for the Netherlands to which it did not consent based on an analogy of this kind. This is particularly so given the debates that took place when the Rome Statute and the Headquarters Agreement were being incorporated into Dutch domestic law. In these debates, concern was expressed by a number of Dutch political parties over the implications of Article 103(4).[387] If the provision was already controversial, extending it by analogy to create broad new obligations for the Netherlands is especially inappropriate. In contrast with the analogy argument, the author proposes that the headquarters agreements for the STL and RMCT be seen as reflecting the law as it stands. The only obligation of the Netherlands stemming from the Rome Statute protection framework is to permit acquitted individuals to remain on Dutch territory as long as their

---

[385] *Case of Waite & Kennedy* v. *Germany*, Application no. 26083/94, Judgment, 18 February 1999 (*Waite and Kennedy*, 18 February 1999).

[386] Göran Sluiter, 'Shared Responsibility in International Criminal Justice: The ICC and Asylum' (2012) 10 *Journal of International Criminal Justice*, 661, 665.

[387] Han Bevers, Niels M. Blokker, and Jaap Roording, 'The Netherlands and the International Criminal Court: On Statute Obligations and Hospitality' (2003) 16 *Leiden Journal of International Law*, 135, 152.

presence at the seat of the Court is necessary, as per Article 29 of the Headquarters Agreement. As to obligations beyond the Rome Statute protection framework, that is another matter. The idea that the Netherlands has an obligation to protect individuals present on its territory should be considered in that context.

In the event that the ICC is unable to find a State to host them on their release, acquitted persons face an uncertain situation. In response, they could seek to rely on the Netherlands' human rights obligations as a way to permit them to remain in the Netherlands upon release. Such obligations stem from Articles 2 and 3 of the ECHR, which include a prohibition on the removal of an individual to a situation where they would be at risk of death or serious harm. As with persons who have been convicted, an application for protection from removal from the host State can be made at two points in time: first, when the acquitted person is waiting to be released from ICC custody; and second, when the acquitted person is outside the ICC Detention Centre and/or is in transit to the point of departure from the Netherlands.

A few days can pass, while arrangements are made, between when the accused person is acquitted and when they are actually released. During that time, the individual might make an application for protection to the Dutch authorities. In Section 6.2.2, it was argued that the decision of the Dutch District Court to allow an application for protection to be made by witnesses detained on the ICC premises did not apply to convicted persons. For acquitted persons, the author argues the opposite: that the reasoning of the District Court applies in the same way for detained witnesses as it does for acquitted persons. The two situations are alike, as in neither case would considering the application for protection interfere with the functioning of the ICC, and in neither case do the individuals have anywhere else to turn because of the structural protection problems arising at this stage in proceedings (discussed in Chapter 3).

The other point in time when an acquitted person can make an application for protection is once they have been released from ICC custody. The obligations of the Netherlands are the same here as they are when a convicted person applies for protection while being transported to the point of departure from the Netherlands. The *Ngudjolo* case shows these obligations in practice. Mathieu Ngudjolo Chui was charged by the ICC with several counts of war crimes and crimes against humanity, alleged to have taken place in the course of an attack on the village of Bogoro in the Eastern DRC on 24 February 2003. His co-defendant, Germain Katanga, was found guilty and sentenced to twelve years' imprisonment, but

Ngudjolo was acquitted of all charges on 18 December 2012. He was released from ICC custody a few days later.

During his trial, Ngudjolo acted as a witness in his own defence. He gave evidence that implicated the DRC government and President Kabila in the planning of the attack on Bogoro. As a result of having provided this evidence, which in particular took the form of a highly incriminating letter, Ngudjolo contended that he would be seen as hostile to the DRC government and would suffer human rights abuses if returned to the DRC.[388] Ngudjolo requested protection within the ICC witness protection programme, but his request for relocation was eventually denied.[389] Following his acquittal, Ngudjolo was released from ICC detention and handed over to the Dutch police, who subsequently transported him to the airport and sought to repatriate him to the DRC. As far as the Dutch authorities were concerned, Ngudjolo had no legal basis for residing on the territory of the Netherlands; as soon as he was released from ICC custody he became an illegal alien.[390] Ngudjolo, who disagreed with the ICC's assessment of his safety situation and not wishing to return to the DRC, applied for protection in the Netherlands once he was in the hands of the Dutch police.[391]

Ngudjolo based his application for protection on both human rights law and refugee law. Both grounds were rejected by the Council of State on 15 October 2014.[392] The rejection was based on two elements. First, the Council held that the Secretary of State was correct to exclude Ngudjolo from refugee protection on the basis Article 1F of the Refugee Convention.[393] This provision allows for the exclusion of an individual from refugee protection on a number of grounds, including that there are serious reasons for considering that they have committed 'a

---

[388] *Ngudjolo*, 21 December 2012, §§27–9.
[389] A certain amount of speculation is necessary to reach this conclusion. Information concerning Ngudjolo's status as an ICC protected witness is ambiguous and hard to come by. Support for this conclusion is found in a note verbale transmitted by the ICC Registry to the Dutch authorities, stating that there was no obstacle to his return to the DRC – ECLI:NL:RVS:2014:3833, Council of State, 15 October 2014 (Council of State, 15 October 2014), §5.2.
[390] *The Prosecutor v. Mathieu Ngudjolo Chui*, ICC-01/04-02/12-22-tENG, Second Addendum to 'Defence Request That the Appeals Chamber Order the Victims and Witnesses Unit to Execute and the Host State to Comply with the Acquittal Judgment of 18 December 2012 Issued by Trial Chamber II of the International Criminal Court', 8 February 2013 (Appeals Chamber) (*Ngudjolo*, 8 February 2013) §§23–4.
[391] *Ngudjolo*, 8 February 2013, §§4–6.
[392] Council of State, 15 October 2014.
[393] Council of State, 15 October 2014, §2.5.

crime against peace, a war crime, or a crime against humanity'. The standard of proof for exclusion under Article 1F is much lower than the criminal standard of proof, and so this exclusion can apply even in case of acquittal. In Ngudjolo's case, the Secretary of State decided that while he may have been acquitted for the attack on Bogoro, there were a number of other instances in which Ngudjolo was implicated in war crimes and crimes against humanity. Second, the Council of State agreed with the Secretary of State's assessment that Ngudjolo would not be at risk of an Article 3 ECHR violation if returned to the DRC,[394] noting that the Registry of the ICC concurred on this point, having communicated this opinion in a note verbale.[395] Despite this negative decision, Ngudjolo did ultimately remain on Dutch territory pending his appeal.[396] Arrangements were made for him to reside in an apartment in The Hague at the expense of the ICC (as such, the hotel situation referred to in Chapter 3 was avoided). When Ngudjolo's acquittal was confirmed on appeal in February 2015, his renewed application for protection from return to the DRC was refused by the District Court of The Hague, and on 11 May 2015 Ngudjolo was returned to the DRC.[397]

Despite the ultimate rejection of Ngudjolo's application, the case shows the Netherlands' ECHR obligations in practice. The Netherlands did not challenge the admissibility of Ngudjolo's application for protection from removal, nor did it challenge the fact that Ngudjolo was subject to Dutch jurisdiction. Instead, the rejection of the claim was based on its merits. As such, it opens the door for acquitted persons in future to apply for protection in the Netherlands, if they face an uncertain future following their acquittal.

6.3.3 Problems in Human Rights Protection

Given that structural problems can make it hard to protect acquitted persons through relocating them to a safe State Party, the role of the Netherlands in the acquittal and release situation is important. States Parties are under no obligation to assist the ICC by hosting an acquitted person, but may become

---

[394] Council of State, 15 October 2014, §4.4.
[395] Council of State, 15 October 2014, §5.2.
[396] *The Prosecutor v. Mathieu Ngudjolo Chui*, ICC-01/04-02/12-69-Red, Registry's Update on the Situation in Relation to Mathieu Ngudjolo Chui, 3 June 2013 (Appeals Chamber), §3.
[397] 'First ICC Acquitted Defendant Returned to DR Congo: Netherlands Rejected Asylum Claim Over Safety Fears', Human Rights Watch, 11 May 2015.

involved by volunteering to do so. The Netherlands *is* obliged to assist the ICC, but only in practical matters such as transporting acquitted individuals to the point of departure from the country. However, through this act of transportation, and potentially merely by the fact that acquitted individuals find themselves on Dutch territory, obligations of the Netherlands under human rights law (and refugee law) may be engaged. As a result, the Netherlands can act as a safety net in cases where structural problems leave gaps in the human rights protection of acquitted persons.

However, relying on the Netherlands to act as a safety net is not a complete solution. In Section 6.2.2 it was noted that if a convicted person's application for protection from removal from the Netherlands was successful, the most likely outcome would be that the ICC would move to designate a different enforcement State, and the convicted person would be transferred there instead. With respect to acquitted persons, the situation may well be different because the individual is likely to remain in the Netherlands. Indeed, if there were a safe State to which the acquitted person could be released, an application for protection to the Netherlands is unlikely to have been made in the first place. The prospect of hosting the acquitted person long term makes the situation very unattractive to the Dutch authorities, which gives rise to its own implementation problem: namely, that the Netherlands is reluctant to allow claims for protection to be made at all. When Ngudjolo was acquitted on appeal, the Dutch authorities sought to remove him with great speed, and it was only quick action by his legal representatives that prevented his removal before a further claim could be made. Indeed, his plane made it to the tarmac at Schiphol Airport before being recalled. A cynical interpretation of the Netherlands' haste is that the authorities were attempting to prevent further claims for protection.

6.3.4 Conclusion

Acquitted persons who cannot return to their home State face an uncertain future. In situations where no State offers to host them, they may turn to the Netherlands for protection upon their release (or even prior to). By invoking the Netherlands' obligations under human rights law, they can seek to prevent their removal to a country where they would face a risk of death or serious harm. However, while they would fall under the Netherlands' jurisdiction, and so be entitled to make such an application, they may encounter implementation problems when doing so. The consequences of a successful application, namely leave to remain in the

Netherlands, make the Dutch authorities reluctant to allow opportunity for such applications to be made.

6.4 Conclusion

The situations addressed in this chapter are already multi-actor in nature, as they each by their nature involve both the ICC and States Parties. The discussions in this chapter demonstrate how a further layer of complexity can be added to these situations when the ICC host State becomes involved. Any situation where accused and witnesses find themselves on the territory of the Netherlands gives rise to the potential for the latter to become involved in their protection. In the case of interim release, it has been argued in Section 6.1 that the role of the Netherlands would be very narrow, coming into play only when an individual has already been released on an interim basis to another State and must return to the Netherlands for the trial proceedings. In the situations of removal to the enforcement State and acquittal and release, the potential role of the Netherlands is broader. If a convicted or acquitted person submits an application for protection to the Dutch authorities at the right moment, the authorities are not free to ignore this.

It was not unforeseen or unintended that the Netherlands would play some role in the protection of individuals appearing before the ICC. We can return here to the example of the Netherlands having an obligation to assist the ICC by transporting individuals to the airport – this can be seen as one link in a chain of actions that leads to their transfer to safety, and by extension to the protection of their rights. However, the situations addressed in this chapter were not necessarily envisaged at the time the Rome Statute and Headquarters Agreement were drafted, or if they were, no provision was made to address them. They involve ascribing to the Netherlands a safety-net role, available in the (admittedly unlikely) event that the ICC fails in its obligation to afford the necessary protection, or where structural gaps in protection leave individuals at risk. In these situations the Netherlands becomes involved because it is obliged to under its human rights law obligations (in particular, those arising beyond the Rome Statute protection framework), and not necessarily because it chooses to. This reluctance to become involved is evident in the way that the Netherlands has responded to claims for protection from ICC acquitted (and, as the next chapter will show, ICC witnesses). It is from this that potential implementation problems arise, with the Netherlands seemingly keen to avoid applications for protection being made, and if they are made, keen to defer to the ICC's assessment of the situation.

The result of host State involvement in situations that are already multi-actor in nature is an elaborate layering of different obligations; while the obligations of the Netherlands and of States Parties have been addressed in separate sections of this book, in reality they will often be in play simultaneously. That being said, host State involvement can provide a degree of protection from the problems that multi-actor protection human rights protection creates, particularly problems connected to structural gaps in protection. Where States Parties fail to volunteer, the host State might be required to step in.

As we turn to discuss host State involvement in the protection of witnesses at the seat of the Court, this picture is complicated further. The role of the Netherlands in this respect will depend on the type of witness in need of protection, and on the particular right at stake.

7

Detained and Non-Detained Witnesses

In the majority of cases, questions concerning the multi-actor protection of the human rights of witnesses fall into the discussion covered in Chapter 4. Arrangements for their protection will be made before a witness travels to the seat of the Court, and will concern either protection within their home State or relocation to a third State. The involvement of the host State is limited to arranging the transport of witnesses within the Netherlands and assisting the Court in accommodating witnesses during their stay.

However, there have been incidents that have rendered the situation more complex by involving the Netherlands substantively in the protection of witnesses. Situations have occurred whereby, once witnesses arrived at the seat of the Court in the Netherlands, they turned away from ICC protection and claimed protection from the Netherlands instead. In light of such developments, this chapter will address the situations in which protecting a witness at the seat of the ICC becomes a complicated multi-actor affair.

There are many reasons why a witness might turn to the ICC host State for protection. It is possible that they no longer trust the ICC to protect them. This distrust might arise if, for example, the ICC is having trouble finding a relocation State. As explored previously, this is a real possibility. Perhaps witnesses are attracted to the higher standard of living in the Netherlands, and see a protection claim while at the ICC as a shortcut to a European residence permit.[398] Or it may be that the terms of the relocation within the ICCPP are not as attractive as protection within the Netherlands, as they would have fewer rights and benefits than with a different protected status.[399]

---

[398] Joris van Wijk, 'When International Criminal Justice Collides with Principles of International Protection: Assessing the Consequences of ICC Witnesses Seeking Asylum, Defendants Being Acquitted, and Convicted Being Released' (2013) 26 *Leiden Journal of International Law*, 173, 184.

[399] The difference in procedural and substantive rights under the ICCPP relocation scheme and under refugee law is explored in Irving, 'Protecting Witnesses at the ICC from Refoulement', 1141, 1147.

Any of these explanations, or a combination, could lead a witness to apply for protection in the Netherlands rather than rely on the ICC protection system.

The sections in this chapter draw a distinction between witnesses that are detained at the seat of the Court and witnesses that are not detained. If a witness is detained in their home State – for example, because they have been convicted of a crime by a domestic court and are serving a custodial sentence – then they travel to the ICC to give evidence subject to special arrangements. One of these arrangements is that they must remain detained while they are at the seat of the Court. Detained witnesses are a relatively small group, but important enough to merit separate consideration in the Rome Statute protection framework. As the issues raised by detained witnesses at the seat of the ICC are especially complex – one commentator has gone so far as to refer to them as forming a legal Gordian knot[400] – two sections of this chapter are dedicated to them. The last section deals with non-detained witnesses.

As in the previous chapters, not all human rights concerns of witnesses can be addressed. Instead, the discussion will focus on a selection of rights. Unlike the other chapters in this study, for the protection of witnesses at the seat of the Court there is a relatively large number of judicial decisions. The rights at the centre of those decisions have guided the selection of rights for consideration in this chapter. To examine the range of issues, this chapter is divided into three sections. The first two sections concern detained witnesses, and consider the same individuals from the perspective of different rights: life, protection from inhuman treatment, and fair trial in Section 7.1, and the right to liberty in Section 7.2. The last section of the chapter (Section 7.3) concerns non-detained witnesses, and deals only with the right to life and protection from inhuman treatment. For each section, after the obligations to protect the rights have been discussed, the analysis turns to the problems in human rights protection that arise from the multi-actor nature of the situation. In contrast to Chapter 6, it is important to explore the obligations of the ICC in detail, as these differ from obligations discussed in earlier chapters.

---

[400] van Wijk, 'When International Criminal Justice Collides with Principles of International Protection', 176.

7.1 Detained Witnesses: Right to Life, Protection from Inhuman Treatment, and Fair Trial

7.1.1 Introduction

Detained witnesses may be a small group, but they are potentially very significant for criminal trials. The very reason for their detention could be that they were in some way involved in the same crimes for which the ICC accused is being tried. This makes them insider witnesses with crucial information. Because of this, they are a significant enough group that special arrangements are made for their appearance in court in the frameworks of various international criminal tribunals.[401] What the respective provisions in these frameworks have in common is that when a detained witness is transferred from a domestic prison facility to the Court or Tribunal, they must remain detained whilst there, and must be returned to the sending State once their presence at the Court is no longer required. The State in which the witness is detained, and which sends the witness to the ICC, will be termed the 'sending State'.

The three rights at the centre of this section are the rights to life, protection from inhuman treatment, and fair trial, as these were the rights at stake in the detained Congolese witnesses case. Given the range of issues that the detained Congolese witnesses case brought to the fore, the analysis and discussion in this section centres around this case, drawing on the judicial decisions that it gave rise to. The facts of that case have been discussed in previous chapters where relevant, but will be set out in full over the course of the following two sections. In 2011, the ICC requested and was granted the transfer to the Court of four witnesses who were in detention in the DRC. These witnesses, three attached to the Katanga case,[402] and one to the Lubanga case,[403] had been arrested by DRC authorities some years earlier on suspicion of involvement in the death of UN peacekeepers and high treason, but had not been formally charged.[404] In May 2011, once the witnesses had finished giving testimony and were set to be transferred back, they

---

[401] Article 93(7) of the Rome Statute; Rule 90bis ICTR RPE; Rule 90bis ICTY RPE; Rule 151 STL RPE.
[402] Floribert Ndjabu Ngabu, Sharif Manda Ndadza Dz'Na, and Pierre-Célestin Mbodina Iribi.
[403] Bède Djokaba Lambi Longa.
[404] Tom de Boer and Marjoleine Zieck, 'ICC Witnesses and Acquitted Suspects Seeking Asylum in the Netherlands: An Overview of the Jurisdictional Battles between the ICC and Its Host State' (2015) 27 *International Journal of Refugee Law*, 573, 575–6.

submitted an application for protection to the Dutch authorities to prevent their return to the DRC.

The witnesses' application was based on the fear that they would be targeted on their return by members of the pro-government militias, that they would be subject to summary execution or disappearance, or that their domestic trial would be nothing but a show trial followed by execution.[405] These risks correspond to the three rights addressed in this section. Counsel for the witnesses argued that the ICC and the Netherlands were obliged to protect these rights by ensuring that the witnesses were not returned to the DRC. The argument was therefore one based on the prohibition on removal aspect of these rights.

If the detained Congolese witnesses had not chosen to involve the Netherlands in the way they did, their case would have remained between the ICC and the sending State (or other State Parties), and so fallen entirely within the realm of Chapter 4. It is the Netherlands' involvement which sets the situation apart. The Dutch courts determined that, as the witnesses were on the territory of the Netherlands, they fell within Dutch jurisdiction, and could therefore ask for protection from removal based on the Netherlands' human rights law obligations.

To establish how the right to life, protection from inhuman treatment, and fair trial are protected in this multi-actor situation, the subsequent section will discuss the obligations of the ICC and the host State in turn. This is followed by the identification of human rights problems that this situation gives rise to. For the period of time in which the detained witness is at the seat of the Court, the sending State does not have any obligations with respect to these rights, as the witness is not on its territory. As such, the sending State is not included in the analysis.

7.1.2 Obligations of the ICC

The starting point for discussing the obligations of the ICC, as with all witnesses, is the overarching protection obligation in Article 68(1). There are two issues at the heart of this discussion. First, if detained witnesses would be at risk of human rights violations in the sending State, is the ICC obliged to refrain from returning them there? And second, if the ICC does have such an obligation, how does this interact with the obligation that the ICC owes to the sending State to return detained witnesses?

---

[405] *Katanga/Ngudjolo*, 22 June 2011, §38.

7.1.2.1 Article 68(1)

If there is an obligation on the ICC to protect detained witnesses by not returning them to the sending State, this must be based on Article 68(1) of the Rome Statute. This provision obliges the ICC to take 'appropriate measures' to protect witnesses. There is nothing in the provision itself that sets limits on what is deemed an appropriate measure. Commenting on the wording of the provision, one academic noted that the broad formulation of the article leaves judges free to propose measures of protection that are not specifically authorised.[406] If returning the witnesses to the sending State would endanger their right to life, to protection from inhuman treatment, and/or to fair trial, to refrain from sending them to that State seems to qualify as an 'appropriate measure' for their protection. There is further support for this interpretation in a decision of Trial Chamber II, in which the judges held that 'as an international organisation with a legal personality, the Court cannot disregard the customary rule of non-refoulement'.[407] Where multiple interpretations of a provision are possible and a choice between them must be made, Article 21(3) requires that preference be given to the interpretation that best protects human rights. In this case, that means interpreting Article 68(1) as requiring the ICC to not return detained witnesses to a situation of risk.

The ICC has an obligation not to return at-risk witnesses, but according to Trial Chamber II in the detained Congolese witnesses case, not all types of risk will engage the protection obligations of the ICC. This pertains to Article 68(1)'s scope, and the question is this: is the ICC obliged to protect witnesses against all types of risk, or only those that are associated with their involvement with the Court? This has been examined already in Chapter 4; however, the situation of witnesses at the seat of the Court is different, and so the question must be considered again. In Chapter 4, when giving an overview of the ICC's general witness protection obligations, the author proposed that the ICC's obligation to protect witnesses applied to all forms of risk that the witness might face, as long as it was not *patently* unconnected to their involvement with the Court. The threshold for such a finding should be high, in effect creating a presumption in favour of protection.

---

[406] Schabas, A Commentary on the Rome Statute, 824.
[407] This should be read as referring to both the refugee law concept of non-refoulement, and the human rights law concept of prohibition on removal, as both are often referred to together under the same term; *Katanga/Ngudjolo*, 9 June 2011, §64.

When witnesses are located at the seat of the Court, the author argues that the scope of Article 68(1) is broader still. It is proposed that a witness cannot be transferred to a State where they would be at risk, even if the risk is patently unconnected with their involvement with the ICC. This is due to the fact that there is an important difference between witnesses located in a State and witnesses located at the seat of the Court. When a witness is in a situation State and is facing a risk of human rights violations, the question is whether or not the ICC is obliged to step in and provide protection. When a witness is at the seat of the ICC, the question is whether or not the Court, through its own actions, is going to expose the individual to a risk of human rights violations by removing them to a certain State.

As discussed in Chapter 4, Trial Chamber II's approach to this question was much more restrictive. It explicitly rejected the broad formulation that the author proposes on the basis that the Rome Statute 'does not place an obligation on the Court to ensure that States parties properly apply internationally recognised human rights in their domestic proceedings'.[408] The author agrees with Sluiter when he argues that Trial Chamber II misidentified the relevant obligation. It is not that the ICC is obliged to ensure that States respect human rights law domestically, but rather that the Court is obliged to not expose an individual to a risk of human rights violations.[409] In the State–State context, any time that a State makes a determination as to whether it can remove an individual on its territory to another State, it must assess the risk to which this could expose the individual. And yet, as the ECtHR held in *Soering*, in so doing 'there is no question of adjudicating on or establishing the responsibility of the receiving country, whether under general international law, under the Convention or otherwise'.[410] The same applies to the ICC–State context: assessing the risk facing a witness does not per se amount to establishing the responsibility of the sending State under international human rights law.

Witnesses at the seat of the ICC, especially detained witnesses, are within the Court's control.[411] There is therefore a direct link between the

---

[408] *Katanga/Ngudjolo*, 9 June 2011, §62.
[409] Sluiter, 'Shared Responsibility in International Criminal Justice', 670. Sluiter is not the only academic commentator to disagree with the Trial Chamber's position – De Boer and Zieck also argue that the ICC's obligation not to expose individuals to risk in another State is not limited to risks incurred through cooperation with the Court (de Boer and Zieck, 'ICC Witnesses and Acquitted Suspects Seeking Asylum in the Netherlands', 578).
[410] *Soering v. United Kingdom*, §90.
[411] Sluiter, 'Shared Responsibility in International Criminal Justice', 670.

ICC's decision to transfer them to a given State and the risk to which that transfer will expose the witnesses. For this reason, Trial Chamber II's approach does not, in the author's opinion, satisfy the Article 21(3) test. In the context of witnesses at the seat of the Court, narrowing the scope of risk to those associated with involvement with the Court allows an individual to be exposed to human rights violations in another State. Such an interpretation and application of the law does not comply with internationally recognised human rights.

7.1.2.2 The Relationship between Articles 68(1) and 93(7)

Article 68(1) is not the only provision governing detained witnesses at the seat of the ICC. Contrary to witnesses at liberty, detained witnesses are subjects of domestic criminal justice, and so the sending State has a strong interest in them being returned. This interest is represented in the Rome Statute in Article 93(7), which sets out the following obligations for the ICC with respect to detained witnesses:

(a) The Court may request the temporary transfer of a person in custody for purposes of identification or for obtaining testimony or other assistance. The person may be transferred if the following conditions are fulfilled:
 (i) The person freely gives his or her informed consent to the transfer; and
 (ii) The requested State agrees to the transfer, subject to such conditions as that State and the Court may agree.
(b) The person being transferred shall remain in custody. When the purposes of the transfer have been fulfilled, *the Court shall return the person without delay to the requested State.* (emphasis added)

This obligation to return detained witnesses can conflict with the obligation in Article 68(1) to not return witnesses to a situation of risk. Discussion must therefore turn to the relationship between these two articles, and in particular, which provision will prevail in case of conflict.

Before discussing this conflict, it is worth exploring how it might be avoided in the first place. If the risk to the detained witnesses in the sending State can be reduced, such that they would be able to return there safely, then the ICC would not need to choose between different obligations. This could be achieved using assurances. Assurances are used often in the extradition context, when the extradition from State A to State B would otherwise be blocked due to concerns about human rights protection in State B. To allay concerns, State B would provide State A with certain assurances, for example, that the individual to be extradited will not be subject to torture or the death penalty.

Assurances were used to this effect in the detained Congolese witnesses case. The ICC went about fulfilling its obligation under Article 68(1) by securing protective measures for the detained witnesses in order that they could return to the DRC safely. For the period between their return from the ICC and the conclusion of their domestic criminal trials, the following assurances were provided by the DRC:

(a) that the witnesses would be detained in a secure prison facility and aprotected from the aggression of other inmates,
(b) that the guards who would be guarding the witnesses were trained according to international standards and selected in consultation between the VWU and the DRC authorities,
(c) that the VWU would maintain regular and direct contact with the guards in order to anticipate any change in the security situation of the witnesses,
(d) that the VWU would regularly visit the detained witnesses to assess their security situation,
(e) that the VWU would monitor any legal proceedings against the detained witnesses.[412]

The measures were designed to be revisited once the trials of the detained witnesses concluded.[413] Trial Chamber II stipulated that assurances of this type are not a substitute for the independent risk analysis that must be conducted by the ICC in order to comply with Article 68(1). However, the Chamber considered that the DRC's assurances should be treated with the greatest respect, be presumed to be in good faith, and be accorded great weight, as they committed the State to both the ICC and the ASP.[414] It was important that the assurances had been given under Part 9 of the Rome Statute, which the Chamber said was based on the principle of mutual trust. In light of this, the Chamber held that the assurances were sufficient to allow the detained witnesses to be returned to the DRC without the Court violating its obligation under Article 68(1).

Diplomatic assurances can be a controversial way of complying with human rights obligations. This is evidenced by the fact that the ECtHR

---

[412] *Katanga/Ngudjolo*, 24 August 2011, §13.
[413] *Katanga/Ngudjolo*, 22 June 2011, §41.
[414] *Katanga/Ngudjolo*, 22 June 2011, §40.

has developed in its case law a set of criteria to determine when they might be relied on and when not. The most recent ECtHR case to discuss the criteria for assurances was *Othman*.[415] For the most part, the assurances provided by the DRC in the detained Congolese witnesses case satisfy these criteria. For instance, the assurances are concrete rather than vague,[416] and compliance can be verified through reliable independent channels, namely the VWU.[417] One criterion which does not appear satisfied is the requirement that the individual had not been ill-treated in the State prior to the assurances being given.[418] The fact that the detained Congolese witnesses had been kept in detention without charge for a number of years certainly points to the existence of previous human rights violations. The ICC is not bound by the ECtHR's rulings, but considering that the Rome Statute protection framework does not mention assurances, and provides no direction for their use, the author suggests that the ECtHR's decisions should guide the practice of the Court and inform the interpretation of Article 68(1).

What happens if the assurances offered by the sending State are not sufficient to discharge the ICC's obligations under Article 68(1)? This possibility is not so far-fetched. If the detained Congolese witnesses situation arose again in the future, the ICC might not be as willing to rely on the sending State's assurances, given that a year and a half after their return to the DRC, three of the Congolese detained witnesses had still not been tried.[419] It is at this point that a conflict will arise between the ICC's obligations under Articles 68(1) and 93(7). The phrasing of both articles is compulsory, so a textual reading alone does not indicate whether the obligation in one is subjugated to the obligation in the other.

If to return a detained witness would violate Article 68(1), this gives rise to two questions. First, does the ICC's obligation to protect a detained witness prevail over its obligation to return that witness to the sending state pursuant to Article 93(7); and second, if so, what type of protective measures is the ICC then obliged to provide for the witness?

The first question can be answered by referring to a decision of Trial Chamber II from 9 June 2011. The detained Congolese witnesses

---

[415] *Case of Othman (Abu Qatada) v. the United Kingdom*, Application no. 8139/09, Judgment, 17 January 2012 (*Othman*, 17 January 2012), §189.
[416] *Othman*, 17 January 2012, §189, subpara (ii).
[417] *Othman*, 17 January 2012, §189, subpara (viii).
[418] *Othman*, 17 January 2012, §189, subpara (x).
[419] 'DR Congo: ICC Convict Faces Domestic Charges', Human Rights Watch, 23 December 2015.

submitted their applications for protection in the Netherlands once they had finished giving their testimony in the *Katanga* and *Lubanga* trials; that was the point at which they would otherwise have been returned to the DRC. In rendering its decision on 9 June 2011, Trial Chamber II therefore faced precisely the situation of deciding whether to go ahead with its return obligation under Article 93(7)(b) or not.

The judges suspended the ICC's obligation to return the detained witnesses to the DRC under Article 93(7)(b), on the basis that to return them would violate the witnesses' human rights. At the time of the decision, the witnesses' applications for protection in the Netherlands were still pending, and it was found that to return them to the DRC before those claims were decided upon would violate the witnesses' right to seek asylum.[420] In this context, the right to seek asylum should be understood as the right to access a mechanism in which the merits of an application for protection, both under human rights law and under refugee law, can be heard (given that the detained Congolese witnesses' applications for protection were made under both of these bodies of law, the Trial Chamber sought to protect access to both). Interpreting Article 93(7) in light of Article 21(3), the Chamber determined that suspension of the witnesses' return was the only approach that conformed to human rights law.[421] Further support for this interpretation can be found in another decision of Trial Chamber II in the same case, in which it held that if the Netherlands granted the detained witnesses' application for protection, the ICC would be unable to return them to the DRC. Instead, Article 21(3) required that the witnesses be handed over to the Netherlands.[422]

These two decisions of Trial Chamber II in the detained Congolese witnesses case demonstrate that, in the ICC's understanding, the rights of a witness prevail over the obligation of immediate return. Suspension of return was ordered so as to not interfere with the ability of the Netherlands to perform its own human rights law obligation of hearing the witnesses' application for protection. This interpretation has been met with academic approval.[423]

---

[420] *Katanga/Ngudjolo*, 9 June 2011, §73.
[421] *Katanga/Ngudjolo*, 9 June 2011, §73.
[422] *Katanga*, 1 October 2013, §21.
[423] It has been called 'an elegant way to permit the witnesses to apply for asylum in the Netherlands' – Dersim Yabasun and Mathias Holvoet, 'Seeking Asylum before the International Criminal Court. Another Challenge for a Court in Need of Credibility' (2013) 13 *International Criminal Law Review*, 725, 727; Sluiter, 'Shared Responsibility in

Towards the end of the 9 June 2011 decision, the Trial Chamber pronounced directly on the relationship between Articles 68(1) and 93(7). The judges held that another reason for the suspension of return was to allow the ICC time to decide whether 'the obligation under Article 93(7) to return the witnesses can be implemented without contravening the Court's other obligations under Article 68'.[424] This clearly subjugates Article 93(7) to 68(1) in case of conflict. The author further agrees with the Chamber that this is the only interpretation of those provisions that conforms to human rights law, and as such the only interpretation that would satisfy the Article 21(3) test.

Complying with Article 68(1) by refraining from returning detained witnesses to the sending State is only the first protective step. As with any other witness in need of protection outside of their own State, another place must be found for them to reside. In other words, they must be relocated.

Some commentators have argued against international relocation as an option for detained witnesses,[425] and others have argued in favour.[426] The legal framework under which relocation would be done has been covered in Chapter 4. The author agrees that relocation abroad is available for detained witnesses, as nothing in the Rome Statute protection framework precludes this. However, it does present a number of difficulties. Given that the potential relocation State did not prosecute and convict the witness itself, and given that it has no agreement with the sending State, there would be no legal basis on which the relocation State could continue to detain the witness. As such, if a witness were relocated to a third State, it would be necessary to release them from detention. And yet, if a witness has been properly tried and convicted on a criminal charge in the sending State, it seems counter-intuitive to simply release them, if indeed any State could be found that would accept a witness under these circumstances. This course of action may be appropriate if the witness's detention at the domestic level was itself a violation of human rights, but making this determination would require the ICC to look in detail at the witness's domestic trial. The ICC has been clear that it is not its role to do this,[427]

International Criminal Justice', 669; Irving, 'Protecting Witnesses at the ICC from Refoulement', 1147.

[424] *Katanga/Ngudjolo*, 9 June 2011, §81.
[425] Yabasun and Holvoet, 'Seeking Asylum before the ICC', 729.
[426] Sluiter, 'Shared Responsibility in International Criminal Justice', 670.
[427] *Katanga*, 1 October 2013, §27.

and one can appreciate the numerous difficulties this would entail. On a practical level, it would require the domestic authorities to turn over the documentation of the trial, which they will most likely be unwilling to do. On a principled level, it would constitute an undue interference by the ICC into the domestic sphere of the State, as it would entail the ICC passing judgment on the quality of domestic proceedings. The legal framework offers no indication as to how to deal with this problem.

Other than internationally relocating detained witnesses using the ICCPP, another way for the ICC to comply with its obligations under Article 68(1) is to present the witnesses to the Dutch authorities in order for them to make an application for protection in the Netherlands. In the detained Congolese witnesses case, this was the protective measure that the witnesses originally requested from the Court.[428] Naturally, this requires that the witnesses make an application to the Netherlands for protection, a course of action which engages the obligations of the Netherlands, to which we now turn.

7.1.3 Obligations of the Host State

7.1.3.1 Obligations within the ICC Protection Framework

The Rome Statute and other ICC documents are silent on the issue of host State involvement in the protection of detained witnesses. Nor is there any relevant provision in the Headquarters Agreement between the ICC and the Netherlands. Given the lack of a public record of the negotiations of the Headquarters Agreement, one can only guess at whether it was considered at all.[429]

Sluiter is one commentator who argues that the Netherlands may have obligations based on the Rome Statute protection framework that stem from its host State relationship with the ICC. As was discussed in previous chapters in other contexts, Sluiter analogises from Article 103(4) of the Rome Statute, which stipulates that the Netherlands must enforce the sentence of a person convicted by the ICC where no enforcement State is found, suggesting that the same approach could be taken in other instances where the ICC needs a territory and the law offers no solution.

---

[428] *Katanga/Ngudjolo*, 9 June 2011, §27. Interestingly when the counsel for the witnesses before the ICC was asked why he had not simply made an application directly to the Dutch authorities (rather than asking the ICC to present the witnesses to the Dutch authorities), he stated that it was beyond the scope of his mandate. Had the counsel gone ahead and done so, possibly there would not be such rich material to analyse (§25).
[429] Sluiter, 'Shared Responsibility in International Criminal Justice', 667.

In support he draws on the 'residual responsibility' of host States for the human rights compliance of international organisations operating on their territory, citing ECtHR case law. However, the author would disagree with Sluiter's suggestion. Article 103(4) very specifically refers to the enforcement of sentences, and such a role should not be imposed on the host State by analogy where the host State is clearly opposed to it. Any obligations on the host State to protect detained witnesses must be found beyond the Rome Statute protection framework.

7.1.3.2 Obligations beyond the ICC Protection Framework

The prohibition on removal and exposure to risk is an important part of the rights to life, protection from inhuman treatment, and fair trial. The Netherlands is obliged to protect these rights pursuant to Articles 2, 3, and 6 of the ECHR. There are two important elements to consider: the substantive right not to be removed to a country where there is a risk of human rights violations, and the procedural right of access to a mechanism for deciding on the application of this right. These rights correspond to obligations for States under whose jurisdiction the individual in question is located.

This issue of jurisdiction is central. If within Dutch jurisdiction, detained witnesses present at the seat of the ICC can apply for protection under human rights law. The Netherlands will be obliged to grant them access to the relevant procedures for determining such an application, and to grant them substantive protection from removal if the application is successful. As this point was substantially argued in the detained Congolese witnesses case, the relevant decision of the Dutch District Court will now be considered in detail.

When the detained Congolese witnesses made their application for protection, they sought protection from removal under both human rights law and refugee law. The Dutch authorities, while initially agreeing to hear their applications, subsequently informed the detained witnesses that the domestic procedures for requesting protection were not available to them because they were not within Dutch jurisdiction. The Dutch authorities stated that instead the applications would be considered using a sui generis procedure, the contents of which were unclear.[430]

---

[430] *The Prosecutor v. Thomas Lubanga Dyilo*, ICC-01/04-01/06-2827, Amicus Curiae Observations by Mr Schüller and Mr Sluiter, Counsel in Dutch Asylum Proceedings of Witness 19, 23 November 2011 (*Lubanga* amicus, 23 November 2011), §7–8.

In arguing that the Netherlands did not have jurisdiction over the detained witnesses, the Dutch government contended that Article 8 of the Headquarters Agreement between the Netherlands and the ICC created a 'carve out' of Dutch jurisdiction with respect to individuals in ICC detention.[431] Article 8 states that 'The premises of the Court shall be under the control and authority of the Court', and that 'no laws or regulations of the host State which are inconsistent with the rules of the Court ... shall be enforceable within the premises of the Court'. Furthermore, the Dutch government invoked Article 88 of the Implementation Act. This is the domestic legislation that incorporates the Headquarters Agreement and the Rome Statute into Dutch law. According to Article 88, Dutch law applicable to the deprivation of liberty shall not apply to those detained at the ICC. As the witnesses were in ICC custody, and had never been detained by the Dutch authorities, the Netherlands contended that they were not under Dutch jurisdiction.[432]

The District Court of The Hague issued a decision on this question in December 2011 which rejected the government's proposed interpretation of Article 8 of the Headquarters Agreement.[433] This decision was mentioned in Chapter 5. It held that the non-applicability of Dutch law to the ICC should be read in a restrictive and functional manner. Dutch law should only *not* apply to the ICC premises where this would interfere with the proper functioning of the ICC. The ICC itself had confirmed that applying Dutch human rights and refugee law to the detained witness would not be an interference,[434] and as such the District Court held that this law applied.[435] As to the argument based on Article 88 of the Implementation Act, the District Court held that the provision concerned law related to the deprivation of liberty, such as habeas corpus proceedings, not to other proceedings that a person deprived of their liberty might bring, such as an application for protection.[436] There was nothing in either the law of the ICC or domestic law that would preclude

---

[431] *The Prosecutor v. German Katanga and Mathieu Ngudjolo Chui*, ICC-01/04-01/07-T-258-ENG ET WT, Transcript of proceedings, 12 May 2011 (*Katanga/Ngudjolo* transcript, 12 May 2011), 72.
[432] *Katanga/Ngudjolo* transcript, 12 May 2011, 72.
[433] The Hague District Court, 28 December 2011, §9.
[434] The Hague District Court, 28 December 2011, §9, made reference to 9 June 2011 decision (*Katanga*, 9 June 2011).
[435] The Hague District Court, 28 December 2011, §9.
[436] The Hague District Court, 28 December 2011, §9.5.

the admissibility of the applications for protection from removal based on human rights law or refugee law.[437]

In addition, the District Court also held that the Netherlands was obliged to admit the detained witnesses to the protection application procedure because they had nowhere else to turn. It distinguished the situation from that of an individual requesting protection in an embassy abroad, stressing the fact that the witness could request protection from no other actor, since the ICC has no territory on which to grant the protection.[438] This argument is, in the author's view, particularly interesting. It has been described as an example of a 'symbiosis' between international criminal justice and a domestic justice system: the District Court acknowledged that the ICC does not operate on Dutch territory in isolation, and that it is appropriate for the Netherlands to step in and address flaws in the ICC protection system.[439]

The decision of the District Court was not appealed by the Dutch State, and so represents the law of the Netherlands on this point. It established that detained witnesses are within Dutch jurisdiction for the purposes of refugee law and Article 3 ECHR, and that therefore the Netherlands is obliged to protect both the procedural and substantive aspects of the prohibition on removal. This case constitutes the 'exception to the exception' mentioned in Chapter 5: the *Longa* case before the ECtHR established that the premises of the ICC is an exception to the territoriality of jurisdiction principle, and the District Court case is an exception to *Longa*.

There are two remaining questions, both relating to how the multi-actor nature of the situation affects the obligations of the Netherlands with respect to the detained witness: first, does the ICC's involvement alter the procedural obligations of the Netherlands, and second, does it impact on the merits of the decision making?

The first question pertains to the *procedure* for assessing the merits of an application for protection from a detained witness – can the Dutch decision maker rely on the ICC's assessment of the witness's security situation, or must it conduct an independent inquiry? In the early stages of the detained Congolese witnesses case, the Netherlands consistently stated that the manner in which it would proceed with the protection request would depend on the decisions of the ICC.[440] The Netherlands

---

[437] The Hague District Court, 28 December 2011, §9.9.
[438] The Hague District Court, 28 December 2011, §9.8.
[439] Sluiter, 'Shared Responsibility in International Criminal Justice', 675.
[440] *Lubanga* amicus, 23 November 2011, §5.

contended that it would be inappropriate to revisit the witness risk assessment conducted by the ICC, and that therefore it would not conduct a risk assessment of its own.[441] This approach was opposed by the ICC in Trial Chamber II's decision on 9 June 2011. The ICC judges determined that it was not for the ICC to conduct a risk assessment in lieu of the State; only the Netherlands could assess the extent of its own obligations.[442]

In practice, it appears from the Dutch decision on the merits of the detained Congolese witnesses' applications that the Netherlands did in fact carry out its own risk assessment. The author considers that this is the correct interpretation of the Dutch obligation, as there is nothing to suggest that this procedural aspect of the right can be outsourced to another actor. The Dutch authorities may not have access to the same information that the ICC used to make its decision, or the Netherlands may have additional information that is relevant to the assessment and which should not be overlooked. In order to comply with its obligations, the Netherlands must always conduct its own assessment. To do otherwise would be to unduly delegate its responsibilities under international law to an international organisation.

The second question pertains to the *substantive* decision on the merits. In the end, the detained Congolese witnesses were not permitted to remain in the Netherlands. The Council of State, the highest court of appeal in the Netherlands on immigration law matters, held that there were no grounds that would preclude their removal. The assurances provided by the DRC to the ICC regarding the witnesses' safety were deemed to remove any risk to the rights protected by Articles 2[443] and 3 ECHR.[444] Just as the ICC had done, the Council of State deemed that the assurances were to be given great weight because they had been given under Part 9 of the Rome Statute.[445] As to Article 6 ECHR, the Council held that the witnesses would suffer no flagrant denial of justice in the DRC.[446]

The Council of State's decision demonstrates that, in the Netherlands' view, Dutch obligations under the ECHR can be satisfied by assurances,

---

[441] de Boer and Zieck, 'ICC Witnesses and Acquitted Suspects Seeking Asylum in the Netherlands', 577–8, citing *Katanga/Ngudjolo*, 9 June 2011, §49.
[442] *Katanga/Ngudjolo*, 9 June 2011, §64.
[443] ECLI:NL:RVS:2014:2427, Council of State, 27 June 2014 (Council of State, 27 June 2014), §11.
[444] Council of State, 27 June 2014, §8.6.
[445] Council of State, 27 June 2014, §8.4.
[446] Council of State, 27 June 2014, §9.3.

even if the assurances were given between the ICC and the sending State and are not addressed to the Netherlands. Although the Council of State did review the assurances in light of the *Othman* criteria, and concluded that they were satisfied,[447] the Netherlands appears to have played no part in the negotiation of the assurances, and has no role in their monitoring. While this does not seem per se problematic, the author would suggest that the evaluation of the assurances in these circumstances should be done with even greater care and taking into account the relationship between the ICC and the sending State, which may differ from the Netherlands' relationship with that State. As one commentator points out, what must be avoided is that the Dutch authorities rely on the fact that the ICC is satisfied with assurances from a sending State, and fails to properly scrutinise them itself.[448]

The detained witness also sought to prevent their removal through refugee law. As will often be the case in these situations, there was ample evidence to satisfy the threshold of Article 1F of the Refugee Convention,[449] which allows States to exclude individuals from refugee protection if there are serious reasons for considering that they have committed a war crime or crime against humanity. In this aspect of the case the Netherlands did not feel the need to be guided by the ICC, using evidence to exclude the witnesses that had been dismissed by the ICC.[450] Following the Council of State's decision on 27 June 2014, the detained Congolese witnesses were returned to the DRC.

7.1.4 Problems in Human Rights Protection

Despite the issues that will be discussed in this section, the Congolese detained witnesses case is a positive departure from previous practice at the ad hoc tribunals. It is often assumed that the situation of detained witnesses applying for asylum in the host State of an international criminal tribunal is an entirely new phenomenon. However, there were two previous cases, one at the ICTR and one at the ICTY.

---

[447] Council of State, 27 June 2014, §8.2.
[448] Sluiter, 'Shared Responsibility in International Criminal Justice', 671.
[449] van Wijk provides details of the detained witnesses' alleged involvement in the conflict in the Ituri district of the DRC and the atrocities involved (van Wijk, 'When International Criminal Justice Collides with Principles of International Protection', 180).
[450] van Wijk, 'When International Criminal Justice Collides with Principles of International Protection', in footnote 125.

Agnes Ntamabyariro was the former Rwandan Justice Minister, and in 2006 she was awaiting trial for genocide in Rwanda when the ICTR ordered her transfer to the Tribunal to testify. During her testimony, she complained of her treatment by the Rwandan authorities, alleging torture and arbitrary detention. According to her lawyer, it was uncontested that she had been illegally kidnapped from Zambia some years earlier and rendered to Rwanda. Fearing to return to Rwanda, she had her counsel deliver a letter to the ICTR President requesting asylum. Disregarding this application, the ICTR transferred Ms. Ntamabyaliro back to Rwanda.[451] The only evidence that this application and return took place is a press release from the witness' lawyer, as no official decisions from the Tribunal appear to exist. Interestingly, it appears that the request was only submitted to the ICTR, and not to Tanzania (the host State of the Tribunal).

Dragan Opačić was convicted to ten years imprisonment by a Bosnian court for war crimes in 1995. Two years later he was transferred to the ICTY to give testimony in the trial of Dušco Tadić. During his testimony he said that he had been abused in Bosnia and pressured into falsely testifying against Tadić. He claimed that, in revealing this, he put himself at risk if returned to Bosnia, and so asked the ICTY that he be permitted to remain in its custody until the Bosnian authorities had revised the judgment against him. This request was rejected and he was returned to Bosnia, with the Tribunal expressing its 'full confidence' that he would not be mistreated. It does not appear that any form of protective measures, similar to those ordered in the detained Congolese witnesses case, was considered by the Tribunal. Following the ICTY's decision, Opačić started summary proceedings before the Dutch courts to block his removal on human rights grounds. The Dutch court held that it had no reason to review the ICTY decision, as the Tribunal had considered the case in light of the ICCPR, which was equivalent to the ECHR. As a last resort he applied for refugee status in the Netherlands, but as in Agnes Ntamabyariro's case, it was not considered and he was returned to Bosnia.[452]

These cases are prime examples of the implementation problems, in particular buck passing, that can arise when multiple actors are involved in protecting a witness. Against this past practice, the extensive consideration

---

[451] 'United Nations Illegally Transfers Asylum Seeker', Press Release of Philippe Larochelle and Avi Singh, Arusha, 13 September 2006. See also van Wijk and Cupido, 'Testifying behind Bars', 1096.
[452] van Wijk and Cupido, 'Testifying behind Bars', 1096–7.

of the detained Congolese witnesses case by both the ICC and the Netherlands is definitely a step in the right direction. Even though the ICC put forward a restrictive interpretation of Article 68(1), in terms of the scope of risk it covers, the Court did prioritise the rights of the detained Congolese witnesses over the obligation to return them under Article 93(7)(b). For the Netherlands' part, even though it fought the applications for protection every step of the way, at least the matter did come before the domestic courts and the applications were fully considered. That being said, there are still important problems that face detained witnesses at the seat of the Court that could compromise their human rights protection.

The ICC and the Netherlands are both obliged, by their respective obligations, to protect detained witnesses from violations of the right to life, protection from inhuman treatment, and fair trial, by refraining from sending them to a State where these rights would be at risk. The two sets of obligations exist in parallel; one does not cancel out the other. The fact that the obligations overlap in this way makes certain implementation problems more likely, in particular buck passing. Each actor may look to the other to protect the right rather than fulfilling its own obligations. Indeed, this can be seen from the conduct of the Netherlands when it sought to rely exclusively on the risk assessment conducted by the ICC instead of carrying out its own. Depending on how one sees the Netherlands' reliance on the assurances given by the DRC to the ICC, this could also be seen as an instance of buck passing. To fully comply with its obligations, it is possible that the Netherlands should have secured assurances itself, rather than delegating this to another actor. Even though the assurances were said to have been evaluated by the Council of State in light of the *Othman* criteria, one can question whether a more stringent approach would have been taken had the assurances been between the Netherlands and the DRC, rather than the ICC and the DRC.

7.1.5 Conclusion

When a detained witness arrives at the seat of the ICC, they may inform the Court that their current level of protection is insufficient, and on this basis claim that they are unable to safely return to the sending State, where their human rights would be at risk. If the witness distrusts the ICC's ability to provide this protection, they may turn to the host State. According to the Dutch courts, the circumstances of detained witnesses are such that they fall under Dutch jurisdiction, allowing them to request protection from removal under the human rights law obligations of the Netherlands. By this action, the witness creates a situation involving both the ICC and the Netherlands: both are involved in the detained witness's protection, and both have obligations to this effect.

As a result of the detained Congolese witnesses case, there are a number of judicial decisions pertaining to this particular situation. The decisions of both the ICC and the Dutch domestic courts have explored the relevant issues in detail. In some instances the author agrees with the outcomes, and in others not. But these divergences relate to the detail of the obligations, and not to the question of whether the obligations exist in the first place. It is established in the case law that the ICC and the Netherlands have parallel obligations to protect detained witnesses. It is this that gives rise to potential implementation problems, mainly buck passing, which were present in the detained Congolese witnesses case. However, the instances of buck passing relating to protection from removal obligations are relatively minor compared to the buck passing in relation to the right to liberty obligations. To this we now turn.

7.2 Detained Witnesses: Right to Liberty

7.2.1 Introduction

The relevance of the right to liberty to detained witnesses is clear, given that they are in detention, but the reason why the protection of this right involves multiple actors requires some explanation. In the detained Congolese witnesses case the right to liberty came to the fore because, while the various legal issues were ironed out with respect to the applications for protection in the Netherlands, the witnesses remained confined to the ICC Detention Centre. Three years elapsed between the detained Congolese witnesses applying for protection and the rejection of their claims and their return to the DRC. Such an extended period of imprisonment raised an important question: how is the right to liberty of detained witnesses protected at the seat of the ICC?

The actors involved are no different between this section and the previous one. The reason why the right to liberty is considered separately is because the focus of this section is on what takes place at the seat of the Court, and not what *could* take place in the sending State upon the witnesses' return. The previous section concerned the prohibition on removal aspect of the rights to life, protection from inhuman treatment, and fair trial; this section concerns respect for the right to liberty on the premises of the ICC itself.

The right to liberty has a number of components. It creates a negative obligation to not arbitrarily detain an individual, but also gives rise to positive obligations, including procedural obligations. The procedural element of the right proved to be the most crucial in the detained Congolese witnesses case, as the most hotly debated issue was which actor had the power and the obligation to review the legality of the detention.

On 24 August 2011, Trial Chamber II determined that, as far as the ICC was concerned, there was no reason for the detained Congolese witnesses to remain at the Court. The ICC was satisfied with the assurances it had secured from the DRC, and did not consider the witnesses to be at risk. The only reason why they were not transferred back to the DRC was because the ongoing protection applications in the Netherlands made their transfer 'impossible from a legal point of view'.[453] The Chamber requested the Registry to enter into consultations with the Netherlands to decide in whose custody the witnesses should remain while their protection claims were pending.[454] Lengthy consultations ensued, but no solution was reached, and the Netherlands refused to take over custody of the witnesses as the ICC often requested. The ICC stressed that the only reason for the detention was the protection applications, and that this detention could not go on indefinitely.[455] Meanwhile, not only the Dutch courts, but also the ECtHR, were issuing decisions on the right to liberty of the detained witnesses. In the end, albeit not pursuant to a judicial decision, the Netherlands did accept the transfer of the witnesses, and held them in immigration detention until they were removed from the country soon afterwards.[456]

In many ways, it is the right to liberty aspect of the detained Congolese witnesses case that remains the most problematic. The issues surrounding the prohibition on removal have been largely resolved (with some notable exceptions); however, for the right to liberty, the matter may have been resolved in practice, but no resolution was found for the legal questions. The discussion in this section hopes to address this by using the detained

---

[453] *Katanga/Ngudjolo*, 24 August 2011, §15.
[454] *Katanga/Ngudjolo*, 24 August 2011, §17.
[455] *The Prosecutor v. Germain Katanga*, ICC-01/04-01/07-3352, Decision on the Request for Release of Witnesses DRC-D02-P-0236, DRC-D02-P-0228 and DRC-D02-P-0350, 8 February 2013 (Trial Chamber II) (*Katanga*, 8 February 2013), §22.
[456] 'ICC transfers three detained witnesses to Dutch custody', ICC Press Release, 4 June 2014.

Congolese witnesses case to examine which actor has an obligation to review the detention of detained witnesses at the seat of the Court, and when this obligation arises. The right to liberty aspect of the detained Congolese witnesses case had not arisen before in international criminal justice, and so information relating to the actors' obligations stems principally from the decisions of different bodies in that case, and from the commentary on these decisions. As before, the discussion of obligations is followed by consideration of the potential issues with human rights protection that can arise due to the multi-actor nature of the situation.

7.2.2 Obligations of the ICC

The question of whether the ICC has the obligation to review the legality of the detention of witnesses on the ICC premises turns on the interpretation of Article 93(7) of the Rome Statute. This provision, in addition to requiring the ICC to return detained witnesses, obliges the Court to keep such witnesses in ICC custody for the duration of their time at the Court. The provision itself says nothing on the power of any actor to review a witness's detention, and neither the drafting history nor the Rome Statute protection framework more broadly provides any guidance.

In two separate decisions in the detained Congolese witnesses case, the majorities at the ICC Trial and Appeals levels held that the ICC had no power, and thereby no obligation, to review the detention of the witnesses. In making this determination the judges employed multiple different arguments. These arguments do not seem to flow from one single underlying rationale, suggesting that the judges making up the majority had different ideas as to how the ICC's obligations should be interpreted. The majority opinions in the Trial and Appeals Chambers were countered by powerful dissents at both levels, which presented compelling alternative views. This section will set out the different elements of the majority opinions and the response of the dissenting judges to each element. This allows for a discussion of the arguments for and against interpreting the ICC's obligations as requiring it to review the detention of detained witnesses.

The first majority argument hinged on the question of which actor the witnesses' detention was attributable to. The majority made a distinction between *detention* and *custody*.[457] The witnesses's *detention* was said to

---

[457] The italics are used to indicate the fact that the way these terms are used in this paragraph is not the same as in the rest of the chapter.

be based on an order from the DRC, with the ICC only maintaining *custody* of the witnesses on the DRC's behalf. The obligation to maintain custody was said to arise from Article 93(7)(b) and Rule 192 RPE. The fact that the ICC still had *custody* over the witnesses even once their testimony concluded was due to the fact that the Netherlands had refused to take over *custody* of them. Right to liberty issues was held to be linked to *detention*, not *custody*,[458] and since the *detention* remained attributable at all times to the DRC, this was the only actor with the capacity to review the witnesses' status.[459] Responding to the argument that reading Article 93(7) in light of Article 21(3) would lead to a different conclusion, the Chamber held that for the ICC to examine the basis of the detention and order release would place the ICC in the position of a human rights court, which it was not intended to be.[460] The majority stressed that nothing the ICC had done amounted to an ICC order for the witnesses' continued *detention*.[461] The ICC's only obligations related to the conditions in its detention centre.[462]

Judges Song and Van den Wyngaert disagreed with this analysis in their individual dissents, made at the Appeal and Trial levels respectively. Both dismissed the *custody–detention* distinction as artificial. The distinction they drew was a different one: they differentiated between the period of detention before Trial Chamber II's 9 June 2011 decision, and the period of detention after. It was in the decision of 9 June 2011 that the Trial Chamber decided to suspend the return of the witnesses pending the outcome of their applications for protection in the Netherlands.[463] This decision was important, because the dissenting judges agree that

[458] The Majority's approach is summarised this way by Judge Song in *The Prosecutor v. Germain Katanga*, ICC-01/04-01/07-3424-Anx, Decision on the Admissibility of the Appeal against the 'Decision on the Application for the Interim Release of Detained Witnesses DRC-D02-P0236, DRC-D02-P0228 and DRC-D02-P0350', Dissenting Opinion Judge Sang-Hyun Song, 20 January 2014 (Appeals Chamber) (*Katanga* (dissent), 20 January 2014), §4, and by Van den Wyngaert in *The Prosecutor v. Germain Katanga*, ICC-01/04-01/07-3405Anx, Decision on the Application for the Interim Release of Detained Witnesses DRC-D02-P-0236, DRC-D02-P-0228 and DRC-D02-P-0350, Dissenting Opinion of Judge Christine Van den Wyngaert, 1 October 2013 (Trial Chamber II) (*Katanga* (dissent), 1 October 2013), §4.
[459] If the Congolese authorities had decided 'to end the pre-trial detention, the Court would be duty-bound to execute such an order for release' (*Katanga*, 1 October 2013, §31).
[460] *Katanga*, 1 October 2013, §27.
[461] *Katanga* (dissent), 1 October 2013, §4.
[462] *Katanga*, 1 October 2013, §28.
[463] See Section 7.1.2.2 on the obligations of the ICC regarding the right to life of detained witnesses, and *Katanga*, 9 June 2011, §73.

prior to this the ICC was indeed detaining the witnesses on behalf of the DRC. Once their return was suspended on 9 June, the situation 'fundamentally changed'.[464] Judge van de Wyngaert argued that following that decision, the ICC became co-responsible for what happened to the detained witnesses while they awaited the outcome of their protection applications.[465] She argued that despite the fact that Article 93(7) continued to provide a legal basis for the detention, this did not mean that the detention had not become arbitrary.[466]

Judge Song's reasoning in his dissent at the Appeals level is largely similar. He considered that the 9 June 2011 decision to suspend the witnesses' return to the DRC effectively suspended the Article 93(7) cooperation agreement between the ICC and the DRC.[467] The Trial Chamber's independent determination that the witnesses should remain in detention during the asylum process, and during consultations between the ICC and the host State, constituted in his opinion, an order for detention.[468] From that point on, the detention became attributable to the ICC, and so the ICC had the obligation to review it.

The second majority argument appears more policy based, focusing on State cooperation and the need to respect State sovereignty. The majority held that to review the detention of the witnesses would be detrimental to cooperation and would erode sovereignty. This was said to overrule other considerations, such as the fact that the ICC had de facto control over the witnesses.[469] Judge Van den Wyngaert counters this in her dissent by stating that State cooperation is not an adequate reason for depriving an individual of their liberty. She considered that maintaining the detention of the witnesses was disproportionate and privileged the DRC's rights over those of the witnesses.[470]

The majority's third argument concerned the existence and relevance of a legal vacuum in protection. In addressing this argument, the majority of Trial Chamber II stressed that the ICC was not the only avenue for review. The detained Congolese witnesses had an alternative forum for

---

[464] *Katanga* (dissent), 1 October 2013, §5.
[465] *Katanga* (dissent), 1 October 2013, §5.
[466] *Katanga* (dissent), 1 October 2013, §15.
[467] *Katanga* (dissent), 20 January 2014, §11.
[468] *Katanga* (dissent), 20 January 2014, §13.
[469] *Katanga*, 1 October 2013, §28 and *The Prosecutor* v. *Mathieu Ngudjolo Chui*, ICC-01/04-02/12-158, Order on the Implementation of the Cooperation Agreement between the Court and the Democratic Republic of the Congo Concluded Pursuant Article 93(7) of the Statute, 20 January 2014 (Appeals Chamber) (*Ngudjolo*, 20 January 2014), §26.
[470] *Katanga* (dissent), 1 October 2013, §17.

their claim, as they could bring review proceedings in the DRC and so would not be left without recourse.[471] This too met with a strong response from Judge Van den Wyngaert. She pointed out that it is precisely the DRC authorities that the detained witnesses were requesting protection from.[472] Details of the alleged violations by the DRC were set out in a complaint by the witnesses to the Human Rights Committee.[473] Furthermore, Judge Van den Wyngaert pointed out that forcing the detained witnesses to seek protection from the DRC would place them in an impossible position, as it would compromise their applications for protection in the Netherlands.[474]

The majorities in both Chambers rejected arguments that used Article 21(3) as a basis for the ICC having an obligation to review the detention. There was little consistency in how the Article was understood, both as between the Appeals and Trial Chambers, and even within the same Chamber. The inconsistency was pointed out by Judge Van den Wyngaert, who in her dissent questioned why Article 93(7) could be set aside in the interests of protecting some rights but not others. The obligation in Article 93(7) to return the witnesses was suspended in order to allow the detained Congolese witnesses to complete their applications for protection in the Netherlands, but the obligation to keep them detained could not be suspended in order to protect their right to liberty. Both Judges Van den Wyngaert and Song described the difference as illogical, given that the provision in question was the same.[475] The Trial Chamber's justification that the prohibition on removal (in particular with regards to torture and inhuman treatment) is jus cogens and the right to liberty is not was rejected in the dissent as unconvincing and unsupported by the text of Article 21(3).[476] Judge Van den Wyngaert criticised the majority for hiding behind the ICC's obligation to another actor to justify violating human rights. Even if the detention was indeed attributable to the DRC at all times, the ICC cannot justify violating human rights on the basis that the violation is being carried out on behalf of another actor. To do so ignored Article 21(3) and unduly deferred to State sovereignty.[477]

---

[471] *Katanga*, 1 October 2013, §33.
[472] *Katanga* (dissent), 1 October 2013, §8.
[473] 'Complaint under the Optional Protocol to the International Covenant on Civil and Political Rights', ICC-01/04-01/06-2827-Anx5, 22 November 2011 (ICCPR Complaint).
[474] *Katanga* (dissent), 1 October 2013, §8.
[475] *Katanga* (dissent), 1 October 2013, §6–7; *Katanga* (dissent), 20 January 2014, §11.
[476] *Katanga* (dissent), 1 October 2013, §6–7.
[477] *Katanga* (dissent), 1 October 2013, §7.

The author agrees with Judges Van den Wyngaert and Song's interpretation of the ICC's obligations much more so than with the majorities' in the Trial and Appeals Chambers. In addition to their arguments, the author would add another that supports their position, based on Article 21(3). The arguments made in both the majority opinions and the dissents regarding Article 21(3) were quite broad and general, only sometimes using it to address whether the ICC can or must review the detention of detained witnesses on its premises. What was not done in the discussed decisions was to apply Article 21(3) as a test that the interpretation of a provision must satisfy. The Article 21(3) test requires interpreters to ask the following question: if the majority's approach to Article 93(7) is correct, is this interpretation and application consistent with internationally recognised human rights? Judge Van den Wyngaert points out that the Trial Chamber majority's approach to human rights and Article 93(7) is inconsistent, subjugates the right to liberty to the interests of the DRC and State sovereignty, and forces detained witnesses to turn to the sending State for protection, thereby jeopardising their ability to seek protection in the Netherlands. The author argues that, in light of this, the majority's approach to Article 93(7) fails the Article 21(3) test.

To say that the ICC is obliged to review the lawfulness of a witness's detention says nothing of the precise nature of this review. There are two alternative shapes that this review could take. The first is that the ICC is obliged to review a detained witness's detention in its entirety, including whether the sending State was violating the right to liberty even before the witness came to the ICC. If the sending State was detaining the witness unlawfully, and the ICC continued to enforce this detention on the sending State's behalf, the ICC could be violating its right to liberty obligations.

Such an approach would be very far reaching; however, it does have some support in a decision of the Human Rights Committee concerning a former Guantanamo Bay detainee.[478] Pursuant to a prison transfer agreement, David Hicks was transferred from Guantanamo Bay to his native Australia, where he served the remainder of a sentence imposed on him by a US military tribunal. He spent seven months in Australian detention and upon his release brought a case before the Human Rights Committee alleging that Australia had violated his right to liberty. The

---

[478] *David Hicks v. Australia*, Communication No. 2005/2010, 16 February 2016 (*Hicks*, 16 February 2016).

Committee determined that there was ample evidence that Hicks's US trial had been a flagrant denial of justice, and as such, it was a 'disproportionate restriction of the right to liberty' for Australia to have enforced the sentence.[479] What this interpretation could mean for the ICC is that it would be obliged to review the detention of a detained witness any time such an individual came to the Court and requested this.

The second alternative is the one proposed in the dissenting opinions, and would mean that the ICC is only obliged to examine the lawfulness of the detention from the point at which the detained witnesses' return to the sending State is suspended. The suspension can be due to an application for protection being transmitted to the Netherlands, or because the ICC is assessing whether it can return the witnesses without violating Article 68(1). In deciding to suspend the return of the detained witnesses to the sending State, the ICC is seen as taking on responsibility for the witnesses. If the detention is maintained, from that point on it is attributable to the ICC. From this follows an obligation on the ICC to ensure that the right to liberty of those witnesses is not violated while they are present on the Court premises.

The standard of review should be arbitrariness, as the right to liberty prohibits arbitrary detention. This is supported by Judge Van den Wyngaert, who sets out some indicators of arbitrariness in her dissenting opinion, including whether there is a foreseen end to the detention, whether the detention is contingent on the decision of another jurisdiction, and whether the detention is proportionate.[480] Finding the detained Congolese witnesses' detention to be arbitrary, Judge Van den Wyngaert would have ordered their release.

The author would argue in favour of the second alternative. The first alternative would be very much against the interpretation of both the majority and the dissents in the decisions discussed, and is, in the author's opinion, unnecessary. In the Guantanamo Bay case, Australia was taking over detention of the individual on a permanent basis; when the ICC hosts detained witnesses in its detention centre it is doing so on a temporary basis and on behalf of the sending State. It makes sense to say that if the ICC delays sending the witness back to the sending State or refuses to do so altogether, the situation is then altered. The ICC's action creates an obligation to ensure the right to liberty, given that the individuals would not otherwise be in the ICC's custody.

---

[479] *Hicks*, 16 February 2016, §4.9.
[480] *Katanga* (dissent), 1 October 2013, §16.

If the ICC found that the detention had become arbitrary, and that therefore the right to liberty was violated, it would be necessary to release the witnesses. Precisely how this is to be implemented is problematic, and we are faced with many of the same concerns that arise with respect to detained witnesses in need of relocation.

7.2.3 Obligations of the Host State

When discussing the obligations of the host State, it must first be ascertained whether the Netherlands has any type of obligations at all with regard to the right to liberty of witnesses detained on ICC premises. Given that they are located on the ICC premises, Dutch jurisdiction over which is generally suspended, and given that they are detained pursuant to arrangements between the ICC and the sending State, it is not obvious that the Netherlands would indeed have any obligations.

Nothing relevant to this discussion can be found in the Rome Statute protection framework, including in the Headquarters Agreement. As such, the Netherlands' obligations are found only under human rights law beyond the protection framework. As the most important human rights instrument under Dutch law, the Netherlands' right to liberty obligations stem from the ECHR, in particular Article 5. For the Netherlands to have an obligation to review the detention of witnesses on ICC premises, which was the main issue of contention in the detained Congolese witnesses case, it must have jurisdiction over them under the ECHR. This is the question that this section will address. As with the discussion of the ICC's obligations above, the main source of information concerning the Netherlands' obligations is the decisions of various courts in the detained Congolese witnesses case.

From early on the ICC attempted to consult with the Netherlands with the aim of transferring the detained Congolese witnesses to the latter's custody.[481] This was also the course preferred by the witnesses themselves (the reason being that under Dutch law detention for individuals seeking protection from removal under human rights or refugee law is limited to eighteen months, and then only in exceptional circumstances. As such, the witnesses stood a chance of being released while their claims were being decided).[482] The Dutch authorities did not want this, and

---

[481] *Katanga/Ngudjolo*, 24 August 2011, §17; *Katanga*, 8 February 2013, §§9–15 and 22; *Ngudjolo*, 20 January 2014, 3.
[482] *Katanga/Ngudjolo*, 9 June 2011, §27.

were adamant that the witnesses were to remain detained at the ICC Detention Centre: 'the position of the Netherlands has consistently been that the witness is to remain in the custody of the Court during the asylum procedure'.[483] The Netherlands even conducted the immigration interviews in the ICC Detention Centre. It was not until the very end, once the applications for protection had been rejected and the removal of the witnesses was imminent, that they were transferred to Dutch custody. Following a final failed attempt to prevent removal, the detained witnesses were returned by the Netherlands to the DRC. The removal was done pursuant to Dutch law, and not as a request of the ICC for transport under the Headquarters Agreement.

The detained Congolese witnesses case went all the way from the District Court of The Hague, to the Dutch Supreme Court, to the ECtHR (although not in that order). These cases were the result of a summary procedure before Dutch courts in which the refusal of the Dutch authorities to take over custody of the witnesses was presented as a tort against those witnesses.[484] The reasoning in these decisions will be analysed in this section.

The District Court of The Hague, on 26 September 2012, was the only judicial institution to rule in favour of the detained Congolese witnesses being transferred to Dutch custody. This was the same court that, one year earlier, held that the witnesses were entitled to apply for protection from removal under Dutch law (the case that established the jurisdiction 'exception to the exception').[485] The court once again used the argument that it was necessary to prevent the formation of a legal vacuum. It held that the detention situation of the witnesses had become unlawful because there was no prospect of a speedy end to the protection proceedings. As the ICC had stated that it could not review the detention, and the DRC was seen as equally unable to do so, the District Court found it to be the responsibility of the Netherlands. The presence of the ICC on Dutch territory was sufficient, in those circumstances, to establish jurisdiction over the witnesses' right to liberty, especially since it was the Dutch proceedings that stood in the way of the witnesses being returned to the DRC. In light of this, the District Court held that the Netherlands was obliged to take over custody of the

---

[483] Note verbale from the Dutch Ministry of Foreign Affairs to the ICC. See *Longa*, 9 October 2012, §22.
[484] de Boer and Zieck, 'ICC Witnesses and Acquitted Suspects Seeking Asylum in the Netherlands', 586.
[485] The Hague District Court, 28 December 2011.

witnesses from the ICC.[486] Unlike the decision on protection from removal described in the previous section of this Chapter, which was not challenged, the Dutch government appealed this decision to the Court of Appeal. Before the appeal could be decided, the ECtHR produced its own decision on the matter.

The ECtHR decision was the result of an application by one of the detained witnesses, Djokaba Lambi Longa, who testified in the *Lubanga* case. The three other witnesses were attached to the *Katanga* case, and it was in respect of these three that the summary tort proceedings for release were brought. The fourth witness, Mr Longa, was not addressed by the District Court decision described in the paragraph above. The application to the ECtHR alleged that the Netherlands had violated Article 5, the right to liberty, and Article 13, the right to a remedy, because Mr. Longa was detained unlawfully on Dutch soil and had been denied the opportunity to seek release. By the time the case was heard by the ECtHR, Mr Longa had withdrawn his application for protection and returned voluntarily to the DRC. Despite this, the ECtHR decided to pronounce on the application anyway. Part of the reason for this was that the ECtHR was aware of the ongoing Dutch proceedings regarding the three *Katanga* witnesses, and it deemed it important to set out its assessment of the matter.[487]

As was explained in Chapter 5, the ECtHR held in the *Longa* case that the Netherlands did not have jurisdiction over the detained witnesses as far as Article 5 ECHR was concerned. While acknowledging that jurisdiction is primarily territorial, the ECtHR cited exceptions established in previous case law and practice to hold that the mere presence of the ICC on Dutch territory was not sufficient to engage Dutch jurisdiction.[488] With the *Longa* decision in hand, the path was paved for the Dutch Court of Appeal and Supreme Court to simply follow the ECtHR without question. Both of these courts held that the Netherlands did not have jurisdiction over the detention of the witnesses, that no legal vacuum existed, and that the Dutch authorities were not obliged to accept the transfer of the witnesses.[489]

---

[486] The Hague District Court, 26 September 2012, decision set out in §38 of *Longa*, 9 October 2012.
[487] *Longa*, 9 October 2012, §57–8.
[488] See also Emma Irving, 'The Relationship between the International Criminal Court and its Host State: The Impact on Human Rights' (2014) 27 *Leiden Journal of International Law*, 479, 483.
[489] ECLI:NL:GHSGR:2012:BY6075, Court of Appeal, 18 December 2012 and ECLI:NL:HR:2014:828, Supreme Court, 4 April 2014.

To conclude, the current state of the law according to the ECtHR in *Longa*, and the Dutch Supreme Court applying *Longa*, is that the Netherlands has no jurisdiction over the detention of witnesses at the ICC Detention Centre, regardless of whether or not they have made an application for protection. However, the author considers that the ECtHR in *Longa* erred in its decision on jurisdiction because it overlooked the fact of the Netherlands' involvement in the witnesses' deprivation of liberty. As per other decisions of the ECtHR, where a State becomes involved in the activities of an international organisation, this engages the State's jurisdiction under the ECHR. The *Kokkelvisserij* case concerned the granting of licenses for cockle collecting in the Wadden Sea in the Netherlands.[490] As the case touched on an issue of EU law, the Dutch court hearing the case made a preliminary reference to the European Court of Justice (ECJ, as it then was). The applicant requested that he be allowed to submit a written response to the opinion of the Advocate General of the ECJ, but this was denied. The Dutch court then followed the instructions of the ECJ and found against the applicant. The applicant brought a claim to the ECtHR against the Netherlands, claiming that his inability to submit his written opinion to the Advocate General violated his Article 6 ECHR right to adversarial proceedings. The Netherlands disputed the possibility of responsibility on the basis that it was an act of the EU, and not of the Netherlands. The ECtHR held that the fact that the Dutch court had made a preliminary reference to the ECJ meant that it was involved in the situation, and so the Netherlands did have jurisdiction. Support can also be found in cases that have reached the opposite conclusion. In *Berić*, the key to the ECtHR finding that there was no jurisdiction on the part of Bosnia-Herzegovina was the fact that the applicants had been removed from their public office by a UN administration, which was following a UN Security Council resolution that required no domestic implementation.[491] Applied to the ICC context, if the Netherlands is in no way involved in the situation of a person detained on the ICC premises, they cannot be said to have jurisdiction; however, as soon as they become in some way involved, jurisdiction would follow.

Returning to the detained Congolese witnesses, if the Netherlands had not been hearing the their applications for protection, they would not have

---

[490] *Kokkelvisserij v. the Netherlands*, Application No. 13645/05, Admissibility Decision, 20 January 2009 (*Kokkelvisserij*, 20 January 2009).

[491] *Dušan Berić and Others v. Bosnia and Herzegovina*, Application nos. 36357/04, 36360/04, 38346/04, 41705/04, 45190/04, 45578/04, 45579/04, 45580/04, 91/05, 97/05, 100/05, 101/05, 1121/05, 1123/05, 1125/05, 1129/05, 1132/05, 1133/05, 1169/05, 1172/05, 1175/05, 1177/05, 1180/05, 1185/05, 20793/05 and 25496/05, Admissibility Decision, 16 October 2007.

been in detention at the ICC. When deciding that the Netherlands should take over custody of the witnesses, the District Court back in September 2012 held that there was jurisdiction due to the fact that 'it is because of the Netherlands asylum proceedings that the [witnesses] cannot be returned to the DRC'.[492] When compared to the ECtHR jurisprudence on what constitutes 'involvement' by a State, this causality between the application for protection proceedings in the Netherlands and the ongoing detention clearly meets the threshold. Relevant precedent on this point, including the *Kokkelvisserij* case,[493] was not considered by the ECtHR in the *Longa* case. Instead, Mr Longa's argument that acceptance of jurisdiction to hear the protection claim gave rise to jurisdiction under the ECHR was rejected on the basis that States are not obliged to allow foreign nationals to await the outcome of protection from removal proceedings on their territory, and that the Convention does not guarantee the right to enter a State of which one is not a national.[494]

The notion that the Netherlands was not involved in the detention of the Congolese witnesses has been described by a commentator as having 'no foothold in reality'.[495] The matter of jurisdiction under the ECHR and the acceptance of the Netherlands to hear the protection claims are necessarily linked: the acceptance set in motion a chain of events 'which had an undeniable impact on the position of the applicant in the ICC's detention facility'.[496] If it were not for the protection claim, the witnesses would not have been so long detained at the ICC. This clearly implicates the Netherlands in their situation. This finding is not confined to the detained Congolese witnesses case, but rather in the author's opinion, represents the correct interpretation of the Netherlands' obligations in future situations of the same type.

7.2.4 Problems in Human Rights Protection

The problem facing detained witnesses with respect to the right to liberty is a structural one. Neither the ICC nor the Netherlands accept that they have an obligation to protect this right, leaving a gap in protection. With

---

[492] The Hague District Court, 26 September 2012.
[493] *Kokkelvisserij*, 20 January 2009.
[494] *Longa*, 9 October 2012, §81–3.
[495] Cedric Ryngaert, 'Oscillating between Embracing and Avoiding Bosphorus: The European Court of Human Rights on Member State Responsibility for Acts of International Organisations and the Case of the EU' (2014) 39 *European Law Review*, 176.
[496] Ryngaert, 'Oscillating between Embracing and Avoiding Bosphorus', 185.

respect to the ICC, the author put forward the dissenting opinions of Judges Van den Wyngaert and Song as reflecting the correct interpretation of the law, and explored how their approach would operate. However, the majority opinions at both the Trial and Appeal levels oppose this view, and they represent the currently accepted approach to the law.

Indeed, the gap in protection at this stage is more pronounced than it is in other multi-actor situations with structural problems. For the situations of interim release, acquittal, and witness protection through relocation, at least the ICC did have an obligation to protect human rights, even if it wasn't able to carry it out without assistance. For this situation, the only actor acknowledged by all sides as having an obligation was the sending State, which is the State from which the detained witnesses were seeking protection. The complaint submitted by the detained Congolese witnesses to the Human Rights Committee details the alleged unlawful detention that had been ongoing for years before their transfer to the ICC to give evidence.[497] As one commentator pointed out, the fact that the extended period of detention at the seat of the Court was due to attempts to secure the witnesses' protection from other human rights abuses strongly suggests that the matter should not be left to the DRC.[498] And yet it has been.

7.2.5 Conclusion

The right to liberty issues that arose in the detained Congolese witnesses case was a result of the extended period of time that it took to resolve the questions surrounding the protection of their rights to life, protection from inhuman treatment, and fair trial. One might assume therefore, that as the legal issues that caused that delay have been resolved, detained witnesses in a similar situation in future would not face the same right to liberty concerns. However, this is not necessarily the case. In the detained Congolese witnesses case, neither the ICC nor the Netherlands accepted that they had an obligation to review the detention, and so if future cases arise (which seems somewhat unlikely) witnesses may still remain detained while their applications for protection from removal under Dutch law are decided, regardless of how long these take.

---

[497] ICCPR Complaint, 5–7.
[498] de Boer and Zieck, 'ICC Witnesses and Acquitted Suspects Seeking Asylum in the Netherlands', 587.

Many commentators have predicted that the chance of detained witnesses being brought to the premises of the ICC again is unlikely. It is foreseen that the ICC, the Netherlands, and any potential sending State will want to avoid a situation similar to the detained Congolese witnesses from ever arising again. Reliance may be had on video link testimony instead. Given that detained witnesses are a relatively small group, this is feasible. However, attempting to avoid protection claims from all witnesses by not bringing them to the seat of the Court is not possible. In the future therefore, questions surrounding the protection of non-detained witnesses at the seat of the Court will continue to be highly relevant, and it is to these that we now turn.

7.3 Non-Detained Witnesses

7.3.1 Introduction

The phenomenon of witnesses arriving at the seat of the ICC and requesting protection in the Netherlands is not limited to detained witnesses. Non-detained witnesses may also turn away from the protection on offer by the ICC, and look to the Netherlands for protection instead. Just such an eventuality occurred in January 2011, when two ICC witnesses filed an application for protection in the Netherlands. Their names and country of origin remain confidential.[499] The success of these applications has paved the way for more witnesses to apply for protection in the Netherlands.

Unlike for the detained witness, the risks to their safety that lead the two non-detained witnesses to apply for protection in January 2011 have not been made public. As such, as with all the other witnesses dealt with in this book, the primary human rights concerns are deemed to relate to the right to life and to protection from inhuman treatment.

The two witnesses who applied for protection in the Netherlands in January 2011 made their claim under both refugee law and human rights law. Thus far, refugee status has not been particularly relevant to the discussion of how to protect human rights because the individuals in question would not have qualified for it. Generally speaking, this is due to their links with criminal activity, which would exclude them from refugee status because of Article 1F of the Refugee Convention. For the category

---

[499] de Boer and Zieck, 'ICC Witnesses and Acquitted Suspects Seeking Asylum in the Netherlands', 596.

of non-detained witnesses however, there is a much stronger chance of success.

Refugee status has a significant advantage as a way of protecting human rights. If an individual is applying for, and is granted, the status of a refugee under the Refugee Convention, this is accompanied by a series of substantive and procedural rights. As human rights law did not originally contain a prohibition on removal, but rather has evolved over time to contain one, there is no regime regulating the status of individuals who cannot be removed. As such, if possible, it is preferable for an individual to acquire refugee status.

The advantages that refugee law can have over human rights law were an important part of why the witnesses chose to turn away from the ICC and look for protection elsewhere. They had been accepted into the ICCPP and were awaiting relocation to a third State when they made their applications in the Netherlands. The ICC had made it clear before they arrived at the Court that they would not be returned to their country of origin.[500] Despite this, the witnesses sought protection in the Netherlands, and they cited three reasons for doing so. First, they argued that it was not clear that they would receive the same procedural and substantive rights if relocated through the ICCPP that they would otherwise be entitled to under international refugee law. For example, they did not know whether they would have access to legal assistance when seeking relocation, or access to review of decisions made about their protective measures, as they would have under the Refugee Convention. Second, they pointed to the restrictive scope of protection under the ICCPP, which following the Trial Chamber's approach to the types of risk is more limited than refugee law.[501] And finally, they raised concerns about the ICCPP's dependence on State cooperation, rendering protection under it always temporary in nature.[502]

For these reasons, the discussion of obligations in the following section looks principally at obligations relating to the granting of refugee status as a way of protecting human rights. Human rights law is, of course, still relevant. However, the human rights law obligations of the Netherlands have been covered extensively already, and this situation requires no significant additions.

---

[500] The Hague District Court, 8 March 2013, §3.
[501] *Katanga/Ngudjolo*, 9 June 2011, §59.
[502] These reasons are listed in The Hague District Court, 8 March 2013, §5; Irving, 'Protecting Witnesses at the ICC from Refoulement'.

7.3.2 Obligations of the ICC

The ICC's obligations are straightforward. Pursuant to Article 68(1), the ICC must protect witnesses, including from removal to a State where they would be at risk. With respect to the witnesses who sought protection in January 2011, the ICC made clear that it considered its obligations under Article 68(1) to continue whether or not the witnesses made an application for protection in the Netherlands, and that the witnesses remained the ICC's responsibility wherever they were located.[503] Beyond this, the relevant obligations of the ICC towards witnesses have been covered elsewhere in this book.

7.3.3 Obligations of the Host State

When an ICC witness applies for protection in the Netherlands, the relevant obligations stem from the human rights and refugee law obligations of the Netherlands beyond the Rome Statute protection framework. As already mentioned, the human rights law obligations need not be considered in detail here, as they have been covered elsewhere in this chapter and this book. It suffices to say that the Netherlands does have jurisdiction over the witnesses under human rights law, and must therefore allow them access to a mechanism to determine their claim and to provide the necessary protection if their claim is successful. When non-detained witnesses come to the Court, they are hosted in accommodation in The Hague and are free to move around as they choose when not needed in proceedings. The fact that they are not held on the ICC premises makes their presence in the Netherlands more straightforward, and as such the question of whether they fall under Dutch jurisdiction is much easier to answer. The existence of jurisdiction has been accepted by the Dutch authorities: in 2002, the Minister of Justice had foreseen the possibility of witnesses applying for asylum in the Netherlands, and had stated that ICC witnesses should be treated as any other alien on Dutch territory.[504]

As far as refugee law is concerned, the Netherlands has not contested that this law applies to non-detained ICC witnesses, and has not contested the access of these individuals to the procedure for requesting refugee status. What the Dutch government has contested is whether ICC

---

[503] The Hague District Court, 8 March 2013, §3.
[504] Letter from the Minister of Justice to the Speaker of the Lower House of Parliament, the Hague, 3 July 2002, 28 098 (R 1704), 28 099, No. 13.

witnesses *qualify* for refugee status under the Refugee Convention. The Dutch government made a number of arguments to this effect when the two witnesses applied for asylum in January 2011. The arguments were not based on the existence or otherwise of risk to the witnesses, but rather on their involvement with the ICC disqualifying them *in principle*.

In arguing that the witnesses did not qualify for refugee status, the Dutch government's first argument was based on Article 1A of the Refugee Convention. The Secretary of State argued that the witnesses were in no danger of being returned to a country where they would be at risk because the ICC was already providing them with protection. As such, they did not have a well-founded fear of persecution within the meaning of the Article 1A.[505] The Dutch Council of State disagreed. It held that what determines whether a person is entitled to refugee status is not whether there is a danger that they will be returned to their country or origin, but whether, if returned, there would be a risk of persecution.[506] Therefore it did not matter that the ICC was involved and was offering an alternative form of protection, what mattered was that there would be a risk if the witnesses were returned. The Council of State stated that the only exceptions to this principle were exhaustively set out in Article 1C to F, none of which applied.[507] It was not open to the Council to create a new exception based on the involvement of an international organisation.

The next argument for exclusion hinged on Article 1D of the Refugee Convention. This provision excludes an individual from refugee status if they are receiving protection from organs or agencies of the UN. The Dutch authorities argued that the ICC is an organisation comparable to the UN, and witnesses protected by the ICC should be excluded under Article 1D by analogy. The Council of State cited the *travaux preparatoires* of the Refugee Convention to reject this argument, stating that the purpose of Article 1D was limited and could not be extended by analogy.[508]

Finally the Secretary of State argued that the witnesses did not qualify as refugees because of the 'safe third country' argument, contained within Dutch and EU law. The argument went that the relocation State to be arranged by the ICC qualified as a safe third country. It was acknowledged

---

[505] ECLI:NL:RVS:2014:627, Council of State, 18 February 2014 (Council of State, 18 February 2014), §6.1.
[506] Council of State, 18 February 2014, §6.2.
[507] Council of State, 18 February 2014, §6.2.
[508] Council of State, 18 February 2014, §11.1.

that the test was not stricto sensu satisfied, as it normally applied where a person was in a safe country before arriving in the Netherlands; all the same the Dutch authorities argued that the spirit of the exception applied. Once again the Council of State dismissed this argument, among other reasons because the protection enjoyed by the alien must be from a known country, which was not the case here as a relocation State had not yet been identified.[509]

The Council of State's interpretation of the Refugee Convention has been met with support from commentators. The arguments of the Secretary of State have been described as elastic and analogous interpretations of the law.[510] What these arguments are said to have in common is their contention that protection by the ICC or by an unknown future relocation State serves to release the Netherlands from its obligation to grant refugee status. As the rejection of each argument by the Council of State shows, the current legal framework does not allow for the Netherlands to be released from its obligations this way.[511] Thanks to the application for protection by the two witnesses in January 2011, the obligations of the Netherlands to protect ICC witnesses from removal by granting them refugee status have been well established.

7.3.4 Problems in Human Rights Protection

In some ways this is an unproblematic area; in the case discussed neither the ICC nor the Netherlands contested the fact that it had obligations to protect the witnesses, and neither is shying away from those obligations. However, there are still two types of implementation problems that may arise.

The obligations of the ICC and the Netherlands overlap, in the sense that they both apply to the same individual at the same time. This can result in one interfering with the implementation of the other. While the protection applications of the witnesses in the case discussed were pending, the ICC pointed out that the existence of these applications in the Netherlands was making it much more difficult to find a willing relocation State within the framework of the ICCPP. Negotiations with one potential relocation State had to be put on hold because the State

---

[509] Council of State, 18 February 2014, §10.2.
[510] de Boer and Zieck, 'ICC Witnesses and Acquitted Suspects Seeking Asylum in the Netherlands', 598 and 560.
[511] de Boer and Zieck, 'ICC Witnesses and Acquitted Suspects Seeking Asylum in the Netherlands', 598 and 560.

considered the Netherlands to be a safe country.[512] This means that, in effect, the burden of protecting witnesses who are unhappy with their ICC protection falls on the Netherlands unless there is some legitimate reason to exclude them.

Whenever there are overlapping obligations, there will be a danger of buck passing, and this is the second potential problem. The efforts of the Dutch government to release itself from responsibility by citing the ICC's involvement are evidence of buck passing attempts. The overlapping nature of the witness protection obligations means that they exist in parallel; the operation of one does not cancel out the other. A consequence of this that has not yet been resolved is the question of when one system of protection takes priority over the other. It is clear that a person cannot be both protected under the ICCPP through relocation *and* protected as a refugee in the Netherlands. The law itself does not offer a solution as to which actor's obligations are primary. It would be detrimental to a witness if each actor ceased their protection efforts in the expectation that the other would continue with theirs.

One sure way to prevent the problems identified in this section is to remove the incentives for witnesses to apply for asylum in the Netherlands. If the protection offered by the ICC were made more certain and transparent, witnesses may not feel the need to turn to the Netherlands. That being said, for some individuals the opportunity to acquire a residence permit in a European country may be such an attractive prospect that no degree of ICC protection could overcome it.[513]

7.3.5 Conclusion

Of the different multi-actor situations covered in this chapter, protecting non-detained witnesses is the least complex. After permitting detained witnesses to apply for asylum in the Netherlands, it was highly unlikely that the possibility would be refused to non-detained witnesses. The earlier case of the detained Congolese witnesses paved the way for non-detained witnesses. That being said, the multi-actor nature of the situation, with both the ICC and the Netherlands having obligations to protect the witnesses, can give rise to implementation problems. Either the implementation of one set of obligations interferes with the ability of

---

[512] The Hague District Court, 8 March 2013, §3.
[513] van Wijk, 'When International Criminal Justice Collides with Principles of International Protection', 184.

the other actor to implement their obligations, or the circumstances allow for inadvertent or deliberate buck passing. Overcoming these issues with respect to non-detained witnesses is in some ways more important than addressing the issues facing detained witnesses. As alluded to in Section 7.2.5, it may be that the situation of detained witnesses never arises again. Non-detained witnesses, however, will continue to come to the Court, and so problems affecting the protection of their rights must be addressed.

7.4 Conclusion

For detained and non-detained witnesses, the fact that they can call on both the ICC and the Netherlands for protection offers opportunities and challenges. Opportunities in the sense that it provides different options, and therefore choices, for what their life will look like once they finish testifying at the ICC. Perhaps they wish to remain in the Netherlands with the well-established and well-understood status of a refugee, rather than moving to an ICC-appointed relocation State. However, with this choice come challenges. The interaction between the ICC protection obligations and those of the Netherlands might dilute the protection on offer, or might create gaps in protection.

The phenomenon of ICC witnesses applying for asylum in the Netherlands highlighted, in many ways, the complex legal questions that can arise in multi-actor situations. In relation to the case of the detained Congolese witnesses, the above sections separated the discussion on the protection of the rights to life, protection from inhuman treatment, and fair trial, from the discussion on the right to liberty. The framework and issues are distinct for these two categories, and each has its own complexities. With respect to the former, as far as the ICC was concerned, it had to determine how to balance competing obligations: the obligation to return detained witnesses to the sending State and the obligation to protect witnesses from threats to their safety. The Netherlands, for its part, faced questions such as whether it had jurisdiction over witnesses located on ICC premises, and how its own obligations under human rights law interacted with the protection obligations of the ICC. While it was determined that each actor did have obligations to protect the witnesses, the fact that these overlap created the possibility for implementation problems. In particular, there was the issue that the Netherlands relied on the assurances that the ICC received from the DRC in order to conclude that the risk faced by the witnesses in the sending State could be managed, and that therefore there were no obstacles to them being returned. This approach can be problematic, as the scope of protection that the ICC must provide is narrower, and the range of information available to each party on which to base their assessment of the situation can be different. Furthermore, it was suggested in Section 7.1.2.2 that the assurances provided to the ICC may not meet the strict requirements for assurances set out by the ECtHR.

Where the right to liberty of the detained witnesses was concerned, the issue was rather that the Netherlands and the ICC both denied that they owed protective obligations to the witnesses at all. The ICC claimed that it was merely maintaining custody of the witnesses on behalf of the DRC, and so lacked the power and authority to review the detention. The Netherlands, recalling the ECtHR decision in *Longa*, argued that the witnesses were outside of Dutch jurisdiction for the purposes of the right to liberty because they were held on the premises of the ICC. The result was a significant gap in protection, whereby no actor was willing to review the legality of the witnesses' detention.

Witnesses that come to the ICC to testify who are not detained present fewer legal complications than detained witnesses. The obligations of the ICC to protect the witnesses remain in place, and the Dutch domestic courts have firmly established that such individuals are entitled to submit applications for protection in the Netherlands. The potential complicating factor, namely whether their status as ICC witnesses would somehow impact on their ability to claim protection from the Dutch authorities, was set aside by the Dutch courts. ICC witnesses may apply for protection, and their involvement with the ICC offers no grounds for refusing this protection if the requirements are otherwise met.

With respect to the rights to life, protection from inhuman treatment, and fair trial of detained witnesses, and these same rights of non-detained witnesses, some clarity has now emerged following the plethora of domestic and ICC decisions. Despite the legal complexities that were raised when the protection claims were originally made, matters are now – for the most part – well understood, and the problems that can arise are more limited. With respect to the right to liberty of detained witnesses however, the difficulties of ensuring their protection from arbitrary detention at the seat of the ICC persist.

Having examined the multi-actor protection of witnesses at the seat of the ICC, this brings to a conclusion the substantive sections of the book. The previous chapters have endeavoured to show how complicated multi-actor human rights protection can be, and the problems that it can lead to in terms of the availability and quality of protection. They have also sought to show that, in some situations, understanding the complex obligations at play can go a long way to preventing and mitigating potential problems. The following chapter explores possible solutions to the problems caused by the multi-actor nature of human rights protection that cannot be easily resolved through a better understanding of the obligations involved.

PART III

Evaluation and Proposals

8

Evaluation and Proposals for Change

Taking Parts I and II together, we can conclude that the involvement of multiple actors in human rights protection at the ICC has the potential to negatively affect the rights of accused and witnesses. A number of the situations discussed in the previous chapters are susceptible to either implementation problems, structural problems, or both. In each instance the precise way in which the problem may manifest may be different, and it won't be the case that problems will always arise in the way discussed, or arise at all. However, the fact that the constellations of different obligations (or lack thereof, as the case may be) leave space for implementation and structural problems is an issue that requires attention.

This chapter will set out possible solutions that could mitigate the deficiencies in protection identified in Parts I and II. Some issues can be addressed with tailored solutions, applicable to specific circumstances; other challenges may benefit from a more systematic approach. There is no one-size-fits-all solution, and putting in place some solutions may cancel out the need for others. What follows are a series of suggestions, some complementary, some alternatives, some supported by the law, and some pushing the boundaries of what is currently accepted.

Before exploring these potential solutions, the chapter will summarise the problems identified in the different multi-actor situations. As the arrest stage presented no issues, it has not been included. Following on from this summary, the first type of solution to be examined will be changes to the law, whether by amendment, re-interpretation, or through changes by analogy. This is accorded first place because it is the solution that is most often turned to when the law is found to be inadequate. This is followed by practical suggestions tailored to specific situations: improving communication, increasing transparency, and considering domestic prosecutions. Thirdly, a proposal is made that sits somewhere between accepted law and not accepted law, possibly leaning towards the latter. The proposal is designed to address implementation problems, and involves a way of choosing between multiple actors with overlapping protection obligations. Fourthly, and pushing the boundaries even further, the author proposes a mechanism to bridge the gaps in protection that arise because of structural problems. This involves a mechanism that would encourage States to voluntarily assist the Court. To bolster this, the fifth section sets out reasons that can be put to States to further motivate them to volunteer.

8.1 Summary of the Problems Identified in the Situations of Multi-Actor Human Rights Protection

The first multi-actor situation analysed in the substantive chapters was the investigative stage of ICC proceedings, and more specifically, interrogations of suspects. At this point in proceedings, the potential issues for human rights protection concern the proper implementation of obligations. In Chapter 3 it was proposed that the actor leading the interrogation is the one that must provide the fair trial protections contained in Article 55 of the Rome Statute (such as the right to an interpreter and to remain silent), but the legal framework appears not to offer a way to determine which actor is leading. In cases of doubt, there is a concern that each actor will assume that the other will provide the protections, with the result that neither does. More cynically, it could be alleged that actors may seek to deliberately obscure which of them is in charge, to enable them to pass the buck.

The situation in which an accused is entitled, under certain circumstances, to interim release, was the first instance where the analysis of the different obligations revealed a structural problem. The ICC is under an obligation to uphold the right to liberty, as protected by the entitlement to interim release, but cannot do so without State assistance; States for their part are not obliged to provide this assistance. This produces a gap in protection that can leave an accused in unnecessary pre-trial detention.

If an accused is convicted, they will be sent to an enforcement State to serve their sentence. This situation was dealt with under both Part I and Part II, as it can involve both States Parties and the ICC host State. States Parties will be involved from the point where they agree to act as an enforcement State. Once a convicted person arrives in the enforcement State, the actors involved in their treatment while in detention will be the enforcement State and the ICC. As between these two actors, the respective roles and obligations of each are clear, and implementation problems are unlikely given the legal framework. The same cannot be said for the situation as between the ICC and the host State. The Netherlands can be potentially involved in the protection of convicted persons during the period between the conviction and their departure from the country. The obligations that the Netherlands has under the ECHR allocate it a safety-net role, such that the Netherlands is precluded from transferring a convicted person to an enforcement State where they would be at risk of harm. However, the Netherlands has demonstrated in its actions to date a reluctance in complying with these obligations. For instance, it may defer to the ICC's risk assessment rather than carry out its own, thereby diluting its safety-net role. In the (admittedly unlikely) situation where the ICC's choice of enforcement State poses a risk to the convicted person, this implementation problem leaves the convicted person vulnerable.

When it comes to accused persons who are acquitted by the ICC, problems can arise when those individuals cannot return to their home state because of safety concerns. This is also a situation that was addressed under Parts I and II, because both States Parties and the ICC host State can potentially be involved. The ICC must uphold the right to liberty of acquitted persons by releasing them immediately, but must also protect them from being sent to an unsafe country. The Court's ability to do this depends on States coming forward and agreeing to allow acquitted persons to reside on their territory. States, however, are under no obligation to do so, which can result in a structural problem. In the practice of the Court to date, namely in the *Ngudjolo* case, the Netherlands stepped in to fill the gap in protection that resulted from this structural problem. In the long term though, this is not a sustainable solution. As mentioned already, implementation problems can arise because of the Netherlands' reluctance to play this role, and it is an inequitable burden on the host State to expect it to.

With respect to witnesses, Part I addressed situations where witnesses could be protected in their home State and situations where their security required relocation abroad. Where a witness remains in their home State (referred to as the situation State), the potential problems concern the implementation of obligations. The confidentiality surrounding witness protection measures means that the discussion of obligations in Chapter 4 was inevitably incomplete; that being said, one assumes that as between the ICC and the situation State there is knowledge of the respective tasks and obligations of each actor, even if the information is not made public. If not, this leaves witnesses vulnerable to deficiencies in the implementation of protection. But there is another implementation problem in addition to this. The way in which the ICC's protection obligation in Article 68(1) of the Rome Statute is currently interpreted makes it difficult to ascertain when a witness will qualify for ICC protection and when they will not. If they do fall under ICC protection, then the situation State need only play a secondary role, supporting the ICC; if they do not fall under ICC protection, then the situation State must take up the primary protective role. According to Trial Chamber II, the risk facing a witness must be connected to their association with the Court, but as the discussion in Chapter 4 showed, this test is difficult to apply in practice. The result of this may be difficulties in establishing, in any given instance, whether the actor in charge of protecting the witness is the ICC or the situation State, with the possible consequence that neither will protect the witness.

The concerns of witnesses whose security situation requires their relocation abroad arise because of structural problems rather than implementation problems. Witnesses can only be relocated if a State agrees to host them, but States are under no obligation to agree to this. The fact that the ICC is the only actor with an obligation to protect the witnesses, but is unable to do so without assistance, leaves a gap in protection. The severity of the risk facing these witnesses means that the potential consequences of this structural problem are correspondingly severe.

Remaining with witnesses, in Part II attention was turned to the situation where a witness arrives at the seat of the ICC to testify, and once there, involve the Netherlands in their protection by submitting an application for protection to the Dutch authorities. The most controversial situations of this type involve detained witnesses, and as the discussion in Chapter 7 showed, different rights are at stake. First, detained witnesses may have concerns about being returned to the State that transferred them to the Court (the sending State). If witnesses distrust the ICC's ability to protect them in the sending State, these concerns may be such as to found an application to the Dutch authorities for protection from removal pursuant to the Netherlands' ECHR obligations. In such a case, the obligations of the ICC remain in effect, meaning that the Netherlands and the ICC are both obliged to protect the detained witnesses. This overlap can lead to implementation problems, including buck passing, which can leave detained witnesses vulnerable to slipping through the cracks in protection. The second right at stake is the right to liberty, as the lengthy process of making arrangements for their protection can cause detained witnesses to remain detained at the ICC Detention

Centre for unjustifiably extended periods. In this situation, the law as it stands leaves a substantial gap in protection: neither the ICC nor the Netherlands accepts that they have an obligation to protect the right to liberty of witnesses. The result is that detention in the ICC Detention Centre can continue, unchallenged, for extended periods.

Not all witnesses who seek protective measures while at the seat of the Court are detained. The final situation of multi-actor human rights protection considered in this study was that of non-detained witnesses at the seat of the Court. These witnesses have also chosen to turn to the Netherlands for protection, rather than rely on the ICC. If they would be at risk if returned to their home State, then the Netherlands is under an obligation not to remove them from the territory. As this creates a situation where, once again, both the ICC and the Netherlands have an overlapping obligation to protect the witnesses, it can lead to implementation problems. The ICC may rely on the Netherlands to provide protection, and the Netherlands may in turn rely on the ICC. The witness is left vulnerable by this, with the possibility that they will not receive protection from either side.

This summary of the implementation and structural problems that face accused and witnesses at the ICC demonstrates the challenges for human rights protection where multiple actors are involved. While some of the problems may be unlikely to occur in practice, or affect only a small number of individuals, the law as it presently stands is ill equipped to deal with these problems when they do arise. The remainder of this chapter is dedicated to exploring ways of mitigating these problems.

8.2 Changes to the Law

8.2.1 Statutory Changes

When the law is unsatisfactory, the first solution that is often considered is whether it can be changed. The summary in Section 8.1 highlights a number of instances where the way in which the law is structured is itself the problem. Structural problems leading to gaps in protection are present in the situations of interim release, acquittal, and witness relocation. If States were obliged to assist the ICC by accepting non-nationals on their territory, as opposed to the ICC having to rely on voluntary assistance, the gaps in protection could be closed. As such, this section considers the possibility of such a change being introduced in the Rome Statute protection framework.

Broadening the scope of the State Party cooperation regime to include an obligation to accept non-nationals on State Party territory would require an amendment to the Rome Statute. The legal hurdles to this are notable: first, a majority of the Assembly of States Parties would have to vote in favour of taking up a proposal for an amendment; second, two-thirds of States Parties would have to vote in favour of adopting an amendment; and third, seven-eighths of States Parties would have to ratify an amendment for it to come into force.[514] The procedure is therefore a complex one for which a high degree of consensus is necessary. For the reasons that will now be set out, this consensus will be difficult to achieve.

One obstacle to reaching consensus for an amendment concerns State sovereignty. Creating a system whereby the ICC can oblige a State to accept non-nationals on its territory would be a significant inroad into State sovereignty. One of the cornerstones of sovereignty is control over territory, including control over who may enter and remain on the territory. The Rome Statute is carefully drafted to accommodate this concern, as can be seen in the double consent regimes that apply to hosting convicted persons for the enforcement of sentences and to the hosting of protected witnesses. Once a State voluntarily agrees to host a convicted person or witness, then applicable obligations are activated regarding their treatment of them; however, the State is at no point compelled to host such individuals. Amending the Rome Statute cooperation framework to make this voluntary assistance compulsory would touch on an area of great sensitivity for States.

Another obstacle to consensus for an amendment is the lack of international precedent for this type of obligatory State cooperation. In the context of international criminal courts and tribunals, one can identify a range of different cooperation regimes in the various courts and tribunals. The ad hoc tribunals (the ICTY and ICTR) benefited from being established by the UN Security Council under Chapter VII of the UN Charter, and therefore cooperation with the tribunals was compulsory for all States. Despite this, neither Tribunal sought to use this power to impose an obligation on States to accept non-nationals on their territory, whether accused persons granted interim release, acquitted persons, or witnesses requiring protection. As was noted in Chapter 4, the judges of ICTR held that a State's obligation to cooperate in the relocation of witnesses and acquitted persons extended to consulting

---

[514] Article 121 of the Rome Statute. This is in fact a deviation from the general practice for multilateral treaties, whereby a State Party will not be bound by an amendment unless they have specifically consented to it, see Schabas, A Commentary on the Rome Statute, 1174.

with the Tribunal only; the State was not required to grant residence or extend special treatment to such individuals. Looking at the hybrid tribunals established over the last twenty years – including the Special Court for Sierra Leone, the Special Tribunal for Lebanon, the Extraordinary Chambers in the Courts of Cambodia, the Specialist Chambers of Kosovo, and so on – no tribunal has been afforded powers to compel cooperation from third States, and particularly not cooperation in the form of accepting non-nationals.

There is therefore, no precedent in the international criminal law context from which to draw inspiration for the necessary amendment to the Rome Statute. Limited precedent can be found beyond the criminal law context, particularly in the practice of the European Union (EU), but the particularities of this practice mean that, ultimately, it doesn't create a precedent for the amendment to the Rome Statute discussed here. Between 2015 and 2017, the EU saw unprecedented numbers of migrants entering EU territory fleeing conflict and violence. Most migrants entered through, and were required to be processed in, Italy or Greece, which were consequently subjected to onerous demands on their resources and infrastructure. To share the burden of the 'migration crisis', the EU Council passed measures to reallocate migrants in need of protection from Italy and Greece to other member States of the EU, with member States being subject to an obligation to accept such migrants.[515]

While the reallocation of migrants in the EU appears to be a relevant precedent for proposing changes to the Rome Statute cooperation regime, it is submitted that the situations are ultimately very different. The Treaty on the Functioning of the European Union, one of the core international instruments on which the EU system currently rests, provides in Article 78(3) for provisional measures to be taken to assist member States that are confronted by an 'emergency situation characterised by a sudden inflow of nationals of third countries'. The measures are therefore designed to be extraordinary in nature, adopted only in emergency situations. Perhaps more importantly, the reallocation measures rest on the notion of solidarity among EU States.[516] The high degree

---

[515] Council Decision (EU) 2015/1601 of 22 September 2015 establishing provisional measures in the area of international protection for the benefit of Italy and Greece, OJ 2015 No. L248/80, 24 September 2015 (Council Decision 2015/1601).

[516] 'The recent crisis situation in the Mediterranean prompted the Union institutions to immediately acknowledge the exceptional migratory flows in that region and call for concrete measures of solidarity towards the frontline Member States', Council Decision 2015/1601, §3.

of integration among EU States, politically and economically, both allows for and requires the availability of measures of this type. Such integration and solidarity is not present either among ICC States Parties inter se or between States Parties and the ICC itself. Ultimately, despite the availability of a legal basis for such measures, and the high degree of EU integration, the reallocation scheme failed to meet its ambitious target: of the 160,000 people that were meant to be relocated over a two-year period, after eighteen months only 12,000 people had been relocated.[517]

A final point, in addition to the concerns about State sovereignty and a lack of relevant precedent, is that the political climate is not conducive to expanding the powers of the ICC. Enthusiasm for a permanent and universal international criminal court has waned somewhat since the adoption of the Rome Statute in 1998. As matters stand, States are more likely to seek to curtail the powers of the ICC than expand them. In 2014, the government of Kenya put forward a proposal to the working group on amendments of the ASP that would prevent the Court from prosecuting Heads of State or their deputies during their term of office.[518] While the proposal was not adopted, it is emblematic of a lack of trust in the ICC on the part of some groups of States, and illustrates the existence of a political climate wherein the chances of an expansive amendment to the Rome Statute are very small.

In conclusion, while statutory change may be the solution that most quickly comes to mind when seeking to address structural issues caused by the law itself, amending the Rome Statute is unlikely to be a viable way of closing the protection gaps in situations of multi-actor human rights protection at the ICC. Two other alternatives, namely interpretation changes and changes by analogy, offer more promise.

8.2.2 Interpretation Changes

The structural problems we see at the interim release, acquittal, and witness relocation stages would need a statutory amendment to resolve,

---

[517] European Parliament Directorate-General for Internal Policies, Policy Department C: Citizens' Rights and Constitutional Affairs, 'Implementation of the 2015 Council Decision establishing provisional measures in the area of international protection for the benefit of Italy and of Greece', PE 583, 2017 (Implementation of the 2015 Council Decision), 7.

[518] United Nations Secretary General, 'Rome Statute of the International Criminal Court, Rome, 17 July 1998, Kenya: Proposal for Amendments', C.N.1026.2013.TREATIES-XVIII.10 (Depositary Notification), 14 March 2014.

but other problems could be addressed by ICC judges adopting a different approach to the existing provisions. This is not amendment by another name, but rather is based on plausible alternative interpretations of the law. The previous chapters identify two instances of this, both concerning witnesses. The details of the arguments were presented in the relevant parts of the substantive chapters, and the following is merely a summary.

The first instance of when an alternative interpretation of the law would ameliorate inadequacies in human rights protection concerns the scope of witness protection. Trial Chamber II in the *Katanga* case held that, in order to trigger the ICC's witness protection obligations under Article 68(1) of the Rome Statute, the risk facing a witness must be connected to their involvement with the Court. In setting out what involvement with the Court means, the Chamber adopted a restrictive approach based on a distinction between three types of risk: (1) risk incurred on account of cooperation with the Court, (2) risk arising from the broader human rights situation in the situation State, and (3) risk of treatment that would amount to persecution such as would found an asylum claim under the Refugee Convention.[519] As discussed, this approach is difficult to apply, especially in borderline cases, with the result that witnesses may be excluded from the protection they need.

The narrow scope of protection would not present such a problem if the State apparatus was able to provide a satisfactory level of protection instead. However, in the case of situation States, the very reason why the ICC needs a witness protection regime is because the State apparatus is lacking. That being said, even where the State does have the capacity, the fact that the current interpretation of Article 68(1) is difficult to apply in practice will leave some witnesses in a grey area, with the possibility that the ICC will assume that it is the State's role to protect them, and the State assuming that it is the ICC's role.

An alternative interpretation of Article 68(1) was proposed in Chapter 4, namely that any risk a witness faces should trigger the ICC's obligations, as long as the risk is not *patently* unconnected with their involvement with the Court. As has already been argued, this is the approach that complies with the Article 21(3) test. Adopting this interpretation instead of the interpretation of Trial Chamber II would make witness protection more inclusive and would reduce the number of witnesses falling into the grey area. By making it clear when the ICC must act to

[519] *Katanga/Ngudjolo*, 9 June 2011, §§59–62.

protect a witness, and when the State must act, this implementation problem for witness protection could be addressed.

The second instance that calls for an alternative interpretation of the law concerns detained witnesses at the seat of the ICC, and involves the obligations of both the ICC and the Netherlands. Chapter 7 discussed the obligations and problems surrounding the right to liberty of detained witnesses for the time that they are detained on ICC premises awaiting the outcome of a protection claim, whether submitted to the ICC, or to the Netherlands, or both. The discussion concluded that, following the majority decisions of the Trial and Appeals Chambers in the detained Congolese witnesses case, there was a gap in protection. Neither the ICC nor the Netherlands was deemed to have any obligations to protect the right to liberty of detained witnesses in those circumstances, effectively leaving the witnesses in a legal limbo and unable to challenge their detention. However unsatisfactory this outcome, it is the current state of the law.

With respect to the ICC's obligations, in Chapter 7 it was argued that the dissenting opinions of Judges Van den Wyngaert and Song in those same ICC decisions represented a sounder interpretation of the law. Under this alternative view, the ICC would have an obligation to review the detention of detained witnesses whose time on ICC premises had been extended due to an application for protection (regardless of the actor to which the application was addressed). In the author's opinion, this is the interpretation that complies with the Article 21(3) test. With respect to the Netherlands' obligations, it was argued that the decision of the ECtHR in *Longa* was incorrect as a matter of law, because it overlooked the fact that the Netherlands was involved in the detained witnesses' situation. This would have been enough to bring them within Dutch jurisdiction, and so activate the Netherlands' right to liberty obligations.

8.2.3 Changes by Analogy

If the *Longa* case were revisited, this would improve human rights protection at the seat of the Court, but the protection would be limited to the particular facts of that case. However, if an entirely different approach to the question of Dutch jurisdiction over individuals on the ICC premises were taken, this would expand the protective role of the Netherlands still further. Such an approach could be based on the analogous application of principles derived from the ECtHR case of *Bosphorus*, something which has not been done before.

EVALUATION AND PROPOSALS FOR CHANGE 219

Before setting out this proposed approach, it is important to stress that it is not proposed that the Netherlands should always have jurisdiction over individuals on the ICC's premises. There are both legal and pragmatic reasons to suspend the host State's jurisdiction over the portion of its territory where the ICC premises are located. Legally speaking, the terms of the Headquarters Agreement place the ICC premises outside of the Netherlands' de jure control: the Dutch authorities cannot enter the premises without permission, carry arms on the premises, and so on. Pragmatically speaking, if the Netherlands always had jurisdiction, and could be potentially responsible for the treatment of individuals located on the premises of the ICC, the Netherlands would be motivated to interfere in the operations of the Court. This would be counter to the distinct legal personality of international organisations. In addition, if such a precedent were established, States would in future be reluctant to host international tribunals at all for fear of incurring liability. That being said, there is a way of balancing the competing concerns of protecting human rights and maintaining the independence of international organisations.

The ECtHR has been dealing with the human rights dimension of the relationship between international organisations and States for some time, and has issued a number of decisions in this regard. While the case law is at times contradictory and problematic,[520] on the whole it reflects a balance between important interests. On the one hand, there is a need to preserve the distinct personality of international organisations, and States' ability to create and use these organisations to further international cooperation. On the other hand, States cannot be permitted to use these organisations to shield themselves from needing to comply with their human rights obligations. The *Bosphorus* case,[521] which is one of the early cases of the ECtHR on this point, developed a satisfactory balance between these interests. The principles that can be distilled from these decisions are termed by the author 'the *Bosphorus* principles', and it is submitted, should be seen as reflecting customary international law.[522]

---

[520] See for example, Tobias Lock, 'Beyond *Bosphorus*: The European Court of Human Rights' Case Law on the Responsibility of Member States of International Organisations under the European Convention on Human Rights' (2010) 10 *Human Rights Law Review*, 529.

[521] *Case of Bosphorus Hava Yollari Turizm Ve Ticaret Anonim Sirketi v. Ireland*, Application no. 45036/98, Judgment, 30 June 2005 (*Bosphorus*, 30 June 2005).

[522] The following examples are evidence of this acceptance. Firstly, the International Law Commission Commentaries on the Articles on the Responsibility of International Organisations (ARIO) cited with approval this case law of the ECtHR, suggesting that the jurisprudence represents general international law on the subject ('Commentaries on the Articles on the Responsibility of International Organisations' (2011) Vol. 2, Part 2,

The principles will be set out first, followed by how they can be applied to the ICC–host State context.

The *Bosphorus* case was brought against Ireland by an airline company.[523] Pursuant to a European Community (EC) Regulation, Ireland was required to impound an aircraft owned by the applicant.[524] The question was whether, in so doing, Ireland had violated Article 1 of Protocol 1 ECHR. The matter of jurisdiction was never at issue, as it was accepted that the action could be attributed to the Irish authorities and the impounding of the aircraft had taken place on Irish territory. The question was whether, in complying with the EC Regulation, Ireland had violated Article 1 of Protocol 1, and it was held that it had not. From the ECtHR's reasoning in the case, the following principles can be discerned.

First, that States are entitled to transfer some element of sovereign power to an international organisation in order to pursue cooperation in certain fields.[525] This is a logical stance, especially as this is the process by which the ECtHR itself came into being. Such a transfer of competence is necessary if international organisations are to fulfil the purposes and functions for which they were created. Second, that where such a transfer is made, it does not follow that States are absolved of the obligations they have under human rights law. The transfer of competence can only be made if human rights can still be secured, and the obligations of the State continue even after the transfer of competence to an international organisation.[526] If this were not the case, it would constitute a significant limitation on the effectiveness of human rights.[527] Of all the cases prior to and subsequent to *Bosphorus* dealing with this issue, this second principle is always constant and invariably reiterated by the ECtHR.[528] The second *Bosphorus* principle has been taken up by the Human Rights Committee with respect to the ICCPR.[529]

Yearbook of the International Law Commission). Secondly, the Human Rights Committee has cited *Case of Matthews* v. *the United Kingdom*, Application no. 24833/94, Judgment, 18 February 1999 (*Matthews*, 18 February 1999), a prelude to the *Bosphorus*, with approval in *Sayadi and Vinck* v. *Belgium*, Communication No. 1472/2006, 29 December 2008 (*Sayadi*, 29 December 2008), §5.8.

[523] *Bosphorus*, 30 June 2005.
[524] *Bosphorus*, 30 June 2005, §110.
[525] *Bosphorus*, 30 June 2005, §152.
[526] The Bosphorus case adopted this principle from previous case law, such as *Waite and Kennedy*, 18 February 1999, §51, and *Matthews*, 18 February 1999, §32.
[527] *Bosphorus*, 30 June 2005, §154.
[528] See *Waite and Kennedy*, 18 February 1999, §51.
[529] *Sayadi*, 29 December 2008, §5.8.

In recognition of the importance that States should not use international organisations to avoid their human rights obligations, *Bosphorus* principle number three requires that whenever a State has discretion in how it implements an obligation imposed on it by an international organisation, the State must use this discretion to secure human rights.[530] As the ECtHR spelt out in a subsequent case, where there is discretion the State must do everything possible to avoid a violation of human rights.[531]

It will sometimes be the case that no discretion exists for a State in carrying out an obligation imposed on it by an international organisation. In such a situation, the potential for conflict between the first and second *Bosphorus* principles is clear. The fourth principle addresses these situations of no discretion, is a compromise between the first two principles, and in deference to the separate legal personality of international organisations,[532] is a way of reconciling them. The fourth principle is as follows: when a State is acting pursuant to an obligation deriving from its membership of an international organisation, its actions are presumed to be justified where the international organisation in question has equivalent or comparable human rights protection to that of the ECHR. The presumption can be rebutted only if, under the circumstances of a particular case, the protection of Convention rights was 'manifestly deficient'.[533] This presumption is called the 'presumption of equivalent protection'. On the facts of *Bosphorus* itself, it was held that the EU did have equivalent human rights protection to that provided under the ECHR, and no manifest deficiency was found. As such, the outcome was that Ireland's impounding of the aircraft was justified, and it was not responsible for any human rights violations that may have occurred.

The proposal of this section is to remedy deficiencies in multi-actor human rights protection by applying the *Bosphorus* principles analogously to the question of host State jurisdiction. The argument is as follows: as the ICC is on Dutch territory, the Netherlands prima facie has jurisdiction over individuals held on the Court's premises. Due to the

---

[530] 'It remains the case that a State would be fully responsible under the Convention for all acts falling outside *its* strict legal obligations' (*Bosphorus*, 30 June 2005, §157).
[531] Case of *Nada v Switzerland*, Application no. 10593/08, Judgment, 12 September 2012, §§196–7.
[532] Cedric Ryngaert and Holly Buchanan, 'Member State Responsibility for the Acts of International Organisations' (2011) 7 *Utrecht Law Review*, 131.
[533] *Bosphorus*, 30 June 2005, §156.

fact that the ICC is an international organisation, Dutch jurisdiction is suspended because competence has been transferred to the Court. However, that transfer is premised on the assumption that the ICC guarantees comparable or equivalent protection to that which the Netherlands is obliged to provide under human rights law. If that assumption is rebutted, then the Netherlands will once again have jurisdiction over individuals on the ICC premises. The assumption would be rebutted if it is found that, in a particular instance, the protection is manifestly deficient.

This approach could improve the human rights protection of individuals located at the seat of the Court, including detained witnesses, convicted persons, acquitted persons, and accused entitled to interim release. It would no longer be necessary to be outside the ICC premises to make a claim for protection. The situation of accused entitled to interim release would show particular improvement.[534] If an accused cannot find a State willing to host them on an interim basis, the law as it currently stands provides no recourse. Being on the ICC premises means the accused is outside Dutch jurisdiction, and so the fact that the ICC is unable to protect their right to liberty is not the Netherlands' concern.[535] However, if the *Bosphorus* principles were applied by analogy, this would not be the end of the story. If an accused in this predicament sought to protect their right to liberty by seeking release onto the territory of the Netherlands, the latter could not outright refuse. It would have to go through the steps dictated by the *Bosphorus* principles. First, by asking whether the ICC provides equivalent protection to that which the Netherlands is required to provide under the ECHR. The answer in this case would be no: the ICC cannot guarantee that an accused entitled to

---

[534] Other situations would also benefit, but in those there comes a point in time when the individual can apply for Dutch protection, which is not the case for the interim release stage. Detained witnesses and acquitted persons fall within the 'exception to the exception' established by the District Court of The Hague, and so can apply for protection from removal from the ICC premises. Convicted persons can apply for protection at the point when the Dutch authorities begin their transport to the point of departure from the Netherlands.

[535] With respect to ICC convicted and acquitted persons, Chapter 6 discussed how at the point at which they leave the ICC Detention Centre and are transported to the airport by the Dutch authorities, they enter Dutch jurisdiction. Once this occurs, they can apply for protection from removal. This is not the case for accused at the interim release stage. These individuals must remain in the ICC Detention Centre until a State agrees to host them. Interim release will in nearly every instance be dependent on the accused residing and remaining in the designated country. As such, if they sought to remain in the Netherlands, this would breach the terms of their release.

interim release will be granted it. Even if the protection were deemed to be equivalent, the next question would be whether protection is manifestly deficient in the circumstances of that particular case. The answer would be yes: the ICC is unable to secure the assistance of a State to host the accused on an interim basis, which compromises the accused's right to liberty.

The result of applying the *Bosphorus* principles by analogy to the host State context could result in better protection of human rights at the seat of the Court. However, there is a downside. Situations that now have a structural problem, such as interim release, may instead acquire an implementation problem. If both the ICC *and* the Netherlands have obligations to protect human rights, an ensuing lack of clarity or a propensity to buck pass may cancel out the positive effect that the solution proposed in this section seeks to achieve. For this reason, broadening the protective obligations of the Netherlands would ideally be combined with the solution proposed in Section 8.4.

8.3 Practical Solutions for Particular Problems

8.3.1 Improved Communication

Leaving to one side proposals for changes in the law, the discussion now turns to more pragmatic solutions that can be put into effect without changes to the legal framework. Some of the implementation problems identified at the different stages could be addressed by means of a relatively simple solution: improved communication between the actors.

As set out in Section 8.2.2, adopting a different interpretation of the scope of risk under Article 68(1) of the Rome Statute would reduce the number of witnesses falling into the grey area between ICC and State protection. In the absence of a change in legal approach, improved communication could help prevent witnesses from being made vulnerable in this way. When an ICC witness appeals to the Court for protection, but the ICC considers that the risk they face is not connected to their involvement with the Court, it should communicate the reported risk to the situation State. The situation State then knows that the witness is not being protected by the ICC, and that it falls to the State to step in. Such communication could be done in practice through, for example, standard channels of communication that are to be used whenever the circumstances described present themselves. It is more than possible – and even likely – that this is already done, but the confidentiality surrounding witness protection means that it is not made public. Even if the broader interpretation of Article 68(1) were adopted, communication of this type would still be helpful to ensure effective witness protection.

Improved communication could also enhance the protection of accused. During interrogations, safeguarding the right to a fair trial is dependent on it being clear which actor is leading the interrogation, as this actor must provide the safeguards. There are a number of ways to achieve this. One is for the parties to confer before the interrogation takes place and specifically agree on the issue. This could be put in writing, so that if problems arise there is no dispute as to which actor was responsible for the suspect. Another option is for the actors to agree that when certain, previously agreed, circumstances are present, one actor is automatically considered to be in charge. For example, whenever a member of the ICC OTP is present, the ICC is presumed to be leading the investigation, regardless of whether it is an ICC staff member asking the questions.

These two situations illustrate the value of more formal communication mechanisms, such as could be set out in written agreements between the parties. Informal, and even behind-the-scenes communication, also has its benefits. Indeed, it is very likely that this is precisely how much of the business between States and the ICC is conducted, but naturally not discussed in the public sphere. One instance where informal communication will be of value is for convicted persons who have not yet been transferred to an enforcement State. If the convicted person believes they will be at risk of harm in the enforcement State designated by the ICC, they may seek protection from removal from the Netherlands. This places the Netherlands in the difficult situation of having to choose between its human rights obligations and its obligations as ICC host State. If the Netherlands informs the ICC of its apprehensions concerning the designated enforcement State, this gives the Court the chance to change the designation before matters come to a head, and so avoid the problem all together.

8.3.2 Greater Transparency in Witness Protection

Witnesses that arrive at the seat of the ICC and request protection, whether detained or non-detained, claim to do so because they lack faith in the ICC's ability to effectively protect them. The ensuing implementation problems, including buck passing, can result in witnesses not getting the protection they need. For this problem there is a particular solution: address the reasons why detained witnesses turn to the Netherlands for protection in the first place. Reducing the Netherlands' involvement in the situation reduces the chance of buck passing.

There are several reasons why a witness turns away from ICC protection. Overall, the lack of transparency surrounding witness protection through the ICCPP can make protection in the Netherlands, with its known guarantees and safeguards, preferable to a system that is largely unknown. As explained in Chapter 7, the non-detained witnesses who applied for protection in the Netherlands cited among their reasons the fact that it was unclear whether they would have the same procedural and substantive rights if relocated through the ICCPP that they would otherwise be entitled to under international human rights and refugee law. The uncertainties they highlighted concerned access to legal assistance during the ICCPP relocation process and access to review of decisions made about their protective measures.[536] If details about the procedures and rights available for witnesses within the ICCPP were accessible and properly communicated to the witnesses, this may go some way to increasing trust in the ICC protection regime. If the ICCPP does not provide the same level of protection as otherwise available under human rights law, the ICC should consider making changes to it.

8.3.3 Domestic Prosecutions

Detained witnesses have a more particular reason for seeking protection from the Netherlands as an alternative to protection from the ICC. If the ICC decides that the risk the detained witness faces in the sending State is severe, and cannot be resolved through the use of assurances, the ICC would be precluded from returning that witness. The question then is, where is the witness to go? They are now in the same position as any other witness seeking relocation, and suffer from the same gap in protection, as States are not obliged to receive them and host them. This problem is difficult enough for witnesses with no criminal history; for detained witnesses, relocating them may be almost impossible. Potential relocation States will be particularly unwilling to host detained witnesses if the crime for which they were convicted in the sending State was a violent one, or a crime that would otherwise indicate that the witness would be a threat to public safety.

---

[536] These reasons are listed in The Hague District Court, 8 March 2013, §5. See also Irving, 'Protecting Witnesses at the ICC from Refoulement'.

A way to lessen a relocation State's concerns could be to arrange for the detained witness to remain detained once they reach the relocation State. If the individual is not at liberty, this lessens the danger that they may pose to society, as well as the political undesirability of hosting the witness. Detention, however, requires a lawful basis. One option could be to cooperate with the sending State, in the sense that the relocation State would be enforcing the sending State's sentence on its behalf. This may not be feasible if the sending State is unhappy with the detained witness not being returned, as will likely be the case. It will also be problematic if the circumstances surrounding the detention in the sending State are alleged to not be human rights compliant; for example if it is alleged that the trial was not fair. Such concerns would have been central if this approach were proposed in the detained Congolese witnesses case. Prior to their transfer to the ICC, the witnesses had been held in detention in the DRC for an extended period without formal charges being brought, a clear violation of their rights.

The other option is for the relocation State to prosecute the witness itself, where a valid basis for jurisdiction exists. This approach is analogous to that taken by countries that find themselves with alleged international criminals on their territory that they cannot extradite. Germany prosecuted a Rwandan man for involvement in the 1994 genocide because it could not extradite him to Rwanda due to human rights concerns. Rather than allow him to live freely in Germany, charges were brought.[537]

While such prosecutions can be a complicated and expensive endeavour, they are, in the author's opinion, a viable option in some situations. The ICC could provide logistical support, cooperating with the domestic judicial system in matters of evidence and testimony. Financial support could be supplied through the Special Fund. Admittedly, this was not the original idea for the money in the Special Fund, but the principle of States being able to host witnesses in a cost-neutral arrangement is maintained. In this set up, witnesses can be protected without compromising the fight against impunity.

8.4 Mechanism for Choosing between Actors

This chapter up until now has, for the most part, dealt with particular issues that can be addressed with particular solutions, whether this involves a change in the law or the use of practical measures. Attention now turns to more general solutions. This section will explore a solution potentially

---

[537] 'Germany gives life sentence to Rwandan for genocide', DW, 29 December 2015.

applicable to all situations in which both the ICC *and* State(s) have an obligation to protect an individual at the same time. For instance, the situation when both the ICC and the Netherlands have an obligation to ensure that acquitted persons are not sent to a State where they would be at risk. It is in these situations that implementation problems arise, either because of a lack of clarity as to which actor must act, or because of deliberate buck passing.

To combat these issues, the author proposes a way of prioritising the obligations of one actor over those of the other. Rather than multiple actors being required to act at the same time, the actors are placed in an ordinal arrangement: one actor becomes the primary duty bearer, the other the secondary duty bearer, and so on. The primary duty bearer will have first responsibility for protecting the individual in a given situation, while the secondary duty bearer need only act where the primary duty bearer fails to do so.

Prioritising obligations and creating an ordinal arrangement of duty bearers removes ambiguity and makes it harder to 'pass the buck'; the primary duty bearer knows it must act, and the other actors know this also. The question then becomes: On what basis is this prioritisation to be done? What criteria determine one actor to be the primary duty bearer and the other the secondary one? No hierarchy is provided by the obligations themselves, as is the case in international law generally, and so it is necessary to look to other principles that may assist. Of the different options, two seem the most plausible: the notion of control and the notion of individual choice.

As an option for organising the ordinal arrangement of obligations, control benefits from both an intuitive appeal and a broad acceptance in international law. It is intuitively appealing that the actor with most control over an individual should be the first to act on an obligation to protect their rights. For example, the State on whose territory an individual is located has more control over the protection of their rights than a different State. This intuitive value is recognised in many areas of international law, in which the criterion of control plays a major role. In human rights law, the exercise of extraterritorial jurisdiction is intrinsically linked to control.[538] In peacekeeping missions and collaborative military action, it has been argued that control is central to allocating responsibility.[539] In the law of

---

[538] For an overview, see Sarah Joseph and Adam Fletcher, 'Scope of Application', in Daniel Moeckli, Sangeeta Shah, and Sandesh Sivakumaran (eds.), *International Human Rights Law* (Oxford University Press 2014), 129–38.

[539] Boutin, Bérénice, *The Role of Control in Allocating International Responsibility in Collaborative Military Operations* (Academisch Proefschrift, 2015).

occupation, the obligations of the occupying State are engaged when a certain degree of control over territory is exercised.[540] In environmental law, responsibility for transboundary harm is tied to the State of origin's control over the territory from which the harm originates.[541] In the law on State responsibility, control can be a deciding factor for the attribution of conduct to a State.[542]

In the context of multi-actor human rights protection at the ICC, the question of which actor has control, or the most control, over an individual will depend on the facts. Detained witnesses seeking protection at the seat of the Court triggers the obligations of both the ICC and the Netherlands. Both actors have protection obligations at the same time to ensure that the witness is not returned to a country where they would be at risk. So which actor is the primary duty bearer that must provide protection to the exclusion of the other actor? In the detained Congolese witnesses case, the control criterion would have indicated the ICC: the witnesses were on ICC premises, the ICC had control over their movement and detention conditions, and the Netherlands could not access the detained witnesses without the permission of the Court.

Even with respect to the same individuals in the same situation, the control criterion can point in different directions depending on the circumstances. Remaining with the detained witnesses, the author concluded in Chapter 7 that, as matters stand, neither the ICC nor the Netherlands accepts the existence of obligations to protect the right to liberty in those circumstances. However, in the previous sections of this chapter, the author argued for an opposite interpretation of the law in which both actors would have such an obligation. While this would remedy the gap in protection, it may produce its own difficulties: if both actors must act, it is possible that neither will. In that case, the author's earlier proposals would fix the structural problem but create an implementation problem. This is where the ordinal arrangement of duty bearers comes in.

With respect to the right to liberty aspects of the detained Congolese witnesses' case, the Netherlands may have lacked physical control over the witnesses but it did have control over the length of the detention. It

---

[540] Tristan Ferraro, 'Determining the Beginning and End of an Occupation under International Humanitarian Law' (2012) 94 *International Review of the Red Cross*, 133.
[541] 'Articles on Prevention of Transboundary Harm from Hazardous Activities with Commentaries' (2001) Vol. 2, Part 2, *Yearbook of the International Law Commission*, 149–50.
[542] Article 8, ILC Articles on State Responsibility.

was due to the lengthy period of time taken to decide on the protection claims, which involved the Dutch government missing several court imposed deadlines, that the period of detention was so long. The ICC had made clear that the witnesses were only held in the ICC Detention Centre because of the ongoing protection applications. This placed the Netherlands in a position of control, and so with respect to the right to liberty, would make it the primary duty bearer according to the control criterion.

Non-detained witnesses seeking protection are in a similar position to detained witnesses vis-à-vis the Netherlands and the ICC, but in their case the notion of control is less helpful for identifying a primary duty bearer. The witnesses are at the seat of the ICC, and the ICC is in the process of finding them a safe place to relocate to, or perhaps has already done so. This would point to the ICC as being the actor with more control over the situation. However, one could equally say that as the witnesses are free on Dutch territory, and since the Dutch legal system is already dealing with their protection requests, the Netherlands has a greater degree of control. In cases such as these, it may be more helpful to use a different criterion to compose the ordinal arrangement.

It is not always appropriate to rely on control to determine how an individual's rights will be protected and by which actor. In some situations, this choice is better left to the right holder. Their preference will dictate the primary duty bearer, and the other duty bearer will automatically assume the role of secondary duty bearer.

Returning to non-detained witnesses, if their protection application is granted *and* a relocation State is found, deferring to their individual choice would mean allowing the witness to decide where they want to live and which protection system to reside under. But this solution is not unproblematic. The fact that the witness has chosen to make an application to remain in the Netherlands makes it likely that this will be their choice. This will place an undue burden on the Netherlands if the relocation State is not as 'attractive' in terms of living standards. Then again the problem may not be as pronounced as one might think. It should not be taken for granted that witnesses would choose to remain in the Netherlands if they are offered a reasonable alternative that was more familiar in terms of language, culture, and tradition. In any case, for individual choice to be meaningful the witness must be presented with a real choice.

Deciding between control and individual choice is ultimately a policy decision, affected by the values that the decision maker considers most important. It may be appropriate to compose the ordinal arrangement differently for different categories of individual, or use both criteria to come up with a solution that reflects the range of concerns involved. This raises the question of who decides what criteria are relevant, and how they are applied in individual instances. The discussion in the following section on how to pinpoint a volunteer State is also highly relevant to determining an ordinal arrangement of obligations, in particular the idea that the ASP could act to set up a decision-making body to this end. To these ideas we now turn.

8.5 Mechanism to Pinpoint a Volunteer State

Having considered a general solution for implementation problems (establishing an ordinal arrangement of obligations), this section explores a general solution for structural problems, namely encouraging States to assist the ICC voluntarily.

As noted in Section 8.2.1, amending the Rome Statute so that States are obliged to assist the ICC in situations where now they need only volunteer would not be feasible. And yet, this means that in the multi-actor situations that suffer from structural gaps in protection, human rights protection will continue to be inadequate. If the author's proposals regarding broadening the jurisdiction of the host State were accepted, then this would go some way to remedying these gaps; but it is not sustainable in the long term, nor is it equitable, to place this disproportionate burden on the Netherlands.

Voluntary assistance can take different forms with different degrees of formality and bindingness. Some of these have been discussed in the substantive chapters. For instance, when a State agrees to host a relocated witness, it may sign a relocation agreement with the Court, but the hosting can also be done under less formal, ad hoc arrangements. The same is true for hosting accused granted interim release, and for taking in at-risk acquitted persons. Flexibility is important when encouraging States to assist the Court. It is for this reason that different options exist for States willing to help with witness relocation: they may act as a relocation State, contribute to the Special Fund, or act as a platform State.

A significant problem with voluntary measures is that they suffer from their own version of buck passing. It is relatively easy to hide among a large number of States Parties, and each potential volunteer State may question why it should be their responsibility to volunteer, when there are so many other States that could also do so. Because of this obstacle, it is helpful to think of criteria to pinpoint which State would be the most appropriate volunteer in any given instance. In this way, the proposal is similar to the mechanism for choosing between multiple duty bearers discussed in the previous section. While the pinpointed State could always still refuse, there would arguably be more pressure on it to act.

The idea here is not to provide a list of definitive criteria for identifying the most appropriate volunteer State, but to put forward some suggestions. Anything more ambitious than this would be outside the scope of this book. Inspiration for these suggestions has been found in refugee law. The problem of how to allocate refugees among different countries is an ongoing issue of a similar nature to the one that faces the ICC. Kritzman-Amir looks at this area of law and distils a number of considerations to guide which State(s) should take more refugees, and which fewer.[543] These can be translated to the context of voluntary measures at the ICC.

The first consideration is absorption capacity, a socio-economic criterion which looks at State gross national product (GNP), life expectancy, land reserves, employment, etc. to determine whether a State could absorb refugees without it having a significant impact on the economy and the State. The second consideration is the existence of special solidarity bonds. These are bonds that might exist between allied countries or between former colonies and colonial powers, which would make a State suitable to take in refugees from that country. The third consideration is whether a State bears responsibility for the immigration, for example because of the exploitation of the mineral, natural, and/or work resources of the other State. In the ICC context, this might be relevant where one State has aggravated the conflict in which the crimes took place. Finally, there are cultural and ethnic considerations. This works two ways. On the one hand, a country may claim that it is too culturally distinct from the refugee to be able to reasonably accommodate them. On the other hand, there may be significant similarities in culture that makes a State or group of States particularly suitable to take an individual in.

Factors that would fall under the first consideration played a role in how the reallocation of migrants was decided during the 'migrant crisis' in the EU. When the decision was made to put in place mandatory reallocation of migrants among EU member States (discussed in

---

[543] Tally Kritzman-Amir, 'Not in My Backyard: On the Morality of Responsibility-Sharing in Refugee Law' (2008–2009) 34 *Brooklyn Journal of International Law*, 355, from 372.

Section 8.2.1), factors were needed to guide how many migrants each State would be required to take in. This was done on the basis of four elements.[544] First, carrying a weight of 40 per cent, was the size of the population, as reflective of the State's capacity to absorb a certain number of incoming migrants. Second, also carrying a weight of 40 per cent, was the State's total gross domestic product (GDP), as reflective of the wealth of the country and therefore of the absorption capability of the economy. Third, with a weight of 10 per cent, was the average number of asylum applications and of resettled refugees over the timeframe of 2010–2014, as reflective of the protection efforts made by the State in the recent past. And finally, also carrying a weight of 10 per cent, was the unemployment rate in the State, as indicative of the capacity to integrate refugees.

In addition to the factors identified by Kritzman-Amir, and those used by the EU, there are particular factors that will be relevant for specific stages of ICC proceedings. For individuals who have been granted interim release and need a place to await their trial, it may be appropriate to focus on the State that surrendered the accused to the Court. This is particularly so if the accused was residing there when they were arrested and surrendered, but less so if the accused was just passing through. For accused that have been acquitted and witnesses in need of relocation, an emphasis may be placed on pinpointing a country with a similar culture and language. This is because these categories of individuals have concluded their involvement with the Court, and need to be able to integrate into their new home on a more permanent basis.

If factors that would guide the pinpointing of a volunteer State could be agreed upon, the next matter to resolve would be designating a decision maker. It is proposed that this role would fall most appropriately to the ASP. In its position as the representative organ of the ICC in which all States Parties have a voice, the ASP could create a mechanism for deciding, following a hearing of the views of the relevant actors, which State is best placed to volunteer to protect the human rights of an individual witness or accused. Creating such a mechanism has the distinct advantage that, instead of each State being addressed in a bilateral manner by either the ICC or the affected individual, and declining to assist based on the State's individual concerns, States could come together to seek a multilateral solution. This mechanism could also determine which factors are to be taken into account when making a decision, and put forward solutions that fit the specific circumstances

---

[544] Implementation of the 2015 Council Decision, 7

of a case. In this sense, the political nature of the ASP is helpful, as the question being dealt with intrinsically concerns matters of politics and policy. Furthermore, it is already established as a forum for States to express their views.

There are numerous options as to the form that the ASP mechanism could take. At one end of the spectrum would be an informal, cooperative forum for the exchange of views, akin to a roundtable discussion. This has the benefit of creating a cooperative atmosphere in which solutions are backed by consensus. At the other end of the spectrum the ASP could set up a more formal mechanism, akin to an adversarial proceeding, in which different States would communicate their views to a decision maker who makes the final determination. While this option would increase the likelihood of pinpointing one particular State, it may alienate States with its forcefulness. Possibly the mechanism used will depend on the particular instance of multi-actor human rights protection being dealt with.

Creating a mechanism like the one described is one step, but getting States to participate in it is another. For this reason, the next section is dedicated to arguments that can be put to States, including the State identified by the ASP mechanism, to encourage and motivate voluntary assistance.

8.6 Reasons for States to Volunteer

Voluntary measures may be a tool to prevent problems with human rights protection, but their utility is limited by the very fact that they are voluntary. Ultimately, there is nothing that can compel a State to agree to them. To really address problems with human rights protection, this section will briefly set out some arguments that can be used to push States into action. These arguments stem from the principle of equity. Equity, meaning 'what is fair and reasonable in the administration of justice',[545] provides two concepts relevant to the ICC context: the principle of estoppel and the duty of care. While these two are related, they will be dealt with separately.

The general principle of estoppel is used to support the following argument: when States came together in Rome to establish the ICC, they announced themselves to be in favour of human rights and against the

---

[545] Francesco Francioni, 'Equity in International Law' (2013) *Max Planck Encyclopedia of Public International Law*, §1.

'unimaginable atrocities that deeply shock the conscience of mankind'.[546] These States established an international criminal justice institution to be the heart of a project aimed at fighting impunity and punishing those who commit gross human rights violations. They are therefore *estopped* from permitting this same project from being the means by which human rights are violated or otherwise compromised.

Estoppel is a concept well known in both common and civil law jurisdictions,[547] though in the latter it is more often termed good faith. Estoppel in the context of judicial proceedings has a narrow application,[548] but such constraint is not called for here. Indeed, a broad notion of estoppel has been used as an argument in a number of contexts. Relating to the ICC, it has been argued that in cases of self-referral under Article 14 of the Rome Statute, the referring State is estopped from challenging the admissibility of the case once the ICC has begun its investigation.[549] Even more interesting, given its similarity to the argument proposed in this section, is the argument with respect to the UN Security Council: through its practice, the UN has created the expectation that its organs will act in compliance with the human rights that the organisation promotes. It should therefore be estopped from permitting the UN Security Council to set up a sanctions regime, such as that in Resolution 1267,[550] that violates individual rights.

[546] Preambular paragraph 2 of the Rome Statute.
[547] In the international arena, the circumstances in which estoppel has been invoked are numerous, and in the 1950s arguments were already being made about its status as a general principle of international law within the meaning of Article 38 of the International Court of Justice (ICJ) Statute. That being said, Cottier and Müller would argue that estoppel does not fit well in the 'straightjacket' of Article 38, but instead should be seen as 'a rule of judge-made public international law, as confirmed and developed by the ICJ on the basis of good faith and equity', Thomas Cottier and Jörg Paul Müller, 'Estoppel' (2007) *Max Planck Encyclopedia of Public International Law*, §10.
[548] 'The principle operates to prevent a State contesting before the Court a situation contrary to a clear and unequivocal representation previously made by it to another State, either expressly or impliedly, on which representation the other State was, in the circumstances, entitled to rely and in fact did rely, and as a result that other State has been prejudiced or the State making it has secured some benefit or advantage for itself', *Case Concerning the Temple of Preah Vihear [Cambodia v. Thailand]*, Merits, ICJ Reports 1962, 15 June 1962, Dissenting Opinion of Sir Percy Spender, 143-4.
[549] William Burke-White and Scott Kaplan, 'Shaping the Contours of Domestic Justice: The International Criminal Court and an Admissibility Challenge in the Uganda Situation' (2009) 7 *Journal of International Criminal Justice*, 257.
[550] UN Security Council Resolution 1267 (1999), S/RES/1267 (1999), 15 October 1999. On the human rights concerns related to the sanctions regime established by this resolution, see for example Lisa Ginsborg and Martin Scheinin, 'You Can't Always Get What You Want: The Kadi II Conundrum and the Security Council 1267 Terrorist Sanctions

Intimately related to this argument, but conceptually distinct, is the idea that States, in creating the ICC, undertook duties of care towards those the project touches. When a company opens a theme park for public enjoyment, they owe a duty of care to those visiting the park to ensure that it is a safe place for said enjoyment. When States set up an international criminal court to pursue justice, they owe a duty of care to those involved in its processes to ensure that it is a safe place for the pursuit of said justice. Another way of conceptualising it is to say that actors have special duties to those entrusted to their care.[551] Parents owe obligations to their children because they brought them into the world. States owe obligations to accused and witnesses because they placed them in the position of being accused and witnesses. The notion of a duty of care is not widely discussed in international law, and it is not argued here that it is an accepted part of general international law. However, it is starting to be used in some areas, such as in the responsibility to protect and protection of the environment,[552] and it is a compelling argument for why States should adopt voluntary measures in the ICC context.

8.7 Conclusion

Mitigating the problems caused by the multi-actor nature of human rights protection at the ICC is certainly possible, it merely requires flexibility, creativity, and acceptance that there is no 'one-size-fits-all' solution. Flexibility would allow the ICC and States to be open to different interpretations of the legal framework and to revisiting existing judicial decisions. This would allow for the changes in interpretation and changes by analogy described in Sections 8.2.2 and 8.2.3, and would alleviate some of the issues that arise because of narrow interpretations of the scope of obligations and the scope of jurisdiction. Creativity would allow for the adoption of new practices tailored to dealing with the

---

Regime' (2011) 8 *Essex Human Rights Review*, 7; Juan Santos Vara, 'The Consequences of *Kadi*: Where the Divergence of Opinion between EU and International Lawyers Lies?', (2011) 17 *European Journal of International Law*, 252; Grant L. Willis, 'Security Council Targeted Sanctions, Due Process and the 1267 Ombudsperson' (2011) 42 *Georgetown Journal of International Law*, 673.

[551] Phillip Pettit and Robert Goodin, 'The Possibility of Special Duties' (1986) 16 *Canadian Journal of Philosophy*, 651.

[552] Louise Arbour, 'The Responsibility to Protect as a Duty of Care in International Law and Practice' (2008) 34 *Review of International Studies*, 445; Mark Allan Gray, 'The International Crime of Ecocide' (1995–1996) 26 *California Western International Law Journal*, 215.

unique problems presented by multi-actor human rights protection. Considering a way to create an ordinal arrangement of duty bearers where there are overlapping obligations is one such practice, as is the creation of a mechanism to pinpoint a volunteer State in cases where the ICC is dependent on voluntary cooperation. Such practices would be a significant shift from the current approach to these issues, but could be implemented in a way that still accounted for the concerns of States.

Crucially, it is important to appreciate that no single solution proposed in this chapter would remedy all types of problems, whether structural or implementation based, that could potentially arise in the different multi-actor situations. There is no 'one-size-fits-all' solution. While some of the ideas explored in this chapter would help to mitigate certain concerns, they would not help with all, and may even lead to new and different problems. As such, a patchwork of measures would be the most promising way of addressing the broadest range of issues.

As has been stressed throughout this book, it is not inevitable that problems in human rights protection will arise in situations involving multiple actors. In the day-to-day work of the ICC, multi-actor situations are regularly handled without issue: new homes are found for witnesses, convicted persons serve sentences in enforcement States, and suspects are interrogated, all without problems arising. However, the fact that the multi-actor nature of protection can create circumstances where rights are not fully protected is a fact of which all actors should be conscious and cautious. As has also been shown by means of the cases discussed in this book, where problems do arise, they can have serious implications for the rights of the individuals involved.

9

Conclusion

This book has addressed the phenomenon of multi-actor human rights protection at the ICC, focusing on the protection of accused and witnesses. The discussion was divided over three parts. Parts I and II considered, respectively, situations involving the ICC and States Parties, and situations involving the ICC and its host State. The aim of these two parts was to identify the relevant obligations incumbent upon each actor in each of the multi-actor situations, and thereby map their respective roles and tasks. With this information, it was then possible to comment on the potential problems that can arise for human rights protection as a result of the involvement of multiple actors. In Part III, solutions were proposed for how these problems might be mitigated or resolved, whether through changes in the current legal framework or institutional innovations.

When the Rome Statute protection framework was being drafted, some of the challenges posed by a multi-actor system of human rights protection were known to the drafters. In the lead up to 1998, the ICTY and ICTR had been functioning for some years, and had already been faced with the difficulties of relying on State cooperation. When it came to establishing a permanent international criminal court therefore, an attempt was made to construct a regime that took account of the involvement of multiple actors. This awareness and anticipation can be seen with regards to some situations involving the ICC and States Parties, and in particular the interrogation and arrest of suspects and the protection of witnesses. Acknowledging that cooperation would be required in these areas, the drafters set up detailed legal frameworks that distribute particular roles among the actors, and delineate the tasks and protective measures that each is required to take. Despite often being complicated to unravel, once properly understood the constellation of obligations provides for comprehensive protection for accused and witnesses in these multi-actor situations. While some implementation problems may arise because the ICC or a State are uncertain as to their obligations – or, more cynically, because they use the multi-actor nature of the situation to 'pass the buck' – the system is designed to work relatively smoothly.

However, not all of the challenges that were foreseen by the drafters were pre-emptively addressed. When it came to other situations involving the ICC and States Parties, namely the situations of interim release, acquittal and release, and the protection of witnesses through relocation to a third State, the drafters of the Rome Statute left structural gaps in the protection framework. The result is that while the ICC is obliged to protect the rights of suspects who are granted interim release or acquitted, and is obliged to protect witnesses by relocating them to a safe third State, there is no corresponding obligation on States to provide the assistance necessary to protect these rights. Despite being aware of the weaknesses of relying on a voluntary system, the type of State assistance required – namely the acceptance of non-nationals onto State territory – touches on an area of such sensitivity for States that they were unwilling to create a system of obligatory cooperation.

Unforeseen at the time the Rome Statute protection framework was drafted was the degree to which the ICC's host State, the Netherlands, would be involved in human rights protection at the Court. Instead of remaining in the background and merely providing practical and logistical assistance to the ICC, the invocation of Dutch human rights and refugee law obligations by ICC acquitted and witnesses placed the Netherlands centre stage. Following some successful claims, it is now the case that whenever an individual is present at the seat of the Court and fears returning to their home State, they may submit an application for protection to the Dutch authorities. Since it was not anticipated that the Netherlands would play this role, it has proven difficult to find an appropriate interaction between the two sets of overlapping protection obligations. This lack of clarity can result in implementation problems with the ICC and the Netherlands each unduly relying on the protection assessments and procedures of the other, with potentially detrimental effects for the individual concerned.

Whether the challenges of multi-actor human rights protection were foreseen or not, and whether they were anticipated in the legal framework or not, the common thread throughout this book is that multi-actor human rights protection at the ICC is a complex affair. On the one hand, it is complex because in some instances the legal frameworks that were put in place to deal with the involvement of multiple actors are detailed and complicated. The frameworks for arrest and surrender and for enforcement of sentences are testament to this, with their thorough allocation of tasks between the ICC and the State Party and their distinction between hands-on and supervisory roles. On the other hand, it is complex because in other instances, rather than a detailed legal framework, there is a lack of legal obligation to protect an individual, either on the part of the State or the Court. Consider in this regard the way that States Parties lack an obligation to host witnesses in need of relocation, or how both the Netherlands and the ICC consider that they have no obligation to protect the right to liberty of witnesses detained on ICC premises.

In situations where legal obligations are lacking, the complexity of multi-actor human rights protection relates to finding ways to mitigate the problems that result from this state of affairs. For example, the ICC has explored some creative solutions in the context of witness relocation, with measures such as relocation agreements, the Special Fund, and the possibility for States to act as platform States. Together, these partial solutions form an interlinking patchwork of protective measures that go some way to remedying a structural gap in protection. In addition to the solutions already being explored by the ICC, Chapter 8 proposed additional measures to address the structural gaps in protection associated with multi-actor human rights protection. Some of the proposed solutions might reduce the complexity of multi-actor protection, but others would certainly add to it. If, for instance, the question of Dutch jurisdiction over the right to liberty of individuals held on ICC premises were approached differently, the legal framework and decision-making process would be a complicated one. Additionally, if a solution such as establishing an institutional mechanism for pinpointing a volunteer State were adopted, this would likely be complicated to operate in practice. And yet, the importance of protecting human rights means that, despite this, finding solutions should remain a priority.

The quest to find solutions to problems arising out of situations involving multiple international actors is not unique to the ICC. From climate change, to responsibility to protect, to joint military operations, to managing refugee flows, there is a growing range of situations of international concern that involve multiple actors. The analysis contained in this book can be positioned against these broader developments at the international level, developments that have led practitioners and scholars to explore how the increasing interconnectedness of legal society impacts traditional notions of international legal obligations and responsibility. These questions prompted the establishment of a substantial research project at the University of Amsterdam, whose aim was to examine notions of shared responsibility in international law.[553] Shared responsibility was understood to cover situations 'where a multiplicity of actors contributes to a single harmful outcome, and legal responsibility for this harmful outcome is distributed among more than one of the contributing actors'.[554]

In a situation where both the ICC and a State have failed to uphold their obligation to protect an accused or witness in a multi-actor situation, would it be possible to speak of them sharing responsibility for the harmful outcome suffered by that individual? The aim of the present book was to examine the *obligations* of the ICC and States in multi-actor situations, and has left unanswered the question of what the *responsibility* of these actors would look like should the obligations not be complied with. Questions of responsibility would arise, in particular, in situations that present implementation problems (given that structural problems are associated with a lack of relevant obligations, it makes less sense to speak of responsibility for breach in that regard). If both the ICC and a State Party were to fail to protect a witness or accused because they were engaged in buck passing, and so trying to avoid complying with their own protection obligations by maintaining that the other should be the one to act, which actor would be responsible? Would this responsibility attach to only one actor, or to both? Would they each be contributing to a 'single

---

[553] André Nollkaemper and Dov Jacobs, 'Shared Responsibility in International Law: A Conceptual Framework' (2013) 34 *Michigan Journal of International Law*, 359. The SHARES Research Project on Shared Responsibility in International Law examined the problem of allocation of responsibilities among multiple States and other actors. The project was directed by Professor André Nollkaemper, who received an Advanced Investigator Grant from the European Research Council for the purpose of the research. The project culminated in a number of edited volumes and individual PhD theses: André Nollkaemper and Ilias Plakokefalos (eds.), *Principles of Shared Responsibility in International Law: An Appraisal of the State of the Art* (Cambridge University Press, 2014); André Nollkaemper and Dov Jacobs (eds.), *Distribution of Responsibilities in International Law* (Cambridge University Press, 2015); André Nollkaemper, Ilias Plakokefalos, and Jessica Schechinger (eds.), *The Practice of Shared Responsibility in International Law* (Cambridge University Press, 2017); Nienke van der Have, *The Prevention of Gross Human Rights Violations under International Human Rights Law* (T. M. C. Asser Press, 2018); Boutin, The Role of Control in Allocating International Responsibility; Nataša Nedeski, *Shared Obligations in International Law* (Academisch Proefschrift 2017). The present monograph is an adaptation of a PhD thesis completed within the SHARES Project.

[554] André Nollkaemper, 'Introduction', in André Nollkaemper and Ilias Plakokefalos (eds.), *Principles of Shared Responsibility in International Law: An Appraisal of the State of the Art* (Cambridge University Press, 2014), 6–7.

harmful outcome'? Would one actor be more responsible than another, and if so, how would this be decided? Having set out the relevant obligations of the different actors, and thereafter identified potential problems in human rights protection, the next step in comprehensively understanding multi-actor human rights protection at the ICC would be to ask how to proceed when the potential problems cease to be hypothetical. The multi-actor nature of protection means that the framework of shared responsibility will be crucial to understanding how responsibility should be distributed among the ICC and States.

As mentioned in the Introduction, the situation of the detained Congolese witnesses was the catalyst for the research that culminated in this book. The 'Gordian knot' of legal issues that the situation gave rise to have been separated out and analysed in different sections of the previous chapters, and the principles distilled from the range of legal decisions associated with the case have formed the basis for understanding other situations of multi-actor human rights protection. While many of the issues raised by the detained Congolese witnesses case were eventually resolved – in particular, it was established that detained ICC witnesses could indeed submit asylum applications to the Dutch authorities – the question of the right to liberty was not. For the author, this episode remains troubling, as it demonstrated a lack of flexibility on the part of the actors involved, and a reluctance to place the protection of human rights above other (notably political) considerations. As the ICC continues to play its role within the global accountability project, and all actors involved settle into the idea of a permanent criminal court, it is hoped that the human rights focus that permeates the ICC's work will translate to all areas, including those where the protection of human rights falls to the cooperation among multiple actors.

BIBLIOGRAPHY

Books

Abels, Denis, *Prisoners of the International Community: The Legal Position of Persons Detained at International Criminal Tribunals* (T. M. C. Asser Press, 2012)

Boutin, Bérénice, *The Role of Control in Allocating International Responsibility in Collaborative Military Operations* (Academisch Proefschrift, 2015)

Clapham, Andrew, *Human Rights Obligations of Non-State Actors* (Oxford University Press, 2006)

Crawford, James, *Brownlie's Principles of Public International Law* (Oxford University Press, 2012)

d'Aspremont, Jean and Droubi, Sufyan (eds.), *International Organizations and the Formation of Customary International Law* (Manchester University Press, forthcoming 2019)

de Meester, Karel, *The Investigation Phase in International Criminal Procedure: In Search of Common Principles* (Academisch Proefschrift, 2014)

Hirsch, Moshe, *The Responsibility of International Organizations Towards Third Parties* (Martinus Nijhoff, 1995)

Nedeski, Nataša, *Shared Obligations in International Law* (Academisch Proefschrift, 2017)

Nollkaemper, André and Jacobs, Dov (eds.), *Distribution of Responsibilities in International Law* (Cambridge University Press, 2015)

Nollkaemper, André and Plakokefalos, Ilias (eds.), *Principles of Shared Responsibility in International Law: An Appraisal of the State of the Art* (Cambridge University Press, 2014)

Nollkaemper, André, Plakokefalos, Ilias, and Schechinger, Jessica (eds.), *The Practice of Shared Responsibility in International Law* (Cambridge University Press, 2017)

Raimondo, Fabian, *General Principles of Law in the Decisions of International Criminal Courts and Tribunals* (Academisch Proefschrift, 2007)

Sands, Philippe and Klein, Pierre, *Bowett's Law of International Institutions* (Sweet & Maxwell, 2009)

Schabas, William, *The International Criminal Court: A Commentary on the Rome Statute* (Oxford University Press, 2010)

Schermers, Henry and Blokker, Niels, *International Institutional Law: Unity within Diversity* (Brill, 2011)
van der Have, Nienke, *The Prevention of Gross Human Rights Violations under International Human Rights Law* (T. M. C. Asser Press, 2018)
Vasiliev, Sergey, *International Criminal Trials: A Normative Theory* (Academisch Proefschrift, 2014)
Weis, Paul, *Nationality and Statelessness in International Law* (Sijthoff & Noordhoff, 1979)
Zeegers, Krit, *International Criminal Tribunals and Human Rights Law: Adherence and Contextualisation*, International Criminal Justice Series (T. M. C. Asser Press, 2016)

Book Chapters

Akande, Dapo, 'International Organisations', in Malcolm D. Evans (ed.), *International Law* (Oxford University Press, 2014)
Bertrand, Anne-Aurore and Schauder, Natacha, 'Practical Cooperation Challenges Faced by the Registry of the International Criminal Court', in Olympia Bekou and Daley Birkett (eds.), *Cooperation and the International Criminal Court: Perspectives from Theory and Practice* (Brill, 2016)
Bitti, Gilbert, 'Article 21 and the Hierarchy of Sources of Law before the ICC', in Carsten Stahn (ed.), *The Law and Practice of the International Criminal Court* (Oxford University Press, 2015)
Chimimba, Trevor Pascal, 'Establishing an Enforcement Regime', in Roy Lee (ed.), *The International Criminal Court: The Making of the Rome Statute – Issues, Negotiations, Results* (Kluwer Law International, 1999)
deGuzman, Margaret, 'Article 21: Applicable Law', in Otto Triffterer and Kai Ambos (eds.), *Rome Statute of the International Criminal Court: A Commentary* (C. H. Beck, 2016)
de Schutter, Olivier, 'Human Rights and the Rise of International Organisations: The Logic of Sliding Scales in the Law of International Responsibility', in Jan Wouters, Eva Brems, Stefaan Smis, and Pierre Schmitt (eds.), *Accountability for Human Rights Violations by International Organisations* (Intersentia, 2010)
Eikel, Markus, 'External Support and Internal Coordination: The ICC and the Protection of Witnesses', in Carsten Stahn (ed.), *The Law and Practice of the International Criminal Court* (Oxford University Press, 2015)
Gallant, Kenneth, 'Individual Human Rights in a New International Organisation: The Rome Statute of the International Criminal Court', in Mahmoud Cherif Bassiouni (ed.), *International Criminal Law – Volume II: Enforcement* (Transnational Publishers, 1999)
Gerards, Janneke and Fleuren, Joseph, 'The Netherlands', in Janneke Gerards and Joseph Fleuren (eds.), *Implementation of the European Convention on Human*

Rights and of the Judgments of the ECtHR in National Case Law: A Comparative Analysis (Intersentia, 2014)

Hall, Christopher and Ryngaert, Cedric, 'Article 59: Arrest Proceedings in the Custodial State', in Otto Triffterer and Kai Ambos (eds.), *Rome Statute of the International Criminal Court: A Commentary* (C. H. Beck, 2016)

Joseph, Sarah and Fletcher, Adam, 'Scope of Application', in Daniel Moeckli, Sangeeta Shah, and Sandesh Sivakumaran (eds.), *International Human Rights Law* (Oxford University Press, 2014)

Khan, Karim, 'Article 60: Initial Proceedings Before the Court', in Otto Triffterer and Kai Ambos (eds.), *Rome Statute of the International Criminal Court: A Commentary* (C. H. Beck, 2016)

Kreß, Claus and Sluiter, Göran, 'Enforcement', in Antonio Cassese, Paola Gaeta, and John R. W. D. Jones (eds.), *The Rome Statute of the International Criminal Court: A Commentary* (Oxford University Press, 2002)

'Imprisonment', in Antonio Cassese, Paola Gaeta, and John R. W. D. Jones (eds.), *The Rome Statute of the International Criminal Court: A Commentary* (Oxford University Press, 2002)

Nollkaemper, André, 'Introduction', in André Nollkaemper and Ilias Plakokcfalos (eds.), *Principles of Shared Responsibility in International Law: An Appraisal of the State of the Art* (Cambridge University Press, 2014)

Pellet, Alain, 'Applicable Law', in Antonio Cassese, Paola Gaeta, and John R. W. D. Jones (eds.), *The Rome Statute of the International Criminal Court: A Commentary* (Oxford University Press, 2002)

Prost, Kimberley, 'Chapter 14: Enforcement', in Roy Lee (ed.), *The International Criminal Court, Elements of Crimes and Rules of Procedure and Evidence* (Transnational Publishers, 2001)

Reinisch, August, 'The Changing International Legal Framework for Dealing with Non-State Actors', in Philip Alston (ed.), *Non-State Actors and Human Rights* (Oxford University Press, 2005)

Scalia, Damien, 'Enforcement', in Paul De Hert, Jean Flamme, Mathias Holvoet, and Olivia Struyven (eds.), *Code of International Criminal Law and Procedure, Annotated* (Larcier, 2013)

Sluiter, Göran, 'Human Rights Protection in the Pre-Trial Phase', in Carsten Stahn and Göran Sluiter (eds.), *The Emerging Practice of the International Criminal Court* (Martinus Nijhoff, 2009)

'International Criminal Tribunals and their Relation to States', in André Nollkaemper, Ilias Plakokefalos, and Jessica Schechinger (eds.), *The Practice of Shared Responsibility in International Law* (Cambridge University Press, 2017)

Stijards, Gerhard, 'Enforcement', in Otto Triffterer (ed.), *Commentary on the Rome Statute of the International Criminal Court: Observers' Notes, Article by Article* (Nomos, 1999)

Swart, Bert, 'Arrest and Surrender', in Antonio Cassese, Paola Gaeta, and John R. W. D. Jones (eds.), *The Rome Statute of the International Criminal Court* (Oxford University Press, 2002)

'Arrest Proceedings in the Custodial State', in Antonio Cassese, Paola Gaeta, and John R. W. D. Jones (eds.), *The Rome Statute of the International Criminal Court* (Oxford University Press, 2002)

van Wijk, Joris and Cupido, Marjolein, 'Testifying behind Bars: Detained ICC Witnesses and Human Rights Protection', in Carsten Stahn (ed.), *The Law and Practice of the International Criminal Court* (Oxford University Press, 2015)

Zappalà, Salvatore, 'International Criminal Proceedings, Investigation', in Antonio Cassese, Paola Gaeta, and John R. W. D. Jones (eds.), *The Rome Statute of the International Criminal Court* (Oxford University Press, 2002)

Journal Articles

Abtahi, Hirad and Koh, Steven Arrigg, 'The Emerging Enforcement Practice of the International Criminal Court' (2013) 45 *Cornell International Law Journal* 1

Akande, Dapo, 'The Effect of Security Council Resolutions and Domestic Proceedings on State Obligations to Cooperate with the ICC' (2012) 10 *Journal of International Criminal Justice* 299

Arbia, Silvana, 'The International Criminal Court: Witness and Victim Protection and Support, Legal Aid and Family Visits' (2010) 36 *Commonwealth Law Bulletin* 519

Arbour, Louise, 'The Responsibility to Protect as a Duty of Care in International Law and Practice' (2008) 34 *Review of International Studies* 445

Arsanjani, Mahnoush, 'The Rome Statute of the International Criminal Court' (1999) 93 *American Journal of International Law* 22

Bevers, Han, Blokker, Niels M., and Roording, Jaap, 'The Netherlands and the International Criminal Court: On Statute Obligations and Hospitality' (2003) 16 *Leiden Journal of International Law* 135

Burke-White, William and Kaplan, Scott, 'Shaping the Contours of Domestic Justice: The International Criminal Court and an Admissibility Challenge in the Uganda Situation' (2009) 7 *Journal of International Criminal Justice* 257

Cassese, Antonio, 'On the Current Trends towards Criminal Prosecution and Punishment of Breaches of International Humanitarian Law' (1998) 9 *European Journal of International Law* 2

Cryer, Robert, 'Royalism and the King: Article 21 of the Rome Statute and the Politics of Sources' (2009) 12 *New Criminal Law Review* 390

Darley, John and Latane, Bibb, 'Bystander Intervention in Emergencies: Diffusion of Responsibility' (1968) 8 *Journal of Personality and Social Psychology* 377

de Boer, Tom and Zieck, Marjoleine, 'ICC Witnesses and Acquitted Suspects Seeking Asylum in the Netherlands: An Overview of the Jurisdictional Battles between the ICC and Its Host State' (2015) 27 *International Journal of Refugee Law* 573

den Heijer, Maarten, 'Whose Rights and Which Rights? The Continuing Story of Non-Refoulement under the European Convention on Human Rights' (2008) 10 *European Journal of Migration & Law* 277

Eikel, Markus, 'Witness Protection Measures at the International Criminal Court: Legal Framework and Emerging Practice' (2012) 23 *Criminal Law Forum* 97

El Zeidy, Mohamed M., 'Critical Thoughts on Article 59(2) of the ICC Statute' (2006) 4 *Journal of International Criminal Justice* 448

Ferraro, Tristan, 'Determining the Beginning and End of an Occupation under International Humanitarian Law' (2012) 94 *International Review of the Red Cross* 133

Ginsborg, Lisa and Scheinin, Martin, 'You Can't Always Get What You Want: The Kadi II Conundrum and the Security Council 1267 Terrorist Sanctions Regime' (2011) 8 *Essex Human Rights Review* 7

Gray, Mark Allan, 'The International Crime of Ecocide' (1995–1996) 26 *California Western International Law Journal* 215

Golubok, Sergey, 'Pre-Conviction Detention before the International Criminal Court: Compliance or Fragmentation' (2010) 9 *Law & Practice of International Courts & Tribunals* 295

Grover, Leena, 'A Call to Arms: Fundamental Dilemmas Confronting the Interpretation of Crimes in the Rome Statute of the International Criminal Court' (2010) 21 *European Journal of International Law* 543

Hafner, Gerhard and Binder, Christina, 'The Interpretation of Article 21(3) ICC Statute Opinion Reviewed' (2004) 9 *Austrian Review of International and European Law* 163

Heller, Kevin Jon, 'What Happens to the Acquitted?' (2008) 21 *Leiden Journal of International Law* 663

Hochmayr, Gudrun, 'Applicable Law in Practice and Theory: Interpreting Article 21 of the ICC Statute' (2014) 12 *Journal of International Criminal Justice* 655

Holá, Barbora and van Wijk, Joris, 'Life after Conviction at International Criminal Tribunals: An Empirical Overview' (2014) 12 *Journal of International Criminal Justice* 109

Irving, Emma, 'The Relationship between the International Criminal Court and its Host State: The Impact on Human Rights' (2014) 27 *Leiden Journal of International Law* 479

'Protecting Witnesses at the International Criminal Court from Refoulement' (2014) 12 *Journal of International Criminal Justice* 1141

Kritzman-Amir, Tally, 'Not in My Backyard: On the Morality of Responsibility-Sharing in Refugee Law' (2008–2009) 34 *Brooklyn Journal of International Law* 355

Lock, Tobias, 'Beyond *Bosphorus*: The European Court of Human Rights' Case Law on the Responsibility of Member States of International Organisations under the European Convention on Human Rights' (2010) 10 *Human Rights Law Review* 529

Mulgrew, Róisín, 'The International Movement of Prisoners' (2011) 22 *Criminal Law Forum* 103

Muller, Clemens A., 'The Law of Interim Release in the Jurisprudence of the International Criminal Tribunals' (2008) 8 *International Criminal Law Review* 589

Nollkaemper, André and Jacobs, Dov, 'Shared Responsibility in International Law: A Conceptual Framework' (2013) 34 *Michigan Journal of International Law* 359

Oosterveld, Valerie, Perry, Mike, and McManus, John, 'Cooperation of States with the International Criminal Court, The Twenty-Fifth Memorial Issue: The Eve of the International Criminal Court: Preparations and Commentary – How the World Will Relate to the Court' (2001–2002) 25 *Fordham International Law Journal* 767

Othman, Mohamed, 'The "Protection" of Refugee Witnesses by the International Criminal Tribunal for Rwanda' (2002) 14 *International Journal of Refugee Law* 495

Pettit, Phillip and Goodin, Robert, 'The Possibility of Special Duties' (1986) 16 *Canadian Journal of Philosophy* 651

Ryngaert, Cedric, 'Oscillating between Embracing and Avoiding Bosphorus: The European Court of Human Rights on Member State Responsibility for Acts of International Organisations and the Case of the EU' (2014) 39 *European Law Review* 176

Ryngaert, Cedric and Buchanan, Holly, 'Member State Responsibility for the Acts of International Organisations' (2011) 7 *Utrecht Law Review* 131

Schabas, William, 'Barayagwiza v. Prosecutor (Decision, and Decision (Prosecutor's Request for Review or Reconsideration)) Case No. ICTR-97-19-AR72' (2000) 94 *American Journal of International Law* 563

Sheppard, Daniel, 'The International Criminal Court and "Internationally Recognized Human Rights": Understanding Article 21(3) of the Rome Statute' (2010) 10 *International Criminal Law Review* 43

Sluiter, Göran, 'Atrocity Crimes Litigation: Some Human Rights Concerns Occasioned by Selected 2009 Case Law' (2010) 8 *Northwestern Journal of International Human Rights* 248

'Shared Responsibility in International Criminal Justice: The ICC and Asylum' (2012) 10 *Journal of International Criminal Justice* 661

'The Surrender of War Criminals to the International Criminal Court' (2002–2003) 25 *Loyola of Los Angeles International & Comparative Law Review* 605

Swart, Bert, 'Commentary on ICTR Decision Barayagwiza v. Prosecutor, Case No. ICTR-97-19-AR72, A. Ch., 3 November 1999' (2001) 2 *Annotated Leading Cases* 197

van Wijk, Joris, 'When International Criminal Justice Collides with Principles of International Protection: Assessing the Consequences of ICC Witnesses Seeking Asylum, Defendants Being Acquitted, and Convicted Being Released' (2013) 26 *Leiden Journal of International Law* 173

Vara, Juan Santos, 'The Consequences of *Kadi*: Where the Divergence of Opinion between EU and International Lawyers Lies?', (2011) 17 *European Journal of International Law* 252

Vasiliev, Sergey, 'Proofing the Ban on "Witness Proofing": Did the ICC Get It Right?' (2009) 20 *Criminal Law Forum* 193

Vatsov, Mihail, 'Security Council Referrals to the ICC and EU Fundamental Rights: A Test for ECJ's Stance in Kadi I' (2012) 25 *Hague Yearbook of International Law* 79

Verhoeven, Joe, 'Article 21 of the Rome Statute and the Ambiguities of Applicable Law' (2002) 33 *Netherlands Yearbook of International Law* 2

Willis, Grant L., 'Security Council Targeted Sanctions, Due Process and the 1267 Ombudsperson' (2011) 42 *Georgetown Journal of International Law* 673

Yabasun, Dersim and Holvoet, Mathias, 'Seeking Asylum before the International Criminal Court. Another Challenge for a Court in Need of Credibility' (2013) 13 *International Criminal Law Review* 725

Young, Rebecca, '"Internationally Recognised Human Rights" before the International Criminal Court' (2011) 60 *International and Comparative Law Quarterly* 189

Reports

Human Rights Watch, 'Courting History: The Landmark International Criminal Court's First Years' (July 2008)

Nick Donovan, 'The Enforcement of International Criminal Court', Aegis (2009)

Chris Mahony, 'The Justice Sector Afterthought: Witness Protection in Africa', Institute for Security Studies, 2010

International Bar Association, 'Witnesses before the International Criminal Court: An International Bar Association International Criminal Court Programme Report on the ICC's Efforts and Challenges to Protect, Support and Ensure the Rights of Witnesses' (July 2013)

ICC Documents

ICC Press Releases

'ICC welcomes UK contribution for relocating at-risk persons in Kenya', ICC Weekly Update, 30 November 2010
'Kenyatta case: Trial adjourned until 7 October 2014', ICC Press Release, 31 March 2014
'Belgium and ICC sign agreement on interim release', ICC Press Release, 10 April 2014
'ICC transfers three detained witnesses to Dutch custody', ICC Press Release, 4 June 2014
'Aimé Kilolo Musamba, Narcisse Arido and Fidèle Babala Wandu released from ICC custody', ICC Press Release, 23 October 2014
'Statement of the Office of the Prosecutor regarding the reported abduction and murder of Mr. Meshak Yebei', ICC Press Release, 9 January 2015
'Kenyatta case: Trial Chamber V(B) terminates the proceedings', ICC Press Release, 13 March 2015
'Statement of the Prosecutor of the International Criminal Court, Fatou Bensouda regarding the unsealing of arrest warrants in the Kenya situation', ICC Press Release, 10 September 2015
'Situation in Kenya: ICC judges unseal an arrest warrant against Paul Gicheru and Philip Kipkoerch Bett', ICC Press Release, 10 September 2015
'Bemba, Kilolo et al. trial opens at the International Criminal Court', ICC Press Release, 29 September 2015
'Thomas Lubanga Dyilo and Germain Katanga transferred to the DRC to serve their sentences', ICC Press Release, 19 December 2015

ICC Decisions

The Prosecutor v. *Thomas Lubanga Dyilo*, ICC-01/04-01/06-424, Decision on the Prosecutor's 'Application for Leave to Reply to "Conclusions de la défense en réponse au mémoire d'appel du Procureur"', 12 September 2006 (Appeals Chamber)
The Prosecutor v. *Thomas Lubanga Dyilo*, ICC-01/04-01/06-447, Decision on a General Framework Concerning Protective Measures for Prosecution and Defence Witnesses, 19 September 2006 (Pre-Trial Chamber I)
The Prosecutor v. *Thomas Lubanga Dyilo*, ICC-01/04-01/06-512, Decision on the Defence Challenge to the Jurisdiction of the Court Pursuant to Article 19(2)(a) of the Statute, 3 October 2006 (Pre-Trial Chamber I)

The Prosecutor v. *Thomas Lubanga Dyilo,* ICC-01/04-01/06-586-tEN, Decision on the Application for the Interim Release of Thomas Lubanga Dyilo, 18 October 2006 (Pre-Trial Chamber I)

The Prosecutor v. *Thomas Lubanga Dyilo,* ICC-01/04-01/06-679, Decision on the Practices of Witness Familiarisation and Witness Proofing, 8 November 2006 (Pre-Trial Chamber I)

The Prosecutor v. *Thomas Lubanga Dyilo,* ICC-01/04-01/06-772, Judgment on the Appeal of Mr Thomas Lubanga Dyilo against the Decision on the Defence Challenge to the Jurisdiction of the Court pursuant to Article 19(2)(a) of the Statute of 3 October 2006, 14 December 2006 (Appeals Chamber)

The Prosecutor v. *Thomas Lubanga Dyilo,* ICC-01/04-01/06-824, Judgment on the Appeal of Mr Thomas Lubanga Dyilo against the Decision of Pre-Trial Chamber I Entitled 'Décision sur la demande de mise en liberté provisoire de Thomas Lubanga Dyilo', 13 February 2007 (Appeals Chamber)

The Prosecutor v. *Thomas Lubanga Dyilo,* ICC-01/04-01/06-924, Second Review of the 'Decision on the Application for Interim Release of Thomas Lubanga Dyilo', 11 June 2007 (Pre-Trial Chamber I)

The Prosecutor v. *Thomas Lubanga Dyilo,* ICC-01/04-01/06-1311-Anx2, Annex 2, Decision on Disclosure Issues, Responsibilities for Protective Measures and Other Procedural Matters, 24 April 2008 (Trial Chamber I)

Situation in the Central African Republic, ICC-01/05-01/08-28, Prosecutor's Application for Request for Provisional Arrest under Article 92, 23 May 2008 (Pre-Trial Chamber III)

The Prosecutor v. *Jean-Pierre Bemba Gombo,* ICC-01/05-01/08-3, Demande d'arrestation provisoire de M. Jean-Peirre Bemba Gombo addressee au Royaume de Belgique, 23 May 2008 (Pre-Trial Chamber II)

The Prosecutor v. *Thomas Lubanga Dyilo,* ICC-01/04-01/06-1401, Decision on the Consequences of Non-Disclosure of Exculpatory Materials Covered by Article 54(3)(e) Agreements and the Application to Stay the Prosecution of the Accused, Together with Certain Other Issues Raised at the Status Conference on 10 June 2008, 13 June 2008 (Trial Chamber I)

The Prosecutor v. *Thomas Lubanga Dyilo,* ICC-01/04-01/06-1486, Judgment on the Appeal of the Prosecutor against the Decision of Trial Chamber I Entitled 'Decision on the Consequences of Non-Disclosure of Exculpatory Materials Covered by Article 54(3)(e) Agreements and the Application to Stay the Prosecution of the Accused, Together with Certain Other Issues Raised at the Status Conference on 10 June 2008', 21 October 2008 (Appeals Chamber)

The Prosecutor v. *Germain Katanga and Mathieu Ngudjolo Chui,* ICC-01/04-01/07-776, Judgment on the Appeal of the Prosecutor against the 'Decision on Evidentiary Scope of the Confirmation Hearing, Preventive Relocation and

Disclosure under Article 67(2) of the Statute and Rule 77 of the Rules' of Pre-Trial Chamber I, 26 November 2008 (Appeals Chamber)

The Prosecutor v. Omar Hassan Ahmad Al Bashir, ICC-02/05-01/09-3, Decision on the Prosecution's Application for a Warrant of Arrest against Omar Hassan Ahmad Al Bashir, 4 March 2009 (Pre-Trial Chamber I)

The Prosecutor v. Germain Katanga and Mathieu Ngudjolo Chui, ICC-RoR217-02/08-8, Decision on 'Mr Mathieu Ngudjolo's Complaint under Regulation 221(1) of the Regulations of the Registry against the Registrar's Decision of 18 November 2008', 10 March 2009 (The Presidency)

The Prosecutor v. Katanga and Ngudjolo, ICC-01/04-01/07-1263, Public Redacted Version of the Defence Motion for a Declaration on Unlawful Detention and Stay of Proceedings (ICC-01/07-01/04-1258-Conf-Exp), 2 July 2009 (Trial Chamber II)

The Prosecutor v. Jean-Pierre Bemba Gombo, ICC-01/05-01/08-475, Decision on the Interim Release of Jean-Pierre Bemba Gombo and Convening Hearings with the Kingdom of Belgium, the Republic of Portugal, the Republic of France, the Federal Republic of Germany, the Italian Republic, and the Republic of South Africa, 14 August 2009 (Pre-Trial Chamber II)

The Prosecutor v. Germain Katanga, ICC-01/04-01/07-1666-Red-tENG, Public Redacted Version of the 'Decision on the Motion of the Defence for Germain Katanga for a Declaration on Unlawful Detention and Stay of Proceedings' of 20 November 2009 (ICC-01/04-01/07-1666-Conf-Exp), 3 December 2009 (Trial Chamber II)

The Prosecutor v. Bemba Gombo, ICC-01/05-01/08-631-Red, Judgment on the appeal of the Prosecutor against Pre-Trial Chamber II's 'Decision on the Interim Release of Jean-Pierre Bemba Gombo and Convening Hearings with the Kingdom of Belgium, the Republic of Portugal, the Republic of France, the Federal Republic of Germany, the Italian Republic and the Republic of South Africa', 2 December 2009 (Appeals Chamber)

The Prosecutor v. Germain Katanga and Mathieu Ngudjolo Chui, ICC-01/04-01/07-2635, Decision on the Prosecutor's Bar Table Motions, 17 December 2010 (Trial Chamber II)

The Prosecutor v. Katanga and Ngudjolo, ICC-01/04-01/07-3003-tENG, Decision on an Amicus Curiae Application and on the 'Requête tenant à obtenir présentations des témoins DRC D02 P 0350, DRC D02 P 0236, DRC D02 P 0228 aux autorités néerlandaises aux fins d'asile' (Articles 68 and 93(7) of the Statute), 9 June 2011 (Trial Chamber II)

The Prosecutor v. Germain Katanga and Mathieu Ngudjolo Chui, ICC-01/04-01/07-3033, Decision on the Security Situation of Three Detained Witnesses in Relation to Their Testimony before the Court (Art. 68 of the Statute) and Order to Request Cooperation from the Democratic Republic of the Congo to Provide Assistance in Ensuring Their

Protection in Accordance with Article 93(1)(j) of the Statute, 22 June 2011 (Trial Chamber II)

The Prosecutor v. *Katanga and Ngudjolo*, ICC-01/04-01/07, Decision on the Security Situation of Witnesses DRC-D02-P-0236, DRC-D02-P-0228, and DRC-D02-P-0350, 24 August 2011 (Trial Chamber II)

The Prosecutor v. *Jean-Pierre Bemba Gombo*, ICC-01/05-01/08-1722, Judgment on the Appeal of Mr Jean-Pierre Bemba Gombo against the Decision of Trial Chamber III of 2 September 2011 Entitled 'Decision on the "Demande de mise en liberté de M. Jean-Pierre Bemba Gombo afin d'accomplir ses devoirs civiques en République Démocratique du Congo"', 9 September 2011 (Appeals Chamber)

The Prosecutor v. *Thomas Lubanga Dyilo*, ICC-01/04-01/06-2827, Amicus Curiae Observations by Mr Schüller and Mr Sluiter, Counsel in Dutch Asylum Proceedings of Witness 19, Public Document, 23 November 2011

The Prosecutor v. *Oman Hassan Ahmad Al Bashir*, ICC-02/05-01/09-139, Decision Pursuant to Article 87(7) of the Rome Statute on the Failure by the Republic of Malawi to Comply with the Cooperation Requests Issued by the Court with Respect to the Arrest and Surrender of Omar Hassan Ahmad Al Bashir, 12 December 2011 (Pre-Trial Chamber I)

The Prosecutor v. *Wiliam Samoei Ruto and Joshua Arap Sang*, ICC-01/09-01/11-446, Prosecution Motion Regarding the Scope of Witness Preparation, 13 August 2012 (Trial Chamber V)

The Prosecutor v. *Laurent Gbagbo*, ICC-02/11-01/11-212, Decision on the 'Corrigendum of the Challenge to the Jurisdiction of the International Criminal Court on the Basis of Articles 12(3), 19(2), 21(3), 55 and 59 of the Rome Statute Filed by the Defence for President Gbagbo (ICC-02/11-01/11-129)', 15 August 2012 (Pre-Trial Chamber I)

Prosecutor v. *Mathieu Ngudjolo Chui*, ICC-01/04-02/12-12, Decision on the Request of the Prosecutor of 19 December 2012 for Suspensive Effect, 20 December 2012 (Appeals Chamber)

The Prosecutor v. *Mathieu Ngudjolo Chui*, ICC-01/04-02/12-15-tENG, Urgent Defence Application for the International Relocation of Mathieu Ngudjolo Outwith the African Continent and His Presentation to the Authorities of One of the States Parties to the International Criminal Court for the Purposes of Expediting His Asylum Application, 21 December 2012 (Appeals Chamber)

The Prosecutor v. *Mathieu Ngudjolo Chui*, ICC-01/04-02/12-22-tENG, Second Addendum to 'Defence Request That the Appeals Chamber Order the Victims and Witnesses Unit to Execute and the Host State to Comply with the Acquittal Judgment of 18 December 2012 Issued by Trial Chamber II of the International Criminal Court', 8 February 2013 (Appeals Chamber)

The Prosecutor v. *Germain Katanga*, ICC-01/04-01/07-3352, Decision on the Request for Release of Witnesses DRC-D02-P-0236, DRC-D02-P-0228 and DRC-D02-P-0350, 8 February 2013 (Trial Chamber II)

BIBLIOGRAPHY 253

The Prosecutor v. *Oman Hassan Ahmad Al Bashir,* ICC-02/05-01/09-151, Decision on the Non-Compliance of the Republic of Chad with the Cooperation Requests Issued by the Court Regarding the Arrest and Surrender of Omar Hassan Ahmad Al-Bashir, 26 March 2013 (Pre-Trial Chamber II)

The Prosecutor v. *Mathieu Ngudjolo Chui,* ICC-01/04-02/12-69-Red, Registry's Update on the Situation in Relation to Mathieu Ngudjolo Chui, 3 June 2013 (Appeals Chamber)

The Prosecutor v. *Mathieu Ngudjolo Chui,* ICC-01/04-02/12-74-Red, Decision on Mr Ngudjolo's Request to Order the Victims and Witnesses Unit to Execute and the Host State to Comply with the Acquittal Judgment of 18 December 2012 Issued by Trial Chamber II of the International Criminal Court, 12 June 2013 (Appeals Chamber)

The Prosecutor v. *Germain Katanga,* ICC-01/04-01/07-3405-tENG, Decision on the Application for the Interim Release of Detained Witnesses DRC-D02 -P-0236, DRC-D02-P-0228 and DRC-D02-P-0350, 1 October 2013 (Trial Chamber II)

The Prosecutor v. *Germain Katanga,* ICC-01/04-01/07-3405Anx, Decision on the Application for the Interim Release of Detained Witnesses DRC-D02-P-0236, DRC-D02-P-0228 and DRC-D02-P-0350, Dissenting Opinion of Judge Christine Van den Wyngaert, 1 October 2013 (Trial Chamber II)

The Prosecutor v. *Jean-Pierre Bemba, Aimé Kilolo Musamba, Jean-Jacques Mangenda Kabongo, Fidèle Babala Wandu and Narcisse Arido,* ICC-01/05-01/ 13-1-Red2-tENG, Warrant of Arrest for Jean-Pierre Bemba, Aimé Kilolo Musamba, Jean-Jacques Mangenda Kabongo, Fidèle Babala Wandu and Narcisse Arido, 20 November 2013 (Pre-Trial Chamber II)

The Prosecutor v. *Germain Katanga,* ICC-01/04-01/07-3424-Anx, Decision on the Admissibility of the Appeal against the 'Decision on the Application for the Interim Release of Detained Witnesses DRC-D02-P0236, DRC-D02-P0228 and DRC-D02-P0350', Dissenting Opinion Judge Sang-Hyun Song, 20 January 2014 (Appeals Chamber)

The Prosecutor v. *Mathieu Ngudjolo Chui,* ICC-01/04-02/12-158, Order on the Implementation of the Cooperation Agreement between the Court and the Democratic Republic of the Congo Concluded Pursuant Article 93(7) of the Statute, 20 January 2014 (Appeals Chamber)

The Prosecutor v. *Germain Katanga,* ICC-01/04-01/07-3436-tENG, Judgment Pursuant to Article 74 of the Statute, 7 March 2014 (Trial Chamber II)

The Prosecutor v. *Omar Hassan Ahmad Al Bashir,* ICC-02/05-01/09-195, Decision on the Cooperation of the Democratic Republic of the Congo Regarding Omar Al Bashir's Arrest and Surrender to the Court, 9 April 2014 (Pre-Trial Chamber II)

The Prosecutor v. *Jean-Pierre Bemba Gombo, Aimé Kilolo Musamba, Jean-Jaques Mangenda Kabongo, Fidèle Babala Wandu and Narcisse Arido,* ICC-01/05-01/

13-588, Decision on 'Narcisse Arido's Request for Interim Release', 24 July 2014 (Pre-Trial Chamber II)

The Prosecutor v. *Jean-Pierre Bemba Gombo, Aimé Kilolo Musamba, Jean-Jaques Mangenda Kabongo, Fidèle Babala Wandu and Narcisse Arido*, ICC-01/05-01/13-612, Decision on the First Review of Jean-Jacques Mangenda Kabongo's Detention Pursuant to Article 60(3) of the Statute, 5 August 2014 (Pre-Trial Chamber II)

Situation in the Central African Republic in the Case of the Prosecutor v. *Jean-Pierre Bemba Gombo, Aimé Kilolo Musamba, Jean-Jaques Mangenda Kabongo, Fidèle Babala Wandu and Narcisse Arido*, ICC-01/05-01/13-703, Decision Ordering the Release of Aimé Kilolo Musamba, Jean-Jaques Mangenda Kabongo, Fidèle Babala Wandu and Narcisse Arido, 21 October 2014 (Pre-Trial Chamber II)

The Prosecutor v. *Paul Gicheru and Philip Kipkoech Bett*, ICC-01/09-01/15-1-Red, Decision on the 'Prosecution's Application under Article 58(1) of the Rome Statute', 10 March 2015 (Pre-Trial Chamber II)

The Prosecutor v. *Jean-Pierre Bemba Gombo, Aimé Kilolo Musamba, Jean-Jaques Mangenda Kabongo, Fidèle Babala Wandu and Narcisse Arido*, ICC-01/05-01/13-969, Judgment on the Appeals against Pre-Trial Chamber II's Decisions Regarding Interim Release in Relation to Aimé Kilolo Musamba, Jean-Jacques Mangenda, Fidèle Babala Wandu, and Narcisse Arido and Order for Reclassification, 29 May 2015 (Appeals Chamber)

The Prosecutor v. *Jean-Pierre Bemba Gombo, Aimé Kilolo Musamba, Jean-Jaques Mangenda Kabongo, Fidèle Babala Wandu and Narcisse Arido*, ICC-01/05-01/13-1151, Decision Regarding Interim Release, 17 August 2015 (Trial Chamber VII)

The Prosecutor v. *Mathieu Ngudjolo Chui*, ICC-01/04-02/12-301-tENG, Decision on the 'Requête en indemnisation en application des dispositions de l'article 85(1) et (3) du Statut de Rome', 16 December 2015 (Trial Chamber II)

The Prosecutor v. *Germain Katanga*, Decision Pursuant to Article 108(1) of the Rome Statute, 7 April 2016 (The Presidency)

The Prosecutor v. *Jean Pierre Bemba Gombo*, ICC-01/05-01/08-3636-Red, Judgment on the Appeal of Mr Jean-Pierre Bemba Gombo against Trial Chamber III's 'Judgment Pursuant to Article 74 of the Statute', 8 June 2018 (Appeals Chamber)

The Prosecutor v. *Jean-Pierre Bemba Gombo, Aimé Kilolo Musamba, Jean-Jaques Mangenda Kabongo, Fidèle Babala Wandu and Narcisse Arido*, ICC-01/05-01/13-2291, Decision on Mr Bemba's Application for Release, 12 June 2018 (Trial Chamber VII)

The Prosecutor v. *Jean-Pierre Bemba Gombo*, ICC-01/05-01/08-320, Fourth Decision on Victims' Participation, 12 December 2018 (Pre-Trial Chamber III)

ICC Assembly of States Parties Documents

Assembly of States Parties, 'Proposed Programme Budget for 2008 of the International Criminal Court', ICC-ASP/6/8, 30 November–14 December 2007

Assembly of States Parties, 'Report on Programme Performance of the International Criminal Court for the Year 2007, Addendum', ICC-ASP/7/8/Add.1, 14–22 November 2008

Assembly of States Parties, 'Report of the Court on the Kampala Field Office: Activities, Challenges and Review of Staffing Levels; and on Memoranda of Understanding with Situation Countries', ICC-ASP/9/11, 6–10 December 2010

Assembly of States Parties, 'Report on Activities and Programme Performance of the International Criminal Court for the Year 2012', ICC-ASP/12/9, 20–28 November 2013

Assembly of States Parties, 'Report of the Court on Cooperation', ICC-ASP/12/35, 20–28 November 2013, 9 October 2013

Assembly of States Parties, 'Report of the Bureau on Cooperation', ICC-ASP/12/36, 20–28 November 2013

Assembly of States Parties, 'Report on Activities and Programme Performance of the International Criminal Court for the Year 2013', ICC-ASP/13/19, 8–17 December 2014

Assembly of States Parties, 'Report of the Bureau on Non-Cooperation', ICC-ASP/13/40, 8–17 December 2014

Assembly of States Parties, 'Report on Activities and Programme Performance of the International Criminal Court for the Year 2014', ICC-ASP/14/8, 18–26 November 2015

Assembly of States Parties, 'Proposed Programme Budget for 2016 of the International Criminal Court', ICC-ASP/14/10, 18–26 November 2015

Assembly of States Parties, 'Report of the Court on Cooperation', ICC-ASP/14/27, 18–26 November 2015

Other ICC Documents

Regulations of the Court, 26 May 2004, ICC-BC/01-03-11

Judicial Cooperation Agreement between the Democratic Republic of the Congo and the Office of the Prosecutor of the International Criminal Court, 6 October 2004

Regulations of the Registry, 6 March 2006, ICC-BD/03-01-06

'Summary Report on the Round Table on the Protection of Victims and Witnesses Appearing before the International Criminal Court', 29–30 January 2009, www.icc-cpi.int/NR/rdonlyres/19869519-923D-4F67-A61F-35F78E424C68/280579/Report_ENG.pdf, last accessed 29 August 2019

The Prosecutor v. Jean-Pierre Bemba Gombo, ICC-01/05-01/08-T-13-ENG, Transcript of proceedings, 29 June 2009 (Pre-Trial Chamber II)
'Summary Report on the Seminar on Protection of Victims and Witnesses Appearing Before the International Criminal Court' (24 November 2010) www.icc-cpi.int/NR/rdonlyres/08767415-4F1D-46BA-B408-5B447B3AFC8D/0/ProtectionseminarSUMMARY.pdf, last accessed 22 February 2016
The Prosecutor v. German Katanga and Mathieu Ngudjolo Chui, ICC-01/04-01/07-T-258-ENG ET WT, Transcript of proceedings, 12 May 2011
'Complaint under the Optional Protocol to the International Covenant on Civil and Political Rights', ICC-01/04-01/06-2827-Anx5, 22 November 2011

ICTR Decisions

Prosecutor v. Jean-Bosco Barayagwiza, Case No. ICTR-97-19-AR72, Decision, 3 November 1999 (Appeal Chamber)
Jean Bosco Barayagwiza v. The Prosecutor, Case No. ICTR-97-19-AR72, Decision (Prosecutor's Request for Review or Reconsideration), 31 March 2000 (Appeals Chamber)
Laurent Semanza v. The Prosecutor, Case No. ICTR-97-20-A, Decision, 31 May 2000 (Appeals Chamber)
Juvénal Kajelijelo v. The Prosecutor, Case No. ICTR-98-44A, Judgment, 23 May 2005 (Appeals Chamber)
The Prosecutor v. André Ntagerura, Case No. ICTR-99-46-A28, Decision on the Motion by an Acquitted Person for Cooperation from Canada, Article 28 of the Statute, 15 May 2008 (Trial Chamber III)
In Re André Ntagerura, Case No. ICTR-99-46-A28, Decision on Motion to Appeal the President's Decision of 31 March 2008 and the Decision of Trial Chamber III of 15 May 2008, 18 November 2008 (Appeals Chamber)

Human Rights Committee Documents

Ng v. Canada, Communication No. 469/1991, 7 January 1994
Mukong v. Cameroon, Communication No. 458/1991, 21 July 1994
Compilation of General Comments and General Recommendations Adopted by Human Rights Treaty Bodies, UN Doc. HRI/GEN/Rev.6, 12 May 2003
Human Rights Committee, 'General Comment 31', U.N. Doc. CCPR/C/21/Rev.1/Add.13, 26 May 2004
Human Rights Committee, 'General Comment 21', HRI/GEN/1/Rev.1, 27 May 2008
Sayadi and Vinck v. Belgium, Communication No. 1472/2006, 29 December 2008

Human Rights Council, 'Annual Report of the United Nations High Commissioner for Human Rights and Reports of the Office of the High Commissioner and the Secretary-General; Right to Truth', A/HRC/12/19, 21 August 2009

David Hicks v. *Australia*, Communication No. 2005/2010, 16 February 2016

European Court of Human Rights Documents

Decisions

Airey v. *Ireland*, Application no. 6289/73, Judgment, 9 October 1979
Case of Soering v. *The United Kingdom*, Application no. 14038/88, Judgment, 7 July 1989
Cruz Varas and Others v. *Sweden*, Application no. 15576/89, Judgment, 20 March 1991
Case of Imbrioscia v. *Switzerland*, Application no. 13972/88, Judgment, 24 November 1993
Vilvarajah and Others v. *United Kingdom*, Application Nos. 13163/87, 13164/87, 13165/87, 13447/87, 13448/87, Judgment, 30 October 1991
Chahal v. *United Kingdom*, Application no. 22414/93, Judgment, 15 November 1996
Case of Matthews v. *the United Kingdom*, Application no. 24833/94, Judgment, 18 February 1999
Case of Waite & Kennedy v. *Germany*, Application no. 26083/94, Judgment, 18 February 1999
Case of Bosphorus Hava Yollari Turizm Ve Ticaret Anonim Sirketi v. *Ireland*, Application no. 45036/98, Judgment, 30 June 2005
Behrami and Behrami v. *France; Saramati* v. *France, Germany and Norway*, Application no. 71412/01, Admissibility Decision, 2 May 2007
Dušan Berić and Others v. *Bosnia and Herzegovina*, Application nos. 36357/04, 36360/04, 38346/04, 41705/04, 45190/04, 45578/04, 45579/04, 45580/04, 91/05, 97/05, 100/05, 101/05, 1121/05, 1123/05, 1125/05, 1129/05, 1132/05, 1133/05, 1169/05, 1172/05, 1175/05, 1177/05, 1180/05, 1185/05, 20793/05 and 25496/05, Admissibility Decision, 16 October 2007
Case of Mirilashvili v. *Russia*, Application no. 6293/04, Judgment, 11 December 2008
Kokkelvisserij v. *the Netherlands*, Application No. 13645/05, Admissibility Decision, 20 January 2009
Galić v. *The Netherlands*, Application no 22617/07, Decision on Admissibility, 9 June 2009
Case of Biełaj v. *Poland*, Application no. 43643/04, Judgment, 27 April 2010

Case of Othman (Abu Qatada) v. *the United Kingdom,* Application no. 8139/09, Judgment, 17 January 2012

Case of Nada v. *Switzerland,* Application no. 10593/08, Judgment, 12 September 2012

Djokaba Lambi Longa v. *The Netherlands,* Application no. 33917/12, Decision, 9 October 2012

Case of Pakshayev v. *Russia,* Application no. 1377/04, Judgment, 13 March 2014

Other

European Court of Human Rights, 'Guide on Article 6: Right to a Fair Trial (Criminal Limb)' (2014)

United Nations

General Assembly Resolution 43/173, A/43/49 (1988), 9 December 1988
General Assembly Resolution 45/111, A/45/49 (1990), 14 December 1990
UN Security Council Resolution 1267 (1999), S/RES/1267 (1999), 15 October 1999
UN Security Council Resolution 1593 (2005), S/RES/1593 (2005), 31 March 2005
UN Security Council Resolution 1970 (2011) S/RES/1970 (2011), 26 February 2011
United Nations Secretary General, 'Rome Statute of the International Criminal Court, Rome, 17 July 1998, Kenya: Proposal for Amendments', C.N.1026.2013. TREATIES-XVIII.10 (Depositary Notification), 14 March 2014

European Union

'Council Decision (EU) 2015/1601 of 22 September 2015 establishing provisional measures in the area of international protection for the benefit of Italy and Greece', OJ 2015 No. L248/80, 24 September 2015

European Parliament Directorate-General for Internal Policies, Policy Department C: Citizens' Rights and Constitutional Affairs, 'Implementation of the 2015 Council Decision establishing provisional measures in the area of international protection for the benefit of Italy and of Greece', PE 583, 2017

International Court of Justice

Reparation for Injuries Suffered in the Service of the United Nations, Advisory Opinion, ICJ Reports 1949, 11 April 1949

Case Concerning the Temple of Preah Vihear [Cambodia v. Thailand], Merits, ICJ Reports 1962, 15 June 1962
Interpretation of the Agreement of 25 March 1951 between the WHO and Egypt, Advisory Opinion, ICJ Reports 1980, 20 December 1980

International Law Commission

'Report of the Commission to the General Assembly on the work of its forty-fifth session' (1993) Vol. 2, Part 2, *Yearbook of the International Law Commission*
'Articles on Prevention of Transboundary Harm from Hazardous Activities with Commentaries' (2001) Vol. 2, Part 2, *Yearbook of the International Law Commission*
'Commentaries on the Articles on the Responsibility of International Organisations' (2011) Vol. 2, Part 2, *Yearbook of the International Law Commission*
'Articles on the Responsibility of International Organisations' (2011) Vol. 2, Part 2, *Yearbook of the International Law Commission*

Treaties

Statute of the International Court of Justice 1946
European Convention on Human Rights 1950
Convention Relating to the Status of Refugees 1951
International Covenant on Civil and Political Rights 1966
Vienna Convention on the Law of Treaties 1969
Convention against Torture and Other Cruel, Inhuman or Degrading Treatment or Punishment 1984
Rome Statute of the International Criminal Court 1998
Headquarters Agreement between the International Criminal Court and the Host State 2002
Negotiated Relationship Agreement with the International Criminal Court and the United Nations 2004
Agreement between the International Criminal Court and the Federal Government of Austria on the Enforcement of Sentences of the International Criminal Court 2005
Agreement between the Government of the United Kingdom of Great Britain and Northern Ireland and the International Criminal Court on the Enforcement of Sentences of the International Criminal Court 2007
Agreement between the Kingdom of the Netherlands and the United Nations concerning the Headquarters of the Special Tribunal for Lebanon 2007

Agreement between the Government of the United Kingdom of Great Britain and Northern Ireland and the Special Court for Sierra Leone on the Enforcement of Sentences of the Special Court for Sierra Leone 2007
Agreement between the International Criminal Court and the Government of the Kingdom of Belgium on the Enforcement of Sentences of the International Criminal Court 2010
Agreement between the International Criminal Court and the Government of the Republic of Finland on the Enforcement of Sentences of the International Criminal Court 2011
Agreement between the Republic of Serbia and the International Criminal Court on the Enforcement of Sentences of the International Criminal Court 2011
Accord entre la Cour pénale internationale et le Gouvernement de la République du Mali concernant l'exécution des peines prononcées par la Cour 2012
Agreement between the Kingdom of Denmark and the International Criminal Court on the Enforcement of Sentences of the International Criminal Court 2012
Agreement between the United Nations and the United Republic of Tanzania concerning the Headquarters of the International Residual Mechanism for Criminal Tribunals 2013
Agreement between the Argentine Republic and the International Criminal Court on the Enforcement of Sentences of the International Criminal Court 2017
Agreement between the Kingdom of Norway and the International Criminal Court on the Enforcement of Sentences of the International Criminal Court 2016
Framework Agreement between the Argentine Republic and the International Criminal Court on Interim Release 2018, ICC-PRES/25-01-18.

Domestic Legislation

International Crimes and International Criminal Court Act 2000, Public Act 2000 No 26, 6 September 2000, New Zealand
International Criminal Court Act 2001, 2001 Chapter 17, 1 September 2001, Great Britain
International Criminal Court Act 2002, Act No. 41 of 2002, Australia

Dutch Domestic Decisions

ECLI:NL:RBSGR:2011:BU9492, District Court of The Hague (sitting in Amsterdam), 28 December 2011
ECLI:NL:GHSGR:2012:BY6075, Court of Appeal, 18 December 2012
ECLI:NL:RBDHA:2013:BZ7942, District Court of The Hague, 8 March 2013
ECLI:NL:RVS:2013:2050, Council of State, 12 November 2013

ECLI:NL:RVS:2014:627, Council of State, 18 February 2014
ECLI:NL:HR:2014:828, Supreme Court, 4 April 2014
ECLI:NL:RVS:2014:2427, Council of State, 27 June 2014
ECLI:NL:RVS:2014:3833, Council of State, 15 October 2014
ECLI:NL:RBDHA:2015:4659, District Court of The Hague, 23 April 2015

News Articles

'Ocampo witnesses now sent to Europe', Property Kenya, 10 March 2011
'80 Kenyan ICC witnesses in safe houses abroad', Mwakilishi, 23 January 2013
Jenny Clover, 'Congo ICC war suspect surrenders at U.S. Embassy in Rwanda', Reuters, 18 March 2013
'Polish jail takes Bosnian war criminal', news.com.au, 22 March 2014
'Acquitted of Rwanda genocide, now left in legal limbo', Daily Mail, 18 December 2014
'Kenyan 'ICC defence witness' in Ruto's trial killed', BBC News, 6 January 2015
'Ex-Liberia president Charles Taylor to stay in UK prison', BBC News, 25 March 2015
'Reporters, witnesses silenced 'one by one' with ICC link deadly in Kenya', AlJazeera America, 24 August 2015
'Germany gives life sentence to Rwandan for genocide', DW, 29 December 2015
'Gbagbo Trial: ICC 'mistakenly' discloses names of witnesses', Africa News, 6 February 2016

Miscellaneous

Letter from the Minister of Justice to the Speaker of the Lower House of Parliament, The Hague, July 2002, 28 098 (R 1704)
'United Nations Illegally Transfers Asylum Seeker', Press Release of Philippe Larochelle and Avi Singh, Arusha, 13 September 2006
Cottier, Thomas and Müller, Jörg Paul, 'Estoppel' (2007) *Max Planck Encyclopedia of Public International Law*
O'Donohue, Jonathan, 'Conditional Release of Bemba Gombo? States object to cooperating with the conditional release of Jean-Pierre Bemba Gombo – another sign of a cooperation crisis?', Amnesty International (reposting from Coalition for International Criminal Court blog (no longer available)), 10 September 2009, available at www2.amnesty.se/icc.nsf/ffc3926fc473d909c12570b90033f05f/89bba55aea0d9a4c0025763500516453
Irving, Emma, 'The Surrender of Ntaganda to the ICC: A Story of Shared Responsibility Success', Shares Project Blog, 3 April 2013

Francioni, Francesco, 'Equity in International Law' (2013) *Max Planck Encyclopedia of Public International Law*
Dzidic, Denis, 'Srebrenica genocide convict sues Britain over attack', Balkan Transitional Justice, 6 November 2014
'First ICC Acquitted Defendant Returned to DR Congo: Netherlands Rejected Asylum Claim Over Safety Fears', Human Rights Watch, 11 May 2015
'DR Congo: ICC Convict Faces Domestic Charges', Human Rights Watch, 23 December 2015
Zimmerman, Dominik (revised by Klamberg, Mark), 'Article 12(3)', Case Matrix Network, 30 June 2016
Stiel, Michael and Stuckenberg, Carl-Friedrich, 'Article 106', Case Matrix Network, 30 June 2016
Daugirdas, Kristina, 'International Organizations and the Creation of Customary International Law' (2018) University of Michigan Public Law Research Paper No. 597

INDEX

acquittal and release, 39, 40, 65, 93, 94, 95, 96, 97, 99, 125, 139, 146, 155, 156, 158, 160, 161, 211, 214, 216, 222, 227, 230
   agreement for the release of accused persons, 99
   implementation problem. *See* implementation problem; acquittal and release
   structural problem. *See* structural problem; acquittal and release
African Charter on Human and People's Rights, 81, 115, 127
Al-Bashir, 25, 50, 64
Argentina, 76, 77, 84, 99
arrest
   arrest and surrender, 4, 30, 31, 37, 39, 40, 48, 49, 50, 54, 55, 56, 59, 60, 61, 62, 63, 64, 65, 92
   arrest warrant, 37, 39, 48, 52, 54, 55, 56, 57, 60, 61, 62, 63, 67, 117, 120
   provisional arrest, 62
assurances, 170
   in the detained Congolese witnesses case, 2, 111, 171, 179, 182, 184
Australia, 55, 189, 190

Barayagwiza, 59, 60, 61
Basic Principles for the Treatment of Prisoners, 89
Belgium, 31, 32, 33, 61, 62, 72, 73, 76, 77, 84, 89, 90, 94, 132, 220
Bemba, 15, 31, 32, 33, 62, 65, 69, 70, 71, 72, 73, 74, 75, 76, 77, 117, 148, 249
Bemba et al., 69, 70, 72, 73, 74, 75, 76, 77, 117, 148
Berić, 194

Blé Goudé, 130
Body of Principles for the Protection of All Persons under Any Form of Detention or Imprisonment, 89
Bosphorus, 195, 218, 219, 220, 221, 222, 223
buck passing, 5, 6, 47, 181, 182, 183, 202, 203, 212, 224, 227, 230, *See* implementation problem

Cameroon, 59, 61, 90
Central African Republic, 62, 69, 103, 107, 116
Chad, 50, 120
Convention Against Torture, 80
conviction, 40, 65, 71, 78, 79, 80, 81, 82, 83, 85, 86, 87, 88, 89, 92, 94, 123, 125, 130, 146, 149, 150, 151, 152, 153, 154, 155, 158, 161, 210, 211, 214, 224
cooperation
   lack of cooperation, 116, 117
   non-State Party, 35
   State Party cooperation, limitations of, 31, 74, 75, 95, 126, 215

Democratic Republic of Congo, 2, 3, 4, 19, 32, 44, 50, 52, 55, 56, 60, 61, 62, 73, 79, 88, 96, 98, 105, 107, 111, 112, 115, 116, 142, 143, 151, 158, 159, 160, 166, 167, 171, 172, 173, 179, 180, 182, 183, 184, 186, 187, 188, 189, 192, 193, 195, 196, 226
detained Congolese witnesses, 1, 3, 105, 111, 115, 142, 151, 152, 166, 167, 168, 171, 172, 173, 175, 176, 178, 179, 180, 181, 182, 183, 184, 185, 187, 188, 190, 191, 192, 194, 195, 196, 197, 202, 218, 226, 228, 241

INDEX

Dutch Council of State, 98, 159, 160, 179, 180, 182, 200, 201
Dutch Court of Appeal, 193
Dutch Minister of Justice, 95, 142, 153, 154
Dutch Supreme Court, 192, 194
duty of care, 233, 235

enforcement of sentences, 39, 78, 80, 82, 86, 93, 123, 146, 149, 150, 155, 157, 176, 210, 214
   agreement on enforcement of sentences, 81, 86, 88, 90
   agreements on, 10
equity, 233
estoppel, 233, 234
European Committee on the Prevention of Torture and Inhuman and Degrading Treatment and Punishment, 84
European Convention on Human Rights, 35, 41, 42, 68, 79, 81, 90, 115, 127, 141, 143, 144, 148, 150, 151, 152, 153, 154, 155, 158, 160, 176, 178, 179, 181, 191, 193, 194, 195, 211, 212, 219, 220, 221, 222
European Court of Human Rights, 23, 35, 41, 42, 79, 90, 141, 142, 143, 144, 148, 151, 155, 157, 169, 171, 172, 176, 178, 184, 192, 193, 194, 195, 218, 219, 220, 221
European Court of Justice, 194
European Union, 43, 194, 195, 200, 215, 216, 221, 231, 232, 235
Extraordinary Chambers in the Courts of Cambodia, 215

gap in protection. *See* structural problem
Gbagbo, 46, 52, 130, 261
Germany, 226
Greece, 215

Headquarters Agreement between the ICC and the Netherlands, 10, 13, 21, 140, 142, 143, 147, 148, 150, 153, 156, 157, 158, 175, 177, 191, 192, 219

Hicks, 189
Human Rights Committee, 34, 66, 80, 90, 188, 189, 196, 220

ICC Assembly of States Parties, 20, 30, 50, 75, 76, 107, 108, 110, 112, 115, 117, 120, 125, 129, 130, 171, 216, 230, 232, 233, 255
ICC Detention Centre, 2, 18, 79, 139, 142, 148, 150, 151, 152, 155, 158, 183, 192, 194, 213, 222, 229
ICC Office of the Prosecutor, 44, 45, 103, 224
ICC Presidency, 15, 18, 20, 80, 81, 82, 83, 84, 85, 86, 88
ICC Registry, 43, 76, 104, 108, 109, 110, 111, 122, 159, 160, 184
ICC Rules of Procedure and Evidence, 10, 11, 13, 17, 35, 42, 43, 45, 57, 60, 63, 68, 69, 70, 78, 80, 83, 88, 89, 94, 104, 105, 118, 122, 166, 186
International Covenant on Civil and Political Rights, 12, 34, 41, 49, 53, 57, 63, 66, 68, 81, 90, 115, 127, 181, 188, 196, 220
implementation problem, 5, 47, 65, 99, 155, 161, 182, 183, 202, 209, 210, 223, 224, 227, 228, 230
   acquittal and release, 161, 211
   detained witnesses
      the right to life, protection from inhuman treatment, and fair trial, 181, 212
   interrogation, 47, 210
   non-detained witnesses, 201, 213
   removal to the enforcement State, 154, 211
   witnesses located in the situation State, 115, 117, 118, 211
interim release, 6, 13, 23, 31, 33, 39, 40, 65, 66, 67, 68, 69, 70, 71, 72, 73, 74, 75, 76, 77, 97, 99, 105, 125, 140, 146, 147, 148, 186, 196, 210, 213, 214, 216, 222, 223, 230, 232
   agreement on interim release, 76, 78
   State cooperation, 70, 78

structural problem. *See* structural
 problem; interim release
International Committee of the Red
 Cross, 84
International Criminal Court
 (Implementation) Act, 140, 142,
 153, 177
International Criminal Court
 Protection Programme, 109,
 110, 111, 121, 127, 128, 164, 175,
 198, 201, 202, 225
International Criminal Tribunal for
 Rwanda, 42, 55, 59, 60, 61, 62,
 63, 93, 94, 95, 96, 97, 98, 114,
 126, 166, 180, 181, 214, 237
International Criminal Tribunal for the
 Former Yugoslavia, 1, 42, 43,
 62, 63, 78, 85, 89, 93, 143, 166,
 180, 181, 214, 237
International Law Commission
 Articles on the Responsibility of
 International Organisations,
 20, 219
international refugee law
 asylum claims, 2, 4, 6, 79, 95, 96, 105,
 132, 143, 151, 152, 154, 173, 176,
 180, 181, 187, 192, 195, 199, 200,
 202, 217, 232
 Refugee Convention, 79, 105, 159,
 180, 197, 198, 200, 201, 217
 refugee status, 126, 181, 197, 198,
 199, 200, 201
International Residual Mechanism for
 Criminal Tribunals, 97, 156,
 157
Investigation, 4, 6, 12, 30, 31, 39, 40, 41,
 42, 43, 44, 45, 46, 47, 48, 50, 67,
 74, 75, 77, 95, 96, 112, 147,
 224, 234
 implementation problem. *See*
 implementation problem;
 interrogation
 interrogation, 30, 40, 41, 42, 43, 44,
 45, 46, 47, 48, 210, 224
Ireland, 42, 83, 84, 90, 219, 220,
 221
Italy, 215
Ivory Coast, 35, 107

Kajelijeli, 55
Katanga, 13, 15, 18, 19, 46, 55, 61, 62,
 65, 79, 88, 105, 106, 112, 115,
 120, 151, 158, 166, 169, 171, 173,
 174, 175, 177, 179, 184, 186, 187,
 188, 190, 191, 193, 198, 217
Kenya, 50, 101, 107, 116, 117, 120, 126,
 132, 216, 261
Kokkelvisserij, 194, 195
Krstić, 85
Kupreškić, 93

Longa, 142, 143, 144, 148, 151, 152, 166,
 178, 193, 194, 195, 218
Lubanga case, 15, 16, 17, 18, 19, 52, 55,
 56, 58, 59, 60, 65, 68, 79, 88, 110,
 113, 114, 116, 118, 166, 173, 176,
 178, 193

Malawi, 50
Mali, 84, 89, 107
Mucić, 43

New Zealand, 55
Ngudjolo, 15, 18, 19, 46, 65, 94, 96, 97,
 98, 99, 106, 112, 120, 151, 153,
 155, 158, 159, 160, 161, 169, 171,
 173, 174, 175, 177, 179, 184, 187,
 191, 198, 211, 217
Ntaganda, 37
Ntagerura, 93, 96, 98, 126
Ntamabyariro, 181

Opačić, 181
Othman, 126, 172, 180, 182

Palestine, 35
prohibition on removal to a situation of
 risk, 79, 95, 121, 123, 124, 144,
 149, 151, 167, 168, 176, 178, 183,
 184, 188, 198

Regulations of the Court, 10, 13, 70,
 76, 88
Regulations of the Registry, 10, 13, 15,
 18, 43, 45, 107, 109, 110, 113
right to fair trial, 8, 9, 15, 17, 19, 22, 23,
 34, 40, 41, 42, 43, 44, 45, 46, 47,

48, 143, 165, 166, 167, 168, 176, 182, 184, 196, 210, 224
right to liberty, 2, 4, 6, 9, 22, 23, 34, 40, 49, 50, 51, 52, 56, 57, 59, 60, 61, 63, 64, 65, 66, 68, 70, 71, 73, 74, 76, 77, 78, 98, 143, 144, 146, 147, 165, 183, 184, 188, 189, 190, 191, 192, 193, 195, 196, 210, 211, 212, 218, 222, 228
right to life, 8, 22, 34, 97, 103, 115, 121, 127, 165, 166, 167, 168, 182, 186, 197
right to protection from torture and inhuman and degrading treatment, 8, 22, 34, 40, 79, 80, 81, 82, 85, 86, 87, 88, 92, 94, 95, 97, 103, 115, 121, 122, 127, 149, 150, 151, 153, 156, 165, 166, 167, 168, 176, 182, 183, 188, 196, 197
Rome Statute
  amendment, 214, 215, 216
  Article 103, 80, 81, 88, 150, 157, 175, 176
  Article 106, 80, 82, 83, 84, 85, 86, 87, 89, 90, 91, 150
  Article 110, 86
  Article 12, 35, 36, 112
  Article 13, 36, 40, 193
  Article 21(3), 11, 15, 16, 17, 18, 19, 20, 24, 25, 30, 33, 34, 45, 50, 53, 54, 56, 60, 69, 72, 73, 74, 75, 81, 87, 91, 92, 95, 97, 106, 111, 112, 115, 124, 126, 127, 168, 170, 173, 174, 186, 188, 189, 217, 218
  Article 55, 12, 30, 42, 43, 44, 45, 46, 47, 48, 50, 56, 60, 62, 63, 210
  Article 58, 48, 60, 63, 67, 70, 116, 147
  Article 59, 30, 50, 51, 52, 53, 54, 55, 56, 57, 58, 59, 60, 63, 66
  Article 60, 50, 66, 67, 68, 69, 70, 72, 73, 74, 77, 147
  Article 64(2), 12, 18, 57
  Article 68, 104, 105, 106, 109, 111, 112, 115, 121, 122, 123, 167, 168, 169, 170, 171, 172, 174, 175, 182, 190, 199, 212, 217, 223, 224
  Article 69, 43, 46
  Article 85, 57, 59, 65
  Article 86, 30, 50, 74, 75, 112, 124, 125, 126
  Article 87, 30, 37, 50, 58, 112, 113, 117
  Article 89, 31, 49, 50, 54, 63
  Article 91, 31
  Article 92, 31, 62, 63
  Article 93, 19, 31, 32, 95, 96, 125, 126, 166, 170, 172, 173, 174, 182, 185, 186, 187, 188, 189
  Article 93(7), 19, 166, 170, 172, 173, 174, 182, 185, 186, 187, 188, 189
  Article 97, 54
  Part 9, 30, 31, 32, 33, 34, 36, 44, 49, 74, 112, 113, 114, 115, 121, 123, 125, 127, 171, 179
  Part 10, 80, 87
Rwanda, 37, 61, 85, 91, 93, 94, 95, 97, 114, 126, 181, 226, 261

Schiphol Airport, 98, 161
Semanza, 59
Soering, 79, 151, 169
sovereignty, 32, 34, 48, 75, 126, 187, 188, 189, 214, 216
Special Court for Sierra Leone, 14, 42, 83, 85, 215
Special Tribunal for Lebanon, 42, 156, 157, 215
Specialist Chambers of Kosovo, 215
State responsibility, 228, 239
  shared responsibility, 240
stay of proceedings, 15, 17, 18, 59, 60, 61, 62
structural problem, 78, 97, 99, 128, 133, 223, 228
  acquittal and release, 97, 156, 211
  detained witnesses
    right to liberty, 195, 213
  interim release, 76, 77, 148, 210
  relocating a witness to a third State, 127, 130, 131, 212

Tanzania, 98, 156, 181
Taylor, 85, 261
The Hague, 2, 66, 85, 95, 135, 141, 143, 144, 148, 151, 152, 160, 177, 178, 192, 193, 195, 198, 199, 202, 225, 261

The Hague District Court, 123, 144, 151, 152, 160, 177, 178, 192, 193, 195, 198, 199, 202, 222, 225
The Netherlands, 225, 229
  as host State, 4, 8, 10, 11, 99, 135, 139, 140, 145, 146, 147, 148, 149, 150, 155, 156, 157, 164, 191, 210, 211, 218, 224, 237, 238
  as State Party, 139, 156
Treaty on the Functioning of the European Union, 215

Uganda, 35, 107, 114, 234
Ukraine, 35
UN Charter, 36, 214
UN High Commissioner for Human Rights, 115
United Kingdom, 55, 73, 79, 83, 84, 85, 86, 90, 125, 132, 151, 169, 172, 220, 261
United Nations, 13, 21, 22, 36, 66, 97, 166, 194, 200, 234
United Nations Security Council, 30, 36, 37, 40, 43, 112, 117, 194, 214, 234, 235

Victims and Witnesses Unit, 94, 103, 104, 106, 107, 109, 110, 111, 112, 120, 122, 159, 171, 172
Vienna Convention on the Law of Treaties, 13, 25

Waite and Kennedy, 157
Witnesses
  agreements on the protection of, 10
  agreements on the relocation of, 122, 123, 124, 126, 127, 128, 129, 130, 131, 133, 230
  assisted move, 109, 110, 111
  detained Congolese witnesses. See detained Congolese witnesses
  detained witnesses, 2, 4, 103, 106, 111, 112, 114, 115, 142, 143, 152, 158, 165, 166, 167, 168, 169, 170, 171, 172, 173, 174, 175, 176, 177, 178, 180, 182, 183, 184, 185, 186, 187, 188, 189, 190, 191, 192, 193, 195, 196, 197, 202, 203, 212, 213, 218, 222, 225, 226, 228, 229, *See* implementation problem; detained witnesses; the right to life, protection from inhuman treatment, and fair trial, *see* structural problem; detained witnesses; right to liberty
  false testimony, 101
  implementation problem. *See* witnesses located in the situation State, non-detained witnesses, implementation problem; detained witnesses; the right to life, protection from inhuman treatment, and fair trial
  in-courtroom protection, 101
  Initial Response System, 103, 107, 108, 109, 111, 112, 113, 114, 116, 118
  internal resettlement, 103, 107, 109, 110, 111, 112, 113, 114, 118, 120, 121, 216
  non-detained witnesses, 197, 199, 202, 203, 204, *See* implementation problem; non-detained witnesses
  platform State, 131, 132, 230
  protective measures in detention, 107, 111, 112, 113, 114
  relocation to third State, 109, 120, 121, 122, 123, 124, 126, 127, 128, 129, 131, 132, 140, 164, 174, 198, 200, 201, 216, 226, 229, 230, *See* structural problem; relocating a witness to a third State
  Special Fund for Relocations, 131, 132, 133, 226, 230
  structural problem. *See* structural problem; relocating a witness to a third State, structural problem; detained witnesses; right to liberty
  witnesses located in the situation State. *See* implementation problem; witnesses located in the situation State